Where the trails are—bill williams

ASHLAND —MEDFORD   AND   BEYOND

How to find nearly 150 recreation trails located in or around the
Rogue River Valley, or on nearby public lands.   The geographical
area covered in this book extends from near the California-Oregon
border, north to the Diamond Lake vicinity. Historical and map
information is included.

Cover design and art work by Bob Sisson

Bob

Independent Printing Co. - 640 Tolman Cr. Road - Ashland, OR

i

ACKNOWLEDGEMENTS

This book became reality due to the contributions of many persons and agencies. The entire manuscript was submitted to Jeffrey M. LaLande, Rogue River National Forest Supervisor's Office for permission to include quotations from the publication "Prehistory and History of the Rogue River National Forest: A Cultural Resource Overview," and from Recreation Opportunity Guides. This book contains 29 sections of maps that were reproduced from the USFS "Rogue River National Forest" map. Others who edited the manuscript, who provided valuable information or gave permission to reproduce their maps include:

U.S. FOREST SERVICE: Rogue River, Winema,and Umpqua National Forest Ranger District personnel.
U.S. BUREAU OF LAND MANAGEMENT: Medford Recreation Dept. staff.
U.S.ARMY CORPS OF ENGINEERS: Rogue River Basin Project staff.
BOISE CASCADE TIMBER AND WOOD PRODUCTS GROUP. Medford office.
CRATER LAKE NATIONAL PARK: Superintendent's office and Crater Lake Natural History Association brochure.
JACKSON COUNTY PARKS AND RECREATION DEPT: Bear Creek Greenway.
MEDFORD PARKS AND RECREATION DEPT: Medford office staff.
THE NATURE CONSERVANCY: Portland office staff.
OREGON FISH AND WILDLIFE: Southwest Regional Office staff.

AUDREY WILLIAMS: Provided much "over the shoulder" advice.
IVAN COLLVER, Ashland computer programmer, helped the author set-up and use word processing equipment.

PLEASE NOTE: The emphasis of this book is to DESCRIBE HOW TO GET TO THE TRAILS AND WHAT EQUIPMENT TO BRING. Although known precautions are listed, the author cannot be responsible for trails that may be hard to follow due to reduced maintenance, abandonment, new roads,logging operations or any other unforeseen conditions. Check with the applicable agencies for the latest trail status.

TABLE OF CONTENTS   PAGE

iii

Collings Mountain Trail

Bill says, "Leave things as you found
them for others to enjoy."

INTRODUCTION

Southern Oregon is a paradise for outdoor enthusiasts! It provides year-round opportunities for hiking and backpacking, horseback riding, and a variety of winter sports! Southern Oregon has less rain than does most parts of the State, and if a person is careful in choosing where and when to go, it is possible to find trails where rain is at a minimum. It is also possible to locate areas above the fog and into the sunshine!

DURING THE WINTER MONTHS, the Applegate Valley and vicinity provide spectacular outdoor experiences! This is a great place to soak up some sunshine and enjoy the open views of the surrounding mountains, or to travel the trails along the Applegate River or Applegate Lake area.

Other favorite winter trails are those at Lost Creek Lake, Table Rocks, Roxy Ann Peak, or the beautiful Lower Rogue River Trail. Ashland generally lifts its head above the Rogue Valley winter fog, and the trails are less muddy due to granite soil.

Mt. Ashland is a favorite for winter sports and is complete with a ski lodge, ski rental facilities, rope tows, chair lifts and trails for cross-country skiing. Contact a Forest Ranger Station for locations of other cross-country ski trails in the Cascade Range.

IN LATE SPRING OR SUMMER, the trails at high elevations begin to open up, but above 7000 feet elevation the snow might not be gone until mid-July. The Pacific Crest National Scenic Trail in this area travels 31 miles through Crater Lake National Park before it continues south another 75 miles along the Cascade Range, crest of the Siskiyou Mountains and on to the Klamath River. This is but a portion of the Pacific Crest National Scenic Trail that extends 2500 miles from Canada to Mexico.

In addition to Crater Lake National Park, southern Oregon boasts several Wilderness Areas: The Rogue-Umpqua Divide, Sky Lakes, Mountain Lakes and Red Buttes. The summit of Mt. McLoughlin at 9495' elevation, is the highest point one can reach in the area covered by this book.

The author has hiked many of these trails during outings conducted by the Oregon-Idaho Conference of the United Methodist Church or by the Rogue Chapter of the Sierra Club. While along on these trips, it became obvious that a book was needed to help find the trailhead locations, because many road junction signs were damaged or missing. Maps are sometimes hard to follow or may need revision, and so an effort is made to present a fairly simple access description to the trailheads, giving directions from nearest mileposts. Every effort will be made to keep this book up-to-date, but changes beyond our control can rapidly happen!

HOW TO USE THIS BOOK

It is very important to BRING MAPS listed in each hike description, and a COMPASS to help you find your way. The U.S. Forest Service has a very excellent leaflet entitled "MAP AND COMPASS." It contains work sheets with practice drills that are easy to understand. It takes the confusion out of using a compass and may save your life!

The U. S. Geological Survey publishes TOPOGRAPHIC MAPS (Topos) that are available from libraries, sporting goods stores, stationary or book stores, and some office suppliers. They can be ordered directly from U. S. Geological Survey, Distribution Section, Federal Center, Denver Colorado 80225. The maps cover every section of the United States in minute detail. An "Index To Topographic Maps of Oregon" is also available from the USGS.

U.S. Forest Service maps are often printed in TOPO form. For the area covered by this book, the Pacific Crest National Scenic Trail, Mountain Lakes Wilderness and Sky Lakes Area maps are all topographic. TOPO MAPS are also available from the Applegate, Ashland, Butte Falls, Prospect, Tiller and Diamond Lake RANGER DISTRICTS.

TOPO MAPS have contour lines that determine elevation and the altitude of peaks, valleys and other landmarks. They also indicate roads, trails, rivers, streams, railroad tracks and other details. MOST ELEVATION DATA IN THIS BOOK WAS ESTIMATED FROM TOPO MAPS AND SHOULD NOT BE CONSIDERED ACCURATE NOR OFFICIAL.

EQUIPMENT NEEDED: In addition to MAPS and COMPASS, the following items are important:

BOOTS OR STURDY SHOES: Waterproof, well fitted with warm socks.
CLOTHING that can be layered, preferably wool.
RAINGEAR. Rainsuits have more wind protection than do ponchos.
EMERGENCY SUPPLIES: First aid,matches,flashlight,bug repellant.
CANTEEN - WATER PURIFICATION: There is no guarantee that any water in the woods is free from Giardia, or other harmful bacteria. The only sure way to avoid sickness is to BRING WATER FROM HOME or to have absolute resolve not to drink any water in the woods unless it has been treated. Water purification tablets are not quite 100% effective. The safest way is to boil the water for at least 10 minutes, or to bring a water filter, available from suppliers of recreation equipment.

The wood tick is much smaller than this but they can be easily seen if they get on you. They are in area all year long.

RULES TO CONSIDER.

SAFETY: Before you leave home, let others know where you are going and stick with the plan! When in the woods, stay with your group, as you may need to rely on each other in case of emergencies! Do not run on the trails or take needless chances. Help may be far away! Drive safely on forest roads and be alert for logging vehicles or other traffic.

OBEY FIRE REGULATIONS. Build fires only where allowed, and make sure they are COMPLETELY OUT before leaving camp. No smoking while traveling, except in vehicles on roads.

OBTAIN PERMITS. Before hiking in the woods, check with the appropriate agencies for fire or wilderness entry permits.

PACK OUT ALL TRASH. Don't bury it. Leave campgrounds cleaner than you found them! Remove litter encountered on the trail.

DO NOT POLLUTE. Keep soaps and other pollutants out of rivers and streams. Bury human waste away from streams or lakes.

PRIVATE PROPERTY. Respect posted signs, stay on the trail.

DON'T CUT ACROSS SWITCHBACKS. This can cause erosion and severe damage to the trails.

LISTEN TO THE WILDERNESS! Leave radios and tape players at home.

ALWAYS BE PREPARED. Bring the equipment listed in the previous paragraph. CARRY DRINKING WATER ON EVERY OUTING!

HAZARDS TO AVOID. Poison oak, deer ticks or an occasional rattlesnake may be encountered while hiking in southern Oregon. Using caution can help minimize these hazards.

POISON OAK is generally found in the lower elevation hills (below
6000 feet) in the Applegate and Rogue River Valleys. Learn to
identify this noxious plant. Its shiny green leaves are in groups
of threes turning to red in late summer. Oils from the plant can
cause an itching rash or blisters. The treatment methods include
scrubbing the skin with naptha or alkaline soap, or by cleansing
with rubbing alcohol. Calamine or other skin lotion may be ben-
eficial if the rash is mild. It may be necessary to seek medical
advice in severe cases.

TICKS can carry Lyme disease,or recently reported cases of H.G.E.
(Human granulocytic ehrlichiosis) and Babesiosis. THESE DISEASES
CAN BE DISABLING OR FATAL IF NOT DIAGNOSED AND TREATED. SEEK THE
LATEST MEDICAL ADVICE.

PREVENTING BITES: Wear long sleeves and pants tucked into boots.
Avoid trail margins, brush and grassy areas when in tick country.
Use tick repellant on clothes and shoes. White clothes help make
ticks visible. Check yourself and pets carefully for ticks.
TREATMENT: Remove attatched tick at once with fine-jaw tweezers,
grasping the tick's mouth-parts as close to the skin as possible,
slowly and gently pulling straight out. AUTHORITIES ADVISE not to
squeeze tick or spray it with oil as it may inject fluid into you.
Wash bite area, hands and apply antiseptic. GET MEDICAL TREATMENT
IF ANY PARTS ARE LEFT IN THE SKIN OR IF COMPLICATIONS DEVELOP.

RATTLESNAKES.   This is not a common problem in southern Oregon,
but an occasional snake may be spotted at lower elevations. During summer months, look for them in shaded areas especially during early morning or late afternoon.   In case of snake bite, the
best treatment is to get the victim to a doctor or a hospital as
soon as possible. Apply cold compresses if available. Loose con-
stricting bands may be placed above the bite, but not so tight as
to stop blood circulation.

WHERE TO GET INFORMATION AND PERMITS.

ROGUE RIVER NATIONAL FOREST.
-Forest Supervisor, P.O. Box 520, 333 W. 8th St., Medford, Or. 97501   Phone (541)858-2200
-District Ranger, Ashland Ranger Station, 645 Washington St., Ashland, Oregon 97520   Phone (541)482-3333
-District Ranger, Butte Falls Ranger Station, P.O. Box 227, Butte Falls, Oregon 97522   Phone (541)865-2700
-District Ranger, Prospect Ranger Station, Prospect, Oregon, 97536   Phone (541)560-3400
-District Ranger, Star Ranger Station, 6941 Upper Applegate Road, Jacksonville, Oregon 97530   Phone (541)899-1812

WINEMA NATIONAL FOREST.
-Forest Supervisor, 2819 Dahlia St., Klamath Falls, Oregon, 97601 Phone (541)883-6714
-Klamath District Ranger, 1936 California Ave., Klamath Falls, Oregon 97601   Phone (541)885-3400

UMPQUA NATIONAL FOREST.
-Forest Supervisor, P.O. Box 1008, Roseburg, Or. 97470   Phone (541)672-6601
-Diamond Lake Ranger District, Toketee Route Box 101, Idleyld Park, Oregon 97447   Phone (541)498-2531
-Tiller Ranger District, Route 2 Box 1, Tiller, Oregon 97484 Phone (541)825-3201

SISKIYOU NATIONAL FOREST.-Supervisor, 200 N.E. Greenfield Road, Grants Pass, Oregon 97526. Phone (541)471-6500
KLAMATH NATIONAL FOREST. -Supervisor, 1312 Fairlane Road, Yreka, California,96097. Phone (916)842-6131

-BUREAU OF LAND MANAGEMENT
3040 Biddle Road, Medford, Or.. 97504.   Phone (541)770-2200
1465 N.E. 7th St., Grant Pass, Or. 97526.   Phone (541)479-7244
-MEDFORD PARKS AND RECREATION DEPT., Medford City Hall, Rm. 140, Medford, Oregon 97501   Phone (541)770-4586
-THE NATURE CONSERVANCY, 1205 N.W. 25th Ave., Portland, Oregon, 97210   Phone (541)228-9561
-OREGON DEPT. OF FORESTRY, 5286 Table Rock Rd., Central Point,Or. 97502 Phone (541)664-3328

-OREGON DEPARTMENT OF FISH AND WILDLIFE, 1495 Gregory Road, White City Oregon.
-PORTLAND DISTRICT, U.S. ARMY CORPS OF ENGINEERS, Lost Creek Project, Trail, Oregon, 97541.
-GEOLOGICAL INFORMATION: BLM staff, 3040 Biddle Road, Medford. USFS Supervisor's Office, 333 West 8th St., Medford, Oregon. Southern Oregon State College, Ashland, Oregon.
-BOTANICAL, BIOLOGICAL INFORMATION: BLM staff, Medford office. USFS Supervisor's Office, 333 West 8th St., Medford, Oregon.

HELPFUL ORGANIZATIONS: Several Rogue Valley organizations have scheduled meetings and field trips. Up-to-date information can be obtained from their chapter newsletters or from the local news media. Chambers of Commerce of the area may also have some listings. The organizations include:

FRIENDS OF THE GREENSPRINGS
MOUNT MAZAMA MUSHROOM ASSOCIATION
NATIVE PLANT SOCIETY OF OREGON
ROGUE VALLEY AUDUBON SOCIETY
ROGUE GROUP SIERRA CLUB
SODA MOUNTAIN WILDERNESS COUNCIL

WHY NOT ADOPT A TRAIL? Outstanding TRAIL MAINTENANCE has been provided by VOLUNTEER GROUPS in our area! Credits to them will be noted as you read through this book. Without their help some of our trails may not have that special "Well-groomed" look, and it is a very rewarding experience to those doing the work! It does make a difference...ask anyone using the trails! To become a part of this vital program, please contact personnel of the USFS Ranger Districts or their Supervisor's office; Bureau of Land Management offices or other agencies listed in this book.

BIKES ARE PERMITTED ON THE FOLLOWING TRAILS:

NOTE: Bikes are not permitted on: Pacific Crest Trail,
Wilderness area trails, National Recreation Trails,
*NOTE MOTOR BIKES ALSO ALLOWED WHEN INDICATED BY *

8

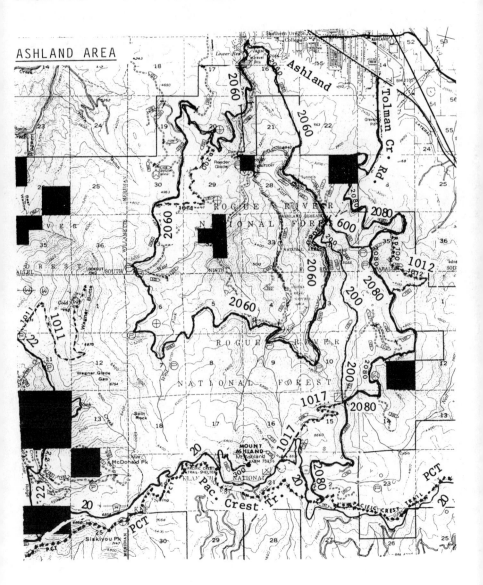

ASHLAND'S LITHIA PARK HIKING TRAILS.

PARK ENTRANCE: Adjacent to downtown Ashland Plaza, just below the Oregon Shakespeare Festival Theaters.
SEASON: All year, EASY TRAILS for hikers or joggers. Bicycles, animals and overnight sleeping prohibited. The park is closed from 11:30 pm to 5:30 am.

FEATURES: Hiking in Ashland's Lithia Park is a very relaxing and educational experience! From the park entrance, the trails extend about one mi. to the far end of the park along both sides of Ashland Creek. Foot-bridges inter-connect, allowing the visitor to create an individualized experience. Picnic and restroom facilities are located throughout the park.

From the upper park boundary, hikers often extend their outing by going 0.2 mi. further south on Granite St. to a newly constructed "Reservoir Trail" leading about 1/4 mile to a park setting along Ashland Creek. This area is used by picnickers and swimmers, and is located at the junction of Granite St. and Glenview Dr....that are often used for more hiking/jogging adventures!

The one mile LITHIA PARK WOODLAND TRAIL also begins from the park entrance and extends past 99 numbered interpretive posts located at various trees and shrubs that have been imported from all over the world. An excellent guide-booklet is available at a very minimal cost from Ashland Parks and Recreation Dept. (located in the park), or from Ashland Chamber of Commerce. A companion booklet entitled "Lithia Park", by Marjorie O'Harra, provides information on the history of Lithia Park and is available from the above locations.

Lithia Park is a very special place that provides various recreational activities for many visitors. Because of its professional landscaping design and maintenance,Lithia Park is included in the National Register of Historic Places.

ENJOY!

BEAR CREEK GREENWAY   (See map on page 27)

NORTH ASHLAND TO TALENT SECTION: 3.7 MILES.
INTERSTATE HIGHWAY 5, EXIT 19, NORTH ASHLAND.   From this interchange, travel toward Ashland, 0.4 mi. to the junction with Hwy.
99. The path leads north from this point but the PARKING AREA is
reached by turning RIGHT onto Hwy. 99 and going 0.7 mi.to a dirt
road leading RIGHT to the parking area and horse arena. The path
leads 3 mi. north to Newbry Park, immediately west of Interstate
Hwy. 5 Exit 21 off-ramps.

"The Bear Creek Greenway is a corridor stretching 30 miles from
Emigrant Lake to the Rogue River.   When completed, this project
will provide a natural greenbelt through the heart of the most
populated land in Jackson County and will link the cities of
Ashland, Talent, Phoenix, Medford and Central Point by a trail
system.   Eventually, the Greenway will include land along the
Rogue River and Little Butte Creek to connect Eagle Point.   The
Greenway will provide a wide range of close-to-home recreation
opportunities including bicycling, horseback riding, hiking, jog-
ging and picnicking.   The Greenway will protect wildlife habitat
throughout the Bear Creek Basin."   (Quote: Jackson County Parks)

AS OF 1996, a paved path for HIKERS and BIKERS runs about 3.7 mi.
from the north end of Ashland to Suncrest Road in Talent; and in
Medford, a 5.6 mi. section is paved from Barnett Road to Pine St.
in Central Point. Fundraising is underway to extend the path from
South Valley View Road to Nevada Street in Ashland.

11

GRIZZLY PEAK TRAIL

GRIZZLY PEAK. (The peak northeast of Ashland that looms over the city) (See maps 21 and 22)

TRAIL BEGINS:	-BLM Road 38-2E-9.2	ELEV. 5200'
TRAIL ENDS:	-Scenic overlook.	ELEV. 5800'
DISTANCE:	-1.5 miles, Moderately easy. Carry water!	
USE:	-Hikers, horses, mountain bikes.	
SEASON:	-Spring to fall, trail can be very muddy just after the snow has melted.	
BRING MAPS:	-Local BLM information.	

ACCESS: From Interstate Hwy. 5, Ashland-Klamath Falls Exit 14, travel 0.6 miles east on State Hwy. 66 to the junction with Dead Indian Memorial Road.   Turn left (northeast) onto this road and follow mileposts to mile 6.6 at the junction with Shale City Road (BLM Road 38-2E-27). Turn left onto 38-2E-27 and go 2.9 mi. to the junction with BLM Road 38-2E-9.2 Turn left onto 38-2E-9.2 and go 3/4 mile to a 3-way road junction.   Road 38-2E-9.2 continues straight ahead uphill 0.9 miles to a parking area on the left.

FEATURES: The trail begins its 1.5 mile journey through the forest and some meadows, before it reaches a trail junction.   Keep straight ahead, a short distance to the overlook that affords views of Mt. Shasta, Black Butte, Mt. Ashland and of the I-5 freeway making its way over Siskiyou Pass.

Backing up to the above trail junction, work has begun to extend the trail about one mile south along the rim-top to "Grizzly",Elevation 5747'. From this rocky viewpoint, there are good views of Ashland and of the mountains to the south.   A future loop trail back to the trailhead is planned.

The BLM advises that "fire danger is high during late summer, refrain from building fires or smoking".

This is one of the more outstanding trails in southern Oregon. It has been reported that because of the altitude, poison oak, ticks or snakes are not in the area. The trail was envisioned by John Ifft, a retired BLM trail planner. With BLM approval,the work was completed in 1991 by Ifft and his crew of 30-40 volunteers.

PACIFIC CREST TRAIL-GROUSE GAP TO FOREST BOUNDARY.

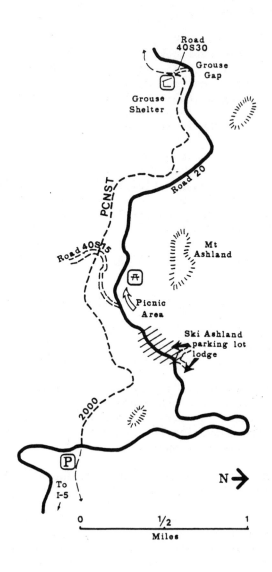

14

PACIFIC CREST NATIONAL SCENIC TRAIL-GROUSE GAP TO FOREST BOUNDARY.
(See map 28)

TRAIL BEGINS:	-Forest Route 20-Grouse Gap.	ELEV. 6400'
TRAIL ENDS:	-Forest Route 20-Forest Boundary.	ELEV. 6200'
DISTANCE:	-3.5 miles (one way), EASY. USE: hikers/horses.	
SEASON:	-June through October.	
BRING MAPS:	-USFS Pacific Crest Trail-Oregon Southern Portion.	
	-USFS Ashland Ranger Dist.-Rogue River Ntl.Forest.	
	-USFS Recreation Opportunity Guide.	

ACCESS   From Ashland Exit 14, drive south on Interstate 5,
             9.0 miles to Mt. Ashland Exit 6.   Turn right and
go 1/4 mi.to Mt. Ashland Access Road (later becoming Forest Route
20). Follow this road 7.2 miles to the NATIONAL FOREST BOUNDARY
SIGN. The Pacific Crest Tr. crosses the road at this point. Look
along the left side of the road for the trail leading to Grouse
Gap. If making a car shuttle, leave one car here and drive to Access #2.

ACCESS # 2
Continue 4 mi. on the same road (from this point posted as Forest
Route 20) to Grouse Gap near milepost 11, at the junction of Road
40S30. The Pacific Crest Trail crosses Road 40S30 at this point,
proceed east along the trail to Access #1.

FEATURES: Beginning at Access #2, the Pacific Crest Trail
                follows along the southern flanks of Mount Ash-
land through a mixed conifer forest, granite rock formations and
small mountain meadows. Mid-summer wildflowers include columbine,
scarlet gilia, Indian paintbrush, mountain gentians and lupine. A
selection of views would include Mt. Shasta, Marble Mountains and
the Trinity Alps. Water from several springs along the trail has
not been tested and may be unsafe to drink.

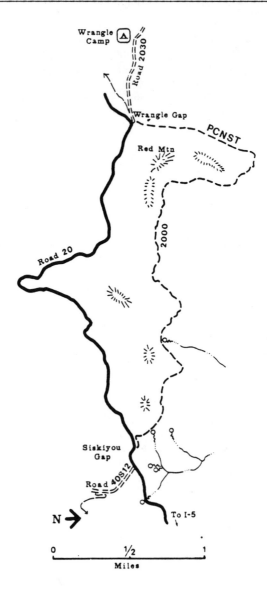

PACIFIC CREST NATIONAL SCENIC TRAIL -WRANGLE GAP TO SISKIYOU GAP.
(See maps 27 and 28)

TRAIL BEGINS:	-Forest Road 20 at Wrangle Gap.	ELEV. 6496'
TRAIL ENDS:	-Forest Road 20 at Siskiyou Gap.	ELEV. 5879'
DISTANCE:	-3.8 miles (one-way)-MODERATE.	
SEASON:	-June through October. USE: hikers/horses.	
BRING MAPS:	-USFS Pacific Crest Trail-Oregon Southern Portion.	
	-USFS Ashland Ranger Dist.-Rogue River Ntl. Forest,	
	-USFS Recreation Opportunity Guide.	

ACCESS #1   From Ashland Exit 14,drive south on Interstate 5,
               9.0 miles to Mt. Ashland Exit 6.   Turn right and
go 1/4 mile to Mt. Ashland Access Road(later becoming Forest Road
20). Follow this road 17 miles (1.0 mile beyond the junction with
Road 22),to where the Pacific Crest Trail crosses Road 20 at Siskiyou Gap. If making a car shuttle, leave one car here and drive
to Access #2.

ACCESS #2   Continue 3.0 miles further on Road 20 to the junction
with Road 2030 at Wrangle Gap.   Park along Road 20 and hike 150'
down Road 2030.   The Pacific Crest Trail leads right (northeast)
to return to Siskiyou Gap (Access #1).

FEATURES: Beginning at Wrangle Gap,the trail contours along
               the flanks of Red Mtn. through a forest of Shasta
red fir and mountain hemlock, and continues to contour the ridge-
line with vistas of Mt. McLoughlin, the Crater Lake Rim, Dutchman
Peak Lookout, Brown Mountain and the rim of Mountain Lakes Wilderness.   The trail contours above Monogram Lakes before beginning its moderate descent to Siskiyou Gap. CARRY WATER,there are
no water sources along the trail.

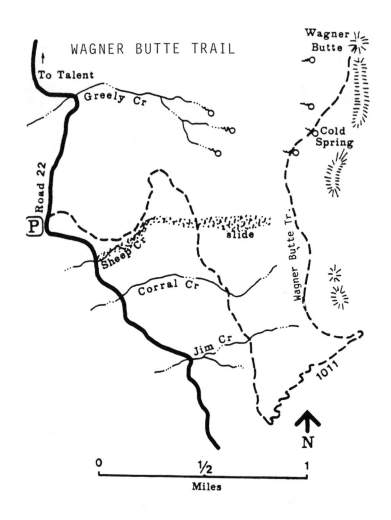

WAGNER BUTTE TRAIL

To Talent

Greely Cr

Road 22

P

Sheep Cr

slide

Corral Cr

Jim Cr

Wagner Butte Tr.

Wagner
Butte

Cold
Spring

1011

N

0	½	1

Miles

WAGNER BUTTE TRAIL #1011.   (Old #972) (Maps 20 and 21)

TRAIL BEGINS:	-Forest Route 22 beyond milepost 10. ELEV. 4960'
TRAIL ENDS:	-Wagner Butte Lookout (former site). ELEV. 7140'
DISTANCE:	-5.2 miles, time up 4 to 5 hours. USE: hiker only.
DIFFICULTY:	-Difficult, steep 15% grade in first .65 mile.
SEASON:	-June through October, wildflowers all summer.
BRING MAPS:	-USFS Ashland Ranger Dist.-Rogue River Ntl. Forest.
	-USFS Recreation Opportunity Guide-Wagner Butte Tr.

ACCESS: From Talent, Oregon, at the intersection of Talent
              Ave. and Main St., travel south on Main Street for
0.4 mile after which Main Street becomes Wagner Creek Road.   Continue south on Wagner Creek Road, which veers left at a junction
beyond milepost 7, and continues 2 miles to a three-way junction.
Keep left onto Forest Road 22 and go 2.0 miles to a large parking
area on the right.   The Wagner Butte Trailhead is on the opposite
(east) side of the road, look for a sign nailed to a tree.

Hike the trail 0.3 mi.to an old road. Turn right and go about 0.6
mile to the northern edge of a meadow.   Look for a "Trail" sign.
It is about 2.3 mi. further to Wagner Glade Gap. Portions of the
trail were hard to follow through hillside meadows or at a large
landslide, but conditions improved after a 1987 trail reconstruction project.   From Wagner Glade Gap, turn left at a sign indicating Wagner Butte 2 miles.   The trail skirts the western slopes
of Wagner Butte and ends at the base of the former Wagner Butte
Lookout site. Find your way to the top by following old blazes or
cairns.

TREES/PLANTS: Noble, white and Douglas-firs, mountain mahogany,
quaking aspen, golden chinquapin, sage, serviceberry, ceanothus,
manzanita and snowbrush.   Wildflowers are abundant.

HISTORY: "WAGNER BUTTE: Named for Jacob Wagner, settler in
               the present area of Talent, Oregon, who later op-
erated the flour mill near the Ashland Plaza." (USFS quote)

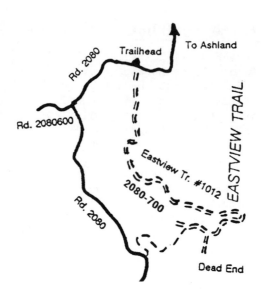

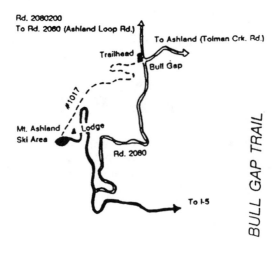

EASTVIEW MOUNTAIN BIKE TRAIL #1012.   (See map 21)

TRAIL BEGINS:	-Lower Trailhead, Road 2080.	ELEV. 4320'
TRAIL ENDS:	-Upper Trailhead, Road 2080.	ELEV. 4720'
DISTANCE:	-2.5 miles.	
USE:	-Mountain bikes, hikers.	
DIFFICULTY:	-More difficult.	
SEASON:	-June thru October.	
BRING MAPS:	-USFS Recreation Opportunity Guide (this trail).	
	-USFS Ashland Ranger Dist.-Rogue River Ntl.Forest.	

ACCESS: From Interstate Hwy 5, Ashland-Klamath Falls Exit
14, travel west on Hwy 66 (Ashland St.) one block
to Tolman Creek Road traffic light. Turn left and follow Tolman
Creek Road 1 mi. before crossing Siskiyou Blvd. Continue up Tolman Creek Road (later becoming Forest Road 2080), 6.5 mi. to the
lower trailhead on the left.   Ample parking is available in the
landing located on the opposite side of Road 2080. Please do not
park in front of the gate at the trailhead on Road 2080700. THE
UPPER TRAILHEAD IS LOCATED 1.5 mile further up Road 2080.

FEATURES: From the lower trailhead on Forest Road 2080 the
first 2.0 miles of Eastview Trail wind up Forest
Road 2080700 (closed to motorized use), with panoramic views of
the upper Bear Creek Valley and Emigrant Lake. At 2.0 miles the
road forks and the route continues to the right another 0.1 mile
before leaving the road. The singletrack trail heads uphill on
the left and meanders another 0.4 miles to meet Road 2080 at the
upper trail terminus. Along the way you'll pass beneath some huge
old sugar pine sentinels.

ROAD 2080 receives a fair amount of vehicle traffic.Bikers should
control their speed when descending this road and be watchful for
oncoming cars or trucks. USFS advises to carry water and a snack
or lunch.
                        -Excerpts USFS Recreation Opportunity Guide.

BULL GAP TRAIL #1017.   (See map 28)

TRAIL BEGINS:	-Mt. Ashland Ski Area.	ELEV. 6620'
TRAIL ENDS:	-Bull Gap, Forest Road 2080.	ELEV. 5520'
DISTANCE:	-2.5 miles.	
USE:	-Mountain bikes, hikers.	
DIFFICULTY:	-More difficult.	
SEASON:	-June thru October.	
BRING MAPS:	-USFS Recreation Opportunity Guide (this trail).	
	-USFS Ashland Ranger Dist.-Rogue River Ntl.Forest.	

ACCESS: From Ashland Exit 14, continue southeast on Inter-
                 state Highway 5, nine miles to Mt. Ashland Exit 6.
This exit leads to the junction with Old Hwy.99 South. Keep right
at this junction and go 0.7 mile to Mt. Ashland Access Road. Turn
onto the Mt. Ashland Access Road and go 7.0 miles to the junction
with Forest Road 2080.

LOWER TRAILHEAD at Bull Gap: Turn right onto Road 2080 and go 3.2
miles to Bull Gap, Trailhead parking with picnic table.
UPPER TRAILHEAD: located near the closed gate at the parking area
between the Mt. Ashland Ski Lodge and the Rental Shop.

FEATURES: Follow the dirt road with blue diamond nordic ski
                 trailblazers, and traverse just below the lodge to
the north. Stay on the road: bikes are prohibited on the ski area
slopes! The blazers leave off when entering the forest just below
the ski area boundary, and the trail is easily followed to Bull
Gap.

CAUTION: The trail is located within the Ashland Watershed,
                 which is the source of the city's water supply. It
is important to give special consideration to its protection. No
camping or campfires allowed. Bicycles must stay on the trail,and
their use is not recommended in rainy weather when soils are wet.
When fire danger is high, the Ashland Watershed may be closed to
all entry but the Bull Gap Trail will remain open.   However,Road
2080200 to the north will be closed; so if you are descending the
15.6 miles to town, use Tolman Creek (2080) Road to the east.(Excerpts USFS Recreation Opportunity Guide).

<u>HOBART BLUFF</u>-Via Pacific Crest National Scenic Trail. (Map 29)

<u>TRAIL BEGINS</u>:-Soda Mountain Road. <u>ELEV.</u> 5300'
<u>TRAIL ENDS</u>: -Hobart Bluff Overlook. <u>ELEV.</u> 5502'
<u>SEASON</u>: -Usually snow-free late May through October. Wild-
flowers abundant May to July.
<u>BRING MAPS</u>: -USFS Pacific Crest Trail-Oregon Southern Portion.
-BLM Transportation Map -Medford District -Klamath
Resource Area.
-BLM Medford District-Pacific Crest Trail Log.
<u>USE</u>: CLOSED TO MOTORIZED/MECHANICAL VEHICLES, INCLUDING
BICYCLES.

<u>ACCESS</u>: From Interstate Hwy. 5, Ashland Exit 14, follow the
mileposts east on State Hwy. 66, 15.7 miles to the
highway summit at Soda Mtn. Road. Turn right onto Soda Mountain
Road and go 4.0 miles to a large meadow on the left, with a parking area and overhead power lines. Look just beyond, along the
road, to where the Pacific Crest Trail leads left, uphill through
the meadow on its 1.0 mile journey to the junction with Hobart
Bluff Viewpoint Trail.

<u>FEATURES</u>: The trail begins with great views of the Greensprings
area and of Mt. Shasta. Wildflowers are plentiful early in the
season. After about 1.0 mile, look left for the junction of the
Hobart Trail leading about 1/2 mile to the viewpoint, where there
are outstanding views of Ashland, Medford and of the Rogue Valley.

To return to the parking area, it will be necessary to take the
trails in the reverse direction.

<u>HISTORY</u>: "State Highway 66.......Known locally as the Green-
springs Highway, this road parallels the 'Old Applegate Trail' which was used during the 1840's by pioneers who
branched off the main Oregon Trail at Fort Hall Idaho and crossed
the sagebrush desert of northern Nevada." (USFS quote)

SISKIYOU CREST MOUNTAIN BIKE ROUTE.   (See maps 27 and 28)

ROUTE BEGINS:	–Mt. Ashland Ski Area Parking Lot.	**ELEV.** 6600'
DISTANCE:	–15 miles (one way).	**HIGH POINT ELEV.** 7418'
USE:	–Mountain bikes.	
DIFFICULTY:	–Moderate (Rd 20) to More Difficult (Rd 800).	
SEASON:	–July thru October.	
BRING MAPS:	–USFS Recreation Opportunity Guide (this route).	
	–USFS Ashland Ranger Dist.–Rogue River Ntl.Forest.	

ACCESS: –From Ashland Exit 14, continue 9 mi. south on Interstate Hwy.5 to Mt. Ashland Exit 6.   Follow the signs 0.7 mile to the Mt. Ashland Access Road.   Turn right onto Mt. Ashland Road and continue 9 mi. to Ski Ashland Parking Lot.

FEATURES: Beginning from the Mt. Ashland Ski Area Parking Lot,the route follows Forest Road 20 for 14 miles along the crest of the Siskiyou Mountains to Jackson Gap. From the Gap, Road 800 ascends on the right 1.5 miles to the summit of Dutchman Peak. Road 20 is a decomposed granite surface, is maintained each year but may be rutted or rockfall in places.   Road 800 to Dutchman Peak is more primitive, and requires some technical ability.

ALONG THE WAY: There is a picnic area and campground 1/2 mi. from the ski area parking lot. Another 1/2 mi. further out is Road 300 to the right, affording a side trip to the summit of Mt. Ashland (Elev. 7533'). Back on Road 20 again at about the 2 mi. point, a short road to the left leads to Grouse Gap Shelter. About 11 mi. out is Wrangle Gap; here Road 2030 goes downhill to the right 1/2 mi. to Wrangle Camp,a good lunch spot with picnic tables, shelter and vault toilet. At the top of Dutchman Peak is one of the very few "cupola style"fire lookouts left in the Pacific Northwest.The lookout was built in 1927.A brochure entitled "The Siskiyou Loop" is available at the Ashland Ranger Station for $1.00. Designed as as an auto tour guide, bikers will find it useful and very interesting.

Please note that the Pacific Crest Trail, which parallels Forest Road 20 most of the route,is closed to bicycles. Bicycles are not allowed on the ski slopes at Mt. Ashland. (Excerpts USFS Recreational Guide).

24

PILOT ROCK CLIMB -From Pacific Crest National Scenic Trail.
(See map 29)

SEASON: -Usually snow-free June through October.

BRING MAPS: -USFS Pacific Crest Trail-Oregon Southern Portion.
                  -BLM Transportation Map -Medford District, Klamath Resource Area.
                  -BLM Medford District-Pacific Crest Trail Log.

CLIMB BEGINS: -Pacific Crest Trail below Pilot Rock. ELEV. 5120'

CLIMB ENDS: -Pilot Rock summit.   ELEV. 5910'

TIME UP: -Approx. 1 hour.

DIFFICULTY: -Easy route through west gully. Careful selection of hand and footholds required in two places in the middle of the route. Hard hats are suggested in case of falling rock from above. CARRY WATER!

ACCESS: From Ashland Exit 14, travel southeast on Interstate Hwy. 5, 9 miles to Mt. Ashland Exit 6. The off-ramp leads to a junction with Old Highway 99S. Keep right at this junction, and continue under the freeway overpass, and go a total of 1.9 miles to Pilot Rock Road 40-2E-33, just beyond the crest of Old Highway 99S. Turn left onto Pilot Rock Road and at:

Mile 2.0 -Turn right onto Road 41-2E-3.

Mile 2.7 -Keep right at an unsigned road junction.

Mile 2.9 -Ridge crest, the Pacific Crest Trail crosses the road, look for trail signs on trees. It is best to park here and hike about 900' east on the Pacific Crest Trail, then follow the uphill road track on the right that leads steeply to the base of Pilot Rock. After reaching the end of the old road,follow the route on the left leading to the mouth of an obvious gully rising to the summit.

After climbing two 6 foot ledges, it is safest to stay along the left wall of the gully for best footing. Several persons have been seriously injured by slipping from the exposed slopes on the right. Views from the summit include just about all of southern Oregon and northern California!

CHAPTER 2 - MEDFORD AREA

BEAR CREEK GREENWAY

MEDFORD TO CENTRAL POINT SECTION: 5.6 MILES.
INTERSTATE HIGHWAY 5, EXIT 27, BARNETT ROAD, SOUTH MEDFORD.   The
bike path begins from the north side of Barnett Road, less than
0.1 mile east of the freeway interchange, continues through Bear
Creek, Hawthorne and Railroad Parks (all with restrooms), before
terminating at Pine St. in Central Point, immediately east of the
INTERSTATE HWY. 5 northbound off-ramp.   From the northbound off-
ramp, turn RIGHT and look immediately for the access road leading
left to Jackson County Expo Park.The path/parking is on the right
JUST AFTER TURNING ONTO THIS ACCESS ROAD.

"The Bear Creek Greenway is a corridor stretching 30 miles from
Emigrant Lake to the Rogue River.   When completed, this project
will provide a natural greenbelt through the heart of the most
populated land in Jackson County and will link the cities of
Ashland, Talent, Phoenix, Medford and Central Point by a trail
system.   Eventually, the Greenway will include land along the
Rogue River and Little Butte Creek to connect Eagle Point.   The
Greenway will provide a wide range of close-to-home recreation
opportunities including bicycling, horseback riding, hiking, jog-
ging and picnicking.   The Greenway will protect wildlife habitat
throughout the Bear Creek Basin."   (Quote: Jackson County Parks)

AS OF 1996, a paved path for HIKERS and BIKERS runs about 3.7 mi.
from the north end of Ashland to Suncrest Road in Talent; and in
Medford, a 5.6 mi. section is paved from Barnett Road to Pine St.
in Central Point. Fundraising is underway to extend the path from
South Valley View Road to Nevada Street in Ashland.

BEAR CREEK GREENWAY

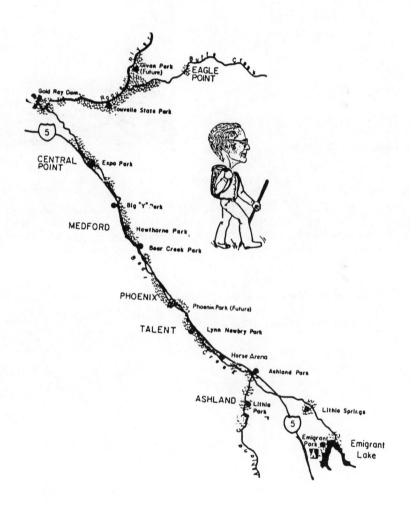

ROXY ANN TRAILS

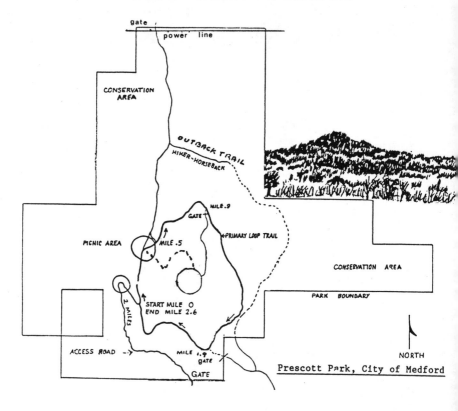

gate
power line

CONSERVATION AREA

OUTBACK TRAIL
HIKER-HORSEBACK

MILE .9
GATE
←PRIMARY LOOP TRAIL

PICNIC AREA
MILE .5

2 MILES

START MILE O
END MILE 2.6

CONSERVATION AREA

PARK BOUNDARY

ACCESS ROAD →

MILE 1.9
GATE

GATE

NORTH

Prescott Park, City of Medford

28

ROXY ANN PEAK HIKING TRAILS-Prescott Park). (Map 13)

SEASON: -Open all year for hikers, mountain bikers, eques-
                 trians. Wildflowers are at their best late spring/
                 early summer, but watch for poison oak or an occa-
                 sional rattlesnake.

BRING MAPS: -See next page.For more information, contact Medford
                 Parks and Recreation Department, Medford City Hall.

ACCESS: From Interstate Highway 5, South Medford Exit 27
                 (Barnett Road), travel east on Barnett Road 1.1 mi.
to the junction with Black Oak Drive.   Turn left onto Black Oak
Drive and continue 1 mile to the intersection of Hillcrest Road.
Turn right onto Hillcrest Road and go 3 1/4 miles to the junction
with Roxy Ann Access Road.   (This point is 0.7 mile beyond milepost 3 on Hillcrest Road.) Turn left onto the access road and go
0.5 mile to a road gate that may be closed, limiting traffic for
EMERGENCY VEHICLES ONLY. PARK SO AS NOT TO OBSTRUCT THE GATE.

FEATURES: Travel 2 miles on the Roxy Ann Access Road from the
                 bottom gate to the PRIMARY LOOP TRAIL. Turn left
                 (clockwise) to the Loop Trail mileage points:
Mile 0.5   Roxy Ann Picnic Area. Just beyond to the left of
                 the loop road is a road track leading north to the
                 OUTBACK TRAIL (for hikers or horses), or further
                 north to the park boundary.
Mile 0.9   -Private Road on right, locked gate.
Mile 1.9   -Keep right at a road junction and gravel pile.
Mile 2.4   -Madrone Ledge Picnic Area.
Mile 2.6   -Back to the beginning of the Primary Loop Trail.
                 The access road leads downhill to the left.

Activities also include nature education, historic site restora-
tion and wildlife protection. The area is closed to hunting, dis-
charge of firearms, livestock grazing and camping. The picnic
area and many of the trails were built by the Civilian Conservation Corps in the 1930s,and more recently by the "Lutheran Evergreens" of Medford.

29

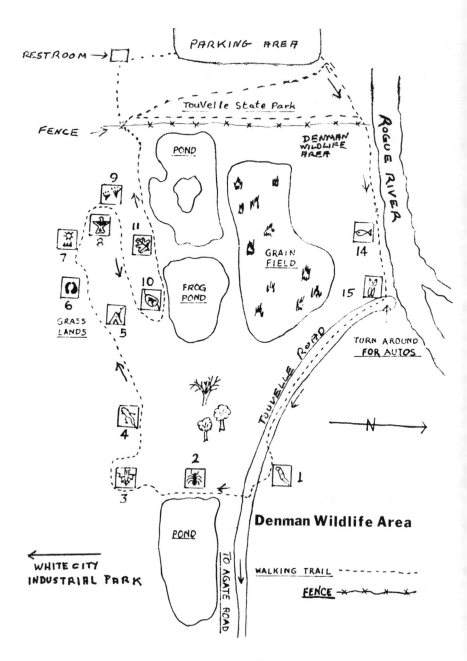

RESTROOM →

PARKING AREA

FENCE →

TouVelle State Park

DENMAN WILDLIFE AREA

Rogue River

POND

9

11

7

8

6

GRASS LANDS

5

10

FROG POND

GRAIN FIELD

14

15

TURN AROUND FOR AUTOS

TouVelle Road

4

N →

2

1

3

Denman Wildlife Area

POND

TO AGATE ROAD

WHITE CITY INDUSTRIAL PARK

WALKING TRAIL -------

FENCE ×—×—×—×

30

TOUVELLE STATE PARK DAY USE AREA and DENMAN WILDLIFE AREA. Map 13
(DAY USE FEES APPLY AT TOUVELLE STATE PARK).

TRAILS BEGIN: -Touvelle State Park.   ELEV.1222'
SEASON: -Open all year. Hunting is conducted during the
              fall and early winter season in the Denman Wild-
              life Area, check schedules.
REFERENCE: -Denman Interpretive Trail Guide.

ACCESS: From Interstate Highway 5, Central Point Exit 32,
              travel east one mile to the traffic light on
Table Rock Road. Turn left (north) onto Table Rock Road and follow mileposts to mile 6.5 to the entrance of TOUVELLE STATE PARK.
Turn right to enter the park and continue to the parking area   at
the end of the road.

FROM THE PARKING AREA THERE ARE TWO GOOD HIKING CHOICES:
(1) 1.5 MILE LOOP HIKE THROUGH THE DENMAN WILDLIFE AREA.
Commence upstream along the banks of the Rogue River a short distance to the fenced boundary of the DENMAN WILDLIFE AREA and hike
along the river to Touvelle Road. Turn right and follow the road
0.3 mi.just before reaching a pond. A low metal sign on the right
indicates the beginning of the Denman Interpretive Trail leading
back to Touvelle State Park. This trail begins along the edge of
a large pond before climbing to a grassy plateau that offers open
views. It then drops to skirt the edges of two more ponds before
reaching the State Park fenced boundary and beyond to the parking
area. See the map and list of interpretive stations on the following pages.

(2)The 1.5 mile loop hike could be broken down into two meaning-
ful hikes that would not involve Touvelle Road: Hiking upstream
along the Rogue River banks to Touvelle Road and return, OR begin
near the parking area restrooms, and hike east to a kiosk at the
fenced boundary of the Denman Wildlife Area. Bark chips mark the
route passing two ponds, climbing a grassy plateau, before dropping to Touvelle Road.

Although this trail is partially covered with bark chips, it may be obscure in a few places. It is advisable to stay on the trail to prevent contacting poison oak and destroying the vegetation.BE AWARE THAT HUNTING IS CONDUCTED IN THE DENMAN WILDLIFE AREA DURING THE FALL AND EARLY WINTER MONTHS for deer, pheasant,quail and water fowl. Otherwise, no firearms are permitted in the area.

FEATURES: 15 interpretive stations are located along the trail and are marked by posts with carved symbols resembling Indian petrographs. They number from Touvelle Road in the clockwise direction:

1. "Earthworm"   (The Agate Desert Soil)
2. "Spider"   (Woodrat Nest)
3. "The Bat"   (Artificial Wildlife Nest Boxes)
4. "Lizard"   (Wedgeleaf Habitat)
5. "Dwelling"   (Urban Valley Development)
6. "Deer Track"   (Rogue Valley Geology)
7. "Grasslands"   (Grassland Habitat)
8. "The Bird"   (Woodpecker Tree)
9. "Rodent Track"(Ground Burrows)
10. "Frog Pond"   (The Pond)
11. "Oak Tree"   (Oak Trees)
12. "Waterfowl"   (Farming For Wildlife)
13. "Bird Tracks" (The Blackberry Habitat)
14. "The Fish"   (The Rogue River Habitat)
15. "The Owl"   (Vandalism and Litter)

HISTORY: The Denman Interpretive Trail, located on the Kenneth Denman Wildlife Management Area, is under the control and management for enhancement of wildlife habitat by the Oregon Department of Fish and Wildlife. Except for 160 acres surrounding the management area's office and shop structure, the 1760 acres came under the General Services Administration control after Camp White Military Reservation was disbanded following World War Two.

Credit has been given to John Ifft, U.S. Bureau of Land Management, for initial trail concept and station post materials. The BLM's Young Adult Conservation Corps crew constructed the trail with coordinating/planning by Oregon Dept. Fish and Wildlife.

Respect the rights of private property owners!

Table Rocks Location Map

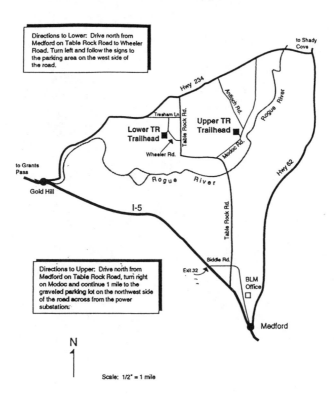

Directions to Lower: Drive north from Medford on Table Rock Road to Wheeler Road. Turn left and follow the signs to the parking area on the west side of the road.

to Shady Cove

Hwy 234

Antioch Rd.

Rogue River

Tresham Ln.

Table Rock Rd.

Lower TR Trailhead

Upper TR Trailhead

Wheeler Rd.

Modoc Rd.

Hwy 62

to Grants Pass

Rogue River

Gold Hill

I-5

Table Rock Rd.

Biddle Rd.

Directions to Upper: Drive north from Medford on Table Rock Road, turn right on Modoc and continue 1 mile to the graveled parking lot on the northwest side of the road across from the power substation.

Exit 32

BLM Office

Medford

N

Scale: 1/2" = 1 mile

34

UPPER TABLE ROCK. (See map 13)

TRAIL BEGINS:	-Modoc Road between mileposts 1 and 2.	ELEV.1294'
TRAIL ENDS:	-Top of Upper Table Rock.	ELEV.2036'
DISTANCE:	-1.25 mi., moderate, hiker only, day use only.	
SEASON:	-All year. High use in spring/limited parking. Low off-season use. Toilet facilities April and May only.	
BROCHURE/MAP:	-U.S. Bureau of Land Management -Recreation Opportunity Guide. Brochure available.	

ACCESS: From Interstate Highway 5, Central Point Exit 32, travel east one mile to the traffic light on Table Rock Road. Turn left (north) onto Table Rock Road and follow mileposts to mile 7.5 at the junction with Modoc Road. Turn right (northeast) onto Modoc Road and go 1.5 mile to the parking area on the left side of the road.

FEATURES: Scenic panorama of the Rogue Valley. Many species of flowers blooming Feb. through May. Unique geologic origin and features. Vernal pools with pacific tree frogs.
HAZARDS: Abundant poison oak, ticks, rattlesnakes, high cliffs.

BLM ADVICE: "No potable water. Please do not pick the wildflowers. Stay on the main trails and out of the sensitive vernal pools". DOGS NOT ALLOWED.

HISTORICAL: Long ago volcanic lava covered the Rogue Valley. Millions of years have eroded most of the lava and much of the underlying sandstone sediment leaving Upper and Lower Table Rocks........Table Rock was once a sanctuary and symbol for the Rogue River Indians; a site for many important meetings. In the early 1850's, settlers and gold prospectors invaded the valley. The Table Rocks afforded the Indians choice places for hiding, ambush, attack, and Indian councils during the years of resistance and war that followed.   The trail was built in 1981 by the Young Adult Conservation Corps.

NOTE: UPPER TABLE ROCK is designated an Outstanding Natural Area. This designation is more oriented toward public use than is Lower Table Rock.

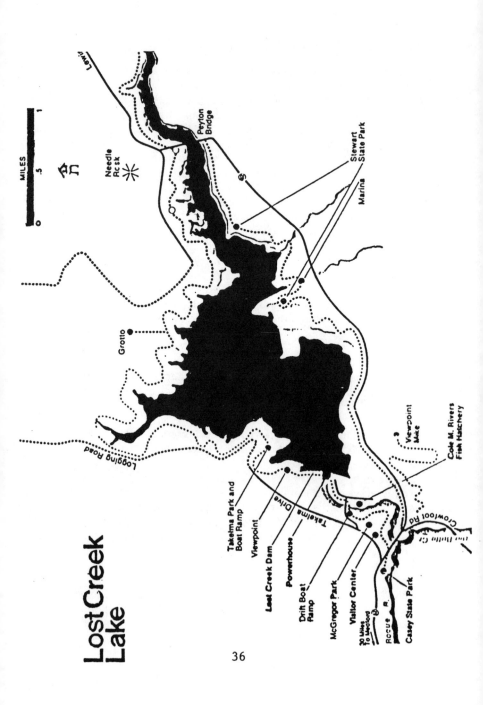

36

CHAPTER 3 - LOST CREEK LAKE AREA

LOST CREEK LAKE-NORTH SHORE TRAIL.   (See map 9)

TRAIL BEGINS:	-Casey State Park, State Highway 62. ELEV. 1538'
TRAIL ENDS:	-Boundary of U.S. Army Corps of Engineers land, 4.5 miles northeast of Peyton Bridge Trailhead.
DISTANCE:	-16.5 miles with access points. Easy grades.
SEASON:	-Open all year.
USE:	-HIKERS on all trails. MOUNTAIN BIKES on all trails except on Stewart Park hiker only trails.
BRING MAPS:	-LOST CREEK LAKE HIKING TRAILS -U.S. Army Corps of Engineers. -See also local road and forest maps.
ACCESS:	From Medford, Oregon, travel north and east on Highway 62 to milepost 29 at Casey State Park.
DESCRIPTION:	Condensed from "LOST CREEK LAKE HIKING TRAILS" brochure, U.S. Army Corps of Engineers.

From the east end of Casey State Park, follow the paved trail to the first junction. North shore hikers should take the right fork and pass under McLeod Bridge. The trail follows the river to McGregor Park and the Visitor Center. Hike through McGregor Park on to the Hatchery/Powerhouse Road and follow painted "paw prints" on the pavement, then cross the fish diversion dam for a possible visit at Cole M. Rivers Fish Hatchery.

The trail begins again in an open field north of the hatchery and then passes through River's Edge Park to the powerhouse. Pass between the two buildings and follow painted "paw prints" to the trail at the base of the dam. The trail then climbs gradually to the top of the dam. Please stay on the developed trail, as this area has restricted access. Follow the painted "paw prints" to Takelma Park. The trail continues 4.3 miles further to where a long arm of the lake reaches the inlet of Lost Creek. (There are two "Lost Creeks" on the lake; the other one is on the south shore.)

From Lost Creek, the trail leads south, then east 3.5 miles to a short spur trail leading to the Grotto, where rock cliffs form the walls of a small canyon. Following heavy rains, a waterfall may be spotted cascading down the far wall. 2.3 miles further along the lakeshore, the trail comes out at the Lewis Road Trailhead and follows the road east for one mile to the Peyton Bridge Trailhead.

Follow the trail under Peyton Bridge to where it enters the Rogue River Gorge. A rest area at the boundary of Corps of Engineers land marks the end of Lost Creek Lake North Shore Trail.

FOR SHORTER HIKES: From Highway 62, the North Shore Trail can be accessed by driving on TAKELMA DRIVE to the following points:

Mile 0.3   -McGregor Park and Visitor Center.
Mile 0.6   -Cole M. Rivers Fish Hatchery.
Mile 2.0   -Lost Creek Dam Viewpoint.
Mile 2.3   -Takelma Park, pavement ends, becoming Road 33-1E-27.
Mile 3.6   -Junction Road 33-1E-23, turn right for trail access.
Mile 5.0   -Rogue River Trail sign on right side of 33-1E-27.
Mile 5.8   -Lost Creek Trailhead, a parking area is on the right.

PEYTON BRIDGE TRAILHEAD is located on Highway 62 near milepost 36 at the north end of Peyton Bridge and the junction of Lewis Road. LEWIS ROAD TRAILHEAD is 1 mile west of Peyton Bridge Trailhead.

NOTES: CARRY DRINKING WATER on long hikes or in warm weather. Camping is permitted only at designated campsites. Check local fire conditions with the Oregon State Dept.of Forestry in Central Point. Phone (541) 664-3328.

LOST CREEK LAKE-SOUTH SHORE TRAIL.   (See map 9)

TRAIL BEGINS:	-Casey State Park, State Hwy. 62.	ELEV. 1538'
TRAIL ENDS:	-Peyton Bridge.	ELEV. 2000'
DISTANCE:	-6.3 miles, gentle grades.	
SEASON:	-Open all year.	
USE:	-HIKERS on all trails. MOUNTAIN BIKES on all trails except Stewart Park hiker only trails.	
BRING MAPS:	-LOST CREEK LAKE HIKING TRAILS -U.S. Army Corps of Engineers. -See also local road or forest maps.	
ACCESS:	From Medford, Oregon, travel north and east on State Hwy. 62 to milepost 29 (Casey State Park).	
DESCRIPTION:	Condensed from "LOST CREEK LAKE HIKING TRAILS" brochure, U.S. Army Corps of Engineers.	

From Casey State Park, follow the paved trail to the first junction.   Take the LEFT fork, cross McLeod Bridge, then turn right to where the trail drops down and passes back under the bridge. Here the trail merges with a gravel road and follows the river. The trail resumes from the end of the road, and after 0.5 mi. ascends to a point above the dam's spillway gates. Further on is a junction with a trail cutting downhill to the left.   This trail leads to the spillway gates and service road on top of the dam. (You may hike the 0.8 mi. length of the dam to reach the intake tower or North Shore Trail.)

The South Shore Trail drops down and remains near the lake's high waterline, and around the bend is a small waterfall where Rumley Creek tumbles to the lake.   In another 2.4 miles the trail enters Stewart State Park day use area. To stay on the South Shore Trail, keep to the three-foot wide trail through the park. Pass the swimming beach and picnic area, then cross the inlet of Lost Creek. There are two "Lost Creeks" draining into the lake; the other one is on the north shore.

Cross the pavement at the boat ramp. The trail parallels the lake shore and crosses Floras Creek. At the junction beyond the creek, the main trail bears to the left; a spur trail to the right leads to Stewart State Park Campground.

The trail passes between the lake shore and the edge of the campground. Where it joins the bike path, hikers should bear to the left and cross Taggarts Creek. The South Shore Trail ends at Peyton Bridge. Hiking across the bridge (0.3 mi.) brings you to the North Shore Trail at Peyton Bridge Trailhead.

For shorter hikes, the South Shore Trail can be accessed by driving to Stewart State Park, either at the picnic area or at the campground. Carry drinking water on long hikes or in warm weather

VIEWPOINT MIKE- LOST CREEK LAKE. (See map 9)

TRAIL BEGINS:	-Big Butte Park, Crowfoot Road.	ELEV. 1550'
TRAIL ENDS:	-Viewpoint Mike.	ELEV. 2550'
DISTANCE:	-2.5 miles, moderate grades.	
SEASON:	Open all year.	
USE:	Hiker, horse, mountain bikes. Motor vehicles not allowed.	
BRING MAPS:	-LOST CREEK LAKE HIKING TRAILS -U.S. Army Corps of Engineers brochure. -See also local road and forest maps.	

ACCESS: From Medford, Oregon, travel north and east on
               State Highway 62 to milepost 29 at Casey State
Park. Continue 0.2 mi. on 62, crossing McLeod Bridge, to Crowfoot Road. Turn right onto Crowfoot Road, and go 0.2 mi. to Big
Butte Park. The Viewpoint Mike Trailhead is directly across the
road.

DESCRIPTION: Condensed from "LOST CREEK LAKE HIKING TRAILS"
               brochure, U.S. Army Corps of Engineers.

The trail to Viewpoint Mike begins across the road from Big Butte
Park and climbs for 2.5 miles to a point overlooking the entire
Lost Creek Lake area. The trail begins with switchbacks through
an oak woodland. It gains elevation above Hwy. 62, providing an
excellent view of the river and fish hatchery below. The trail
ends at the viewpoint where you can rest and enjoy the view.

The panorama from this height includes views of the lake, the dam
and intake tower. Massive Flounce Rock, weathered by the ages to
a reddish color, rises above the north shore of the lake. Toward
the northeast, you can see the rim of Crater Lake. CARRY DRINKING
WATER as none is available along the trail.

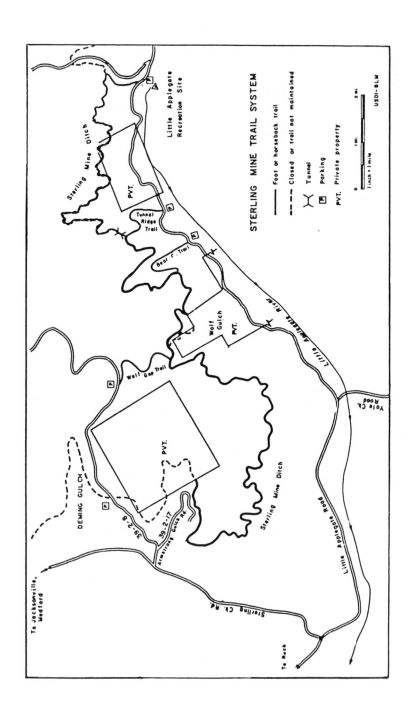

STERLING MINE TRAIL SYSTEM

— Foot or horseback trail

— — — Closed or trail not maintained

⋊ Tunnel

🅿 Parking

PVT. Private property

0   1 mi.   2 mi.

1 inch = 1 mile

USDI-BLM

Little Applegate Recreation Site

Sterling Mine Ditch

PVT.

Tunnel Ridge Trail

Bear C. Trail

Wolf Gulch PVT.

Wolf Gap Trail

Little Applegate River

Yale Cr. Road

PVT.

DEMING GULCH

39-2-17

39-2-17

Armstrong Gulch Rd.

Sterling Mine Ditch

Little Applegate Road

To Jacksonville, Medford

Sterling Ck. Rd.

To Ruch

42

CHAPTER 4 - JACKSONVILLE/RUCH AREA

STERLING MINE TRAIL SYSTEM.

"The Sterling Mine Ditch, about 20.0 miles long and 3 feet deep, was started and completed in 1877 by nearly 400 workers, many of them being Chinese laborers. The ditch carried water from Little Applegate River to operate hydraulic jets for the Sterling Mine Company at the town of Sterlingville. The ditch continued to be used for gold mining through the 1930's." (BLM quote)

THE LITTLE APPLEGATE RIVER was once known by local settlers as Applegate Creek. The name was officially changed to the present form after the year 1900, in order to avoid confusion with the Applegate Creek of the South Umpqua River. (USFS information)

A trail system follows the route of the ditch, and the U.S. Bureau of Land Management advises to "Carry drinking water at all times of the year, please observe Oregon Department of Forestry fire regulations (telephone 664-3328) and respect property rights on adjoining private lands." The lower 2 mi. of trail below Deming Gulch are not open for public use.

See the text on the following pages for trailheads that provide access to the ditch:
1. Little Applegate Trailhead, Little Applegate Road.
2. Deming Gulch Trailhead, Deming Gulch Road.
3. Tunnel Ridge Trailhead, Little Applegate Road.
4. Bear Gulch Trailhead, Little Applegate Road.
5. Wolf Gap Trailhead-TEMPORARILY ABANDONED, no reconstruction date given.

SEASON: —All year. Ideal during late winter or early spring
             before poison oak leafs out. It is hard to avoid.
USE: —Hiker/horse, mountain bikes, no motorized vehicles.
             —Moderate grades.
BRING MAPS: —BLM brochure and map STERLING MINE TRAIL SYSTEM.
             —BLM Medford District Transportation Map, Jackson-
             ville Resource Area.
             —(This area is not on National Forest land, but is
             shown on USFS Rogue River National Forest maps.)

DEMING GULCH-STERLING MINE DITCH ACCESS. (See maps 19 & 20)

ROUTE BEGINS: -Road 39-2-8 (at Deming Gulch).
DISTANCE: -About 16 miles to Little Applegate Trail.
USE: -Hiker/horse/mountain bike. WATCH FOR POISON OAK.

ACCESS: From Jacksonville, travel southwest on Hwy. 238,
                 2.9 miles and turn left on Cady Road.   Continue
1/2 mile on Cady Road to the junction with Sterling Creek Road.
Turn right onto Sterling Creek Road and go 8.7 miles to Armstrong
Gulch Road 39-2-17.   Turn left onto Armstrong Gulch Road and go
0.3 mi. to the junction with Road 39-2-8 on the left. Take 39-2-8
0.6 miles, and look closely along the RIGHT side of the road for
the Sterling Mine Ditch. There may be no signs.

FEATURES: Estimated distances along the ditch as it heads
                 southwest from Road 39-2-8 are:
Milepoint
   1.5   -Ditch crosses Armstrong Gulch Road. 39-2-17.

   8.0   -WOLF GAP TRAIL leading uphill left to Wolf Gap.
                 TEMPORARILY ABANDONED.

   9.0   BEAR GULCH TRAIL leads right 1 mile to Little
                 Applegate Road.

  11.0   TUNNEL RIDGE TRAIL leads right 1 mile to Little
                 Applegate Road.

  16.0   LITTLE APPLEGATE TRAIL leads right, one mile to
                 Little Applegate Road.

Poison oak is found along
trails up to about 5000
ft. altitude.

BEAR GULCH TRAIL, Sterling Mine Ditch.   (See map 19 and 20)

TRAIL BEGINS: -Little Applegate Road.
TRAIL ENDS: -Sterling Mine Ditch.
DISTANCE: -1 mile, moderately uphill.
                  USE: hiker/horse/mountain bikes.   WATCH FOR
                  POISON OAK.

ACCESS: From the town of Ruch, Oregon, travel 2.8 miles
                  south on Upper Applegate Road to the junction of
Little Applegate Road. Turn left on Little Applegate Road and go
9.1 miles to a parking area on the left at Bear Gulch Trailhead.
It is about 1 mile from the trailhead to Sterling Mine Ditch.

FEATURES: After reaching the ditch, two options are avail-
                  able; (1). By TURNING RIGHT, a loop trip is pos-
sible by going about 2.0 miles to the Tunnel Ridge Trail leading
1.0 mile to Little Applegate Road. At the road, turn right (west)
and go 0.6 mile back to the starting point at Bear Gulch Trailhead. The total loop distance is 5 miles and requires 3 to 4 hrs.

(2). TURNING LEFT from the Bear Gulch Trail,it is about 1.0 mile
along the ditch to the Wolf Gap Trail (TEMPORARILY ABANDONED) and
about 8 miles further to the Deming Gulch Trailhead on Rd. 39-2-8.

45

TUNNEL RIDGE TRAILHEAD, Sterling Mine Ditch. (See map 19 and 20)

TRAIL BEGINS: —Little Applegate Road.
TRAIL ENDS: —Sterling Mine Ditch.
DISTANCE: —1 mile. Moderate uphill grades.
USE: hiker/horse/mountain bike.
WATCH FOR POISON OAK.

ACCESS: From Ruch, Oregon, take the Upper Applegate Road 2.8 miles to Little Applegate Road. Follow this road 9.8 miles to a parking area on the right, at a former picnic ground. The Tunnel Ridge Trailhead is directly across the road.

FEATURES: The trail continues to the ridge, providing many interesting views. Where the trail reaches the ditch, there is a tunnel dug by Chinese laborers to divert water through the hillside. A loop trip is possible by turning left (west) along the ditch, nearly 2.0 miles to the Bear Gulch Trail, and following it about 1.0 mile to Little Applegate Road. Turn left (east) and follow the road 0.6 mile back to the Tunnel Ridge parking area.

Another loop trip is possible by TURNING RIGHT at the tunnel and traveling about 5 miles east to the Little Applegate Trailhead. A portion of this trail climbs high above the ditch to avoid private property and later rejoins and follows the ditch to a signed junction of a trail leading 1.0 mi.to the Little Applegate Trailhead on Little Applegate Road. Turn right (west) along the road and go about 1.7 miles back to the Tunnel Ridge Trailhead.

Not very often do you see
these things but when you
do just give them room
and they will move out of
your way.

46

<u>LITTLE APPLEGATE TRAILHEAD</u>, Sterling Mine Ditch. (See map 19,20)

<u>TRAIL BEGINS:</u>   -Little Applegate Road.
<u>TRAIL ENDS:</u>   -Sterling Mine Ditch.
<u>DISTANCE:</u>   -1.0 mile, gentle uphill grade.
                 <u>USE:</u> hiker/horse/mountain bike.

<u>ACCESS:</u>   From the town of Ruch, Oregon, go 2.8 miles south
                on the Upper Applegate Road to the junction with
Little Applegate Road.   Turn onto Little Applegate Road and follow the mileposts to mile 11.6, at the Little Applegate Trailhead
on the left side of the road.   Parking is available at the Little
Applegate Picnic Ground, about 100 yards further.

<u>FEATURES:</u>   This is the eastern-most BLM public access to the
                Sterling Mine Ditch.   It is about 1.0 mile to the
ditch.   To reach Tunnel Ridge, TURN LEFT (WEST) at the ditch and
go about 5.0 miles.   A portion of the trail rises above the ditch
to avoid private property.

A loop trip is possible by taking the Tunnel Ridge Trail one mile
down to Little Applegate Road.   Turn left (east) on this road and
go 1.7 miles back to Little Applegate Trailhead.

              A left-over from the old days.
              A gold seeker's "SLUICE BOX".

47

GIN LIN TRAIL #917. (See map 19)

TRAIL BEGINS: -Flumet Flat Campground.   ELEV. 1700'
TRAIL ENDS: -Flumet Flat Campground.
DISTANCE: -3/4 mile interpretive loop trail. Easy, hikers
              only. Trail open all year.

REFERENCES: USFS interpretive brochure "Gin Lin Trail."
              USFS "Rogue River National Forest" map. Both
publications available at Star Ranger Station or the USFS Supervisor's Office in Medford.

ACCESS: From the town of Ruch, Oregon, travel south on Up-
              per Applegate Road and follow mileposts to mile
8.6 at the junction with Palmer Creek Road. Turn right onto Palmer Creek Road and continue 0.8 mile just beyond the entrance to
Flumet Flat Campground. Turn right to the parking area and trailhead.

FEATURES   The Gin Lin Trail has 14 numbered "stations" that
              are keyed to the information and diagrams of the
brochure, available at the Star Ranger Station or the USFS Supervisor's Office in Medford. You will see evidence of mining ditches, dug more than 100 years ago by Chinese laborers, to divert
water from Palmer Creek to a mining site where hydraulic pressure
was used to loosen gravel and cobbles from nearby slopes. Sluice
boxes were used to separate the materials washed down from the
hillside, with the resulting collection of gold dust and mine
tailings. WATCH FOR POISON OAK or an occasional rattlesnake.

HISTORICAL   Gin Lin was a Chinese mining boss who purchased min-
                ing claims   along   Palmer   Creek in 1881 after being
successful in other local mining operations.   More than a million
dollars worth of gold dust   were deposited by him in the Jacksonville Bank.   The actual fate of Gin Lin is uncertain.
(Condensed from USFS interpretive brochure)

GIN LIN TRAIL

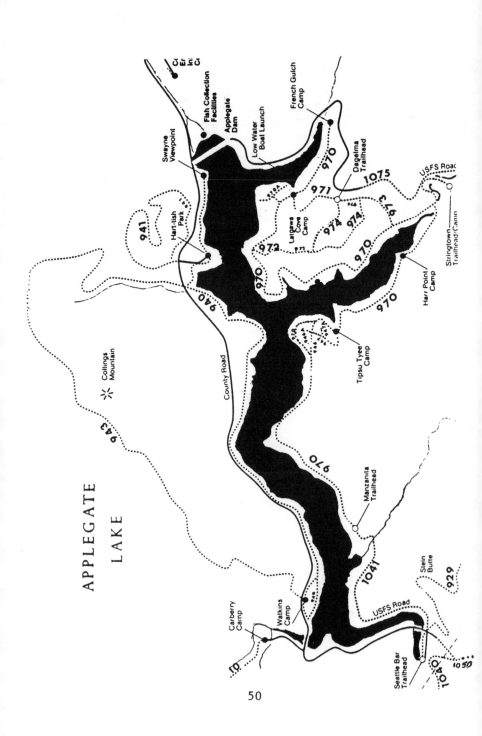

APPLEGATE
LAKE

* Collings Mountain

Fish Collection Facilities

Swayne Viewpoint

Applegate Dam

Low Water Boat Launch

French Gulch Camp

Hart-tish Park

Dagelma Trailhead

1075

USFS Road

941

971

Latgawa Cove Camp

974

974

973

972

970

Stringtown Trailhead/Camp

Harr Point Camp

970

970

970

943

County Road

940

Tipsu Tyee Camp

970

Manzanita Trailhead

1041

Stein Butte

929

Carberry Camp

Watkins Camp

USFS Road

1040

1050

Seattle Bar Trailhead

1040

50

CHAPTER 5 - APPLEGATE AREA   (see map 26)

SEASON: -Open all year.
CAMPS: -ROAD ACCESS: Carberry, French Gulch, Stringtown,
                Watkins. HIKE-IN: Harr Point, Latgawa, Tipsu-
                Tyee. Schedule/facility info at Star Ranger Sta.
MAPS: -AVAILABLE AT STAR RANGER STATION, 6941 Upper
                Applegate Road.
                -U.S. Army Corps of Engineers brochure "APPLEGATE
                LAKE"
                -Applegate Ranger Dist. -Rogue River Ntl. Forest.
                -USFS Recreation Opportunity Guides.
TRAIL USAGE: -HIKERS on all trails. HORSES, Collings Mountain,
                Stein Butte, Dakubettede. MOUNTAIN BIKES on all
                trails. MOTOR BIKES on Stein Butte Trail.

TRAILHEADS:

SWAYNE VIEWPOINT. Near milepost 15, Upper Applegate Road. Drinking water, restrooms, interpretive viewpoint. DAKUBETEDE TRAIL
940 begins here.

HART-TISH PARK. Near milepost 16 on Upper Applegate Road. Check
with Star Ranger Sta. for park schedules/facilities. DAKUBETEDE
TRAIL 940, GROUSE LOOP TRAIL 941, and the north end of COLLINGS
MOUNTAIN TRAIL 943 can be accessed from this park.

WATKINS PICNIC GROUND.   Just beyond milepost 18 on Upper Applegate Road.   Check with Star Ranger Station for park schedules
and facilities. DAKUBETEDE TRAIL 940, and the south end of COL-
LINGS MTN. TRAIL 941 can be accessed here.

SEATTLE BAR.   Beyond milepost 18 on Upper Applegate Road, turn
left at the junction with Carberry Creek Road and continue to
milepost 20 at Seattle Bar.   Check with Star Ranger Station for
schedules/facilities. STEIN BUTTE TRAIL 929 begins here.

MANZANITA: From Seattle Bar Trailhead drive 2 miles north on Manzanita Creek Road. No facilities. PAYETTE TRAIL 970 begins here.

FRENCH GULCH: From Swayne Viewpoint, cross over Applegate Dam on Squaw Creek Road 1075 to the trailhead just beyond milepost 1. Check with the Star Ranger Station for camp schedules/facilities. PAYETTE TRAIL 970 begins here.

DAGELMA: From Swayne Viewpoint, cross over Applegate Dam and continue on Squaw Cr. Road 1075, 2.2 miles to the trailhead parking area on the right. No facilities. CALSH TRAIL 971, SINNS BAR TRAIL 972, OSPREY TRAIL 973 and PROSPECTORS LOOP TRAIL 974 begin here.

STRINGTOWN: From Dagelma Trailhead, continue on Squaw Cr. Road just beyond milepost 3. The trailhead is on the right. This is an access point for the PAYETTE TRAIL. Check with Star Ranger Station for camp schedules/facilities.

HIKING TRAIL DESCRIPTIONS.
Detailed "USFS Recreation Opportunity Guides" are available from Star Ranger Station or from Forest Supervisor's Office in Medford.

DAKUBETEDE TRAIL 940. 4.8 miles, moderately easy. Hiker/horse/ mountain bike. From SWAYNE VIEWPOINT, the trail begins just behind the restrooms and continues southwest along the lakeshore to HART-TISH PARK COPPER BOAT RAMP and ends at WATKINS PICNIC GROUND. CARRY WATER.

An 18 mile mountain bike loop can be made: starting at the Swayne Viewpoint and using the Dakubetede and Payette Trails.

GROUSE LOOP TRAIL 941.
2.8 MILES, moderately easy, ELEV. GAIN 700'. Hiker/mountain bike.
At HART-TISH-PARK, the trailhead is at the upper end of the picnic area. Cross the highway to the trail beginning. The clockwise direction is suggested for ease of travel. There are good
views of Applegate Lake, Elliott Creek Ridge and the Red Buttes
to the south. CARRY WATER.

COLLINGS MOUNTAIN TRAIL 943.
7 mi., difficult, ELEV. GAIN 1040'. Hiker/horse/mountain bike.
The northern end of the trail begins from the upper end of the
Hart-tish Park picnic area. The trail crosses the highway to the
edge of a guardrail then continues 1/2 mile to a miner's cabin,
an inactive "Bigfoot trap", a mine adit and then climbs to the
crest of a ridge. About 2 miles south along the ridge, the trail
passes along the west slopes of Collings Mtn. and then drops down
to Watkins Picnic Ground (the southern end of the trail), passing
through a wildlife foraging area and the site of a 1981 forest
fire burn. A 3 mile hike back to Hart-tish Park can be made via
the Dakubetede Trail 940. CARRY WATER.

The "Bigfoot" trap was installed by a Eugene-based wildlife research organization in 1974 for the unsuccessful efforts in cap-
turing the elusive "Bigfoot." The use of the trap was discontin-
ued in 1976.

STEIN BUTTE TRAIL 929. 5.0 mile plus 2.5 mile on New London Trail
to Road 1050 if you are doing a shuttle arrangement. Difficult,
hiker,horse,mountain and motor bikes. ELEVATION GAIN 2331 feet.
From SEATTLE BAR, the trail climbs up the west end of Elliott Cr.
Ridge, passing a 19th Century water diversion ditch that was used
by the Seattle Mining Company. It then follows an old haul road
past a marble deposit before reaching the top of Elliott Creek
Ridge. The trail then follows the ridge to a point just north of
Stein Butte summit, look for rock cairns and a faint trail on the
right for a side-trip to the summit. A lookout tower existed at
this location between the years 1936 and 1968. ELEVATION 4400'.

After returning to the main trail, proceed 0.5 mile to a saddle just east of Stein Butte at the junction with NEW LONDON TR. #928 and ELLIOTT RIDGE TR. #969.

The New London Trail, formerly a continuation of the Stein Butte Trail, leads 2.6 miles downhill (south), passing two 20th Century mine adits before reaching Elliott Creek Road.

Stein Butte,Elliott Ridge and New London Trails are maintained by Motorcycle Riders Assn.

PAYETTE TRAIL 970.   Easy trail, hikers/mountain bikes.
9.2 MILES.....From FRENCH GULCH TRAILHEAD TO MANZANITA TRAILHEAD. The distance can be shortened by using the Stringtown Trailhead access. Hiker campgrounds are located at Latgawa Cove, Harr Point and at Tipsu Tyee. CARRY WATER.

Latgawa Cove Camp is 0.7 mi. from French Gulch Trailhead. Just beyond, Calsh Trail 971 leads left to the Dagelma Trailhead, and Viewpoint Trail 970A Leads RIGHT to a viewpoint.   Payette Trail 970 follows the lakeshore to the Squaw Creek Arm of the lake and on beyond Tipsu Tyee Campground. Near the mouth of the lake's Squaw Arm, CUTOFF TRAIL 946 is a short-cut to the Payette Trail that ends at Manzanita Trailhead. Midway along the Cutoff Trail, SQUAW POINT TRAIL 946A leads to a viewpoint.

HARR RIDGE TRAIL 947 runs from Tipsu Tyee Campground to the mid-point of the Cutoff Trail. Culy Trail 947A branches off from the Harr Ridge Trail and leads to a viewpoint overlooking Tipsu Tyee Campground and the Squaw Creek Arm of the lake.

OUTDOOR STUDY AREA TRAILS FROM DAGELMA TRAILHEAD. Hiker/mtn. bike.
CALSH TRAIL 971: Leads 0.7mi. to Payette Trail near Latgawa Camp.
SINNS BAR TRAIL 972: 0.8 mi. long, links the Prospectors Loop and
   Payette Trails. (RATED EASY)
OSPREY TRAIL 973: Leads 0.6 mi. to the Payette Trail. (EASY)
PROSPECTORS LOOP TRAIL 974: 1.6 miles long, begins and ends at
   Dagelma Trailhead.

WHERE THE NAMES CAME FROM: Excerpts from USFS Applegate Ranger District Recreation Opportunity Guides.

HART-TISH: Chief Hart-tish was the leader of the Dakubetede Indians that inhabited the Applegate Valley and resisted the influx of miners into their territory following the discovery of gold in southern Oregon.

COPPER VISITOR CENTER: Commemorates the Copper Store built in the 1920's near the mouth of Carberry Creek before construction of the dam. The site of the store is now under water.

COLLINGS MOUNTAIN: Named for two prospectors, the Collings brothers, who mined in the Applegate Dam vicinity.

WATKINS: The name of a prospector who mined near the mouth of Carberry Creek in the 1850's.   A small community post office and schoolhouse were named for Watkins.

SEATTLE BAR: Commmemorates the Seattle Mining Co. (of Washington) which conducted hydraulic mining operations above the confluence of Carberry Creek and Applegate River during the 1890's.

DAKUBETEDE: A band of Indians that lived in the Applegate Valley.

TIPSU TYEE: A bearded Shasta Indian Chief.

STEIN BUTTE: Believed to be named for a prospector who mined in this vicinity during the early gold rush years.

DAGELMA: Named for "Dagelma" or "River Takelma" Indians.

CULY: Named for the family of George and Pamelia Culy, settlers in the mining community of Steamboat in the 1880's.

SINNS BAR: Named for a Chinese prospector who mined the gravel bars along the Applegate River during the early gold rush years.

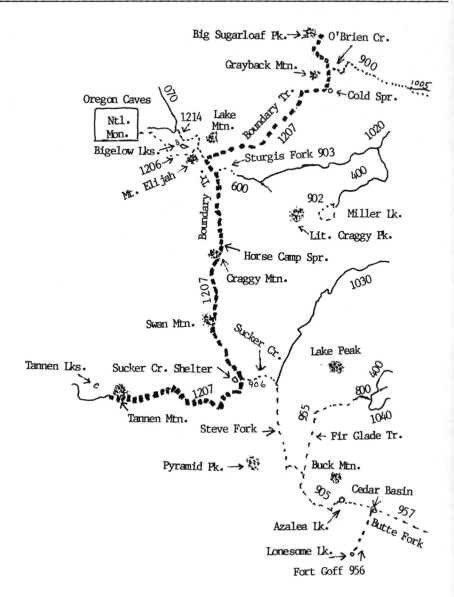

56

O'BRIEN CREEK TRAIL #900. (See map 18)

TRAIL BEGINS:	—Forest Road 1005,near mileposts 2 & 4 ELEV. 4080'
TRAIL ENDS:	—Boundary Trail 1207. ELEV. 6240'
DISTANCE:	—About 3.3 mi, difficult.
SEASON:	—Usually snow-free July through September.
USE:	—Hiker/horse/mountain and motor bike.
CONNECTING TR.	—Boundary National Recreation Trail 1207.
BRING MAPS:	—Applegate Ranger Dist.—Rogue River Ntl. Forest.

ACCESS: From the town of Ruch, Oregon, travel west on Hwy.
238, 7 miles to the town of Applegate. Cross the
bridge and turn left onto Thompson Creek Road, which later becomes Forest Route 10. Follow this route 12 miles to the junction
with Forest Road 1005. Turn right onto 1005 and travel 2.1 miles
to the junction with Forest Road 300, where a one mile extension
of Trail 900 offers a trailhead with trailer turn-around. HORSES
SHOULD USE MILE 4 TRAILHEAD UNTIL IMPROVEMENTS ARE MADE SOMETIME
AFTER 1995,AT WHICH TIME THE MILE 4 TRAILHEAD COULD BE ABANDONED.
CHECK WITH STAR RANGER STATION.

FEATURES: About 2 miles from the lower trailhead at a junction, keep right to bypass Grayback Snow Shelter
and Krause Cabin where Grayback Meadows is undergoing vegetation
repair for soil stabilization. No unauthorized horse use.   From
the above junction, it is 1.2 mi. to BOUNDARY NATIONAL RECREATION
TRAIL 1207 at the base of Grayback Mountain.   The Boundary Trail
is a popular route to Oregon Caves or for sidetrips to Windy Gap
or Sugarloaf Peak. CARRY WATER!   Treatment of water is essential
since many cattle graze in the area.

HISTORY: "Grayback Snow Shelter was built for winter-time
Forest Service snow surveyors who measured the wa-
ter content of snowpacks for irrigation supply projections (built
ca. 1944).   Krause Cabin was built by a local cattleman as a
round-up time 'line shack.' It was completed in August (V-J Day)
1945. 'Graybacks' were the lice that so plagued the early miners! They gave this name to a number of features." (USFS quote)

57

MILLER LAKE TRAIL #902. (See map 25)

TRAIL BEGINS:	-End of Road 1020/400. ELEV. 4834'
TRAIL ENDS:	-Miller Lake.
DISTANCE:	-0.6 mile to lake, about 2 mile loop around lake. Moderate grades. USE: hiker/horse. Highpoint ELEV. about 5200'
SEASON:	-Usually snow-free June thru October.
BRING MAPS:	-Applegate Ranger District-Rogue River Ntl. Forest.

ACCESS: From the town of Ruch, Oregon, travel west on Hwy. 238 for 7 miles to the town of Applegate.   Cross the bridge and turn left onto Thompson Creek Road which later becomes Forest Route 10. Continue southwest on Thompson Creek Road, 12 miles to the junction with Forest Road 1020. Follow Road 1020 4.4 miles to the junction with Road 1020/400. Keep left onto Road 400 and go 3 mi. to the end of the road at the Miller Lake Trailhead.

FEATURES: From the parking area, the trail climbs, crossing an old road (also leading to the lake). Upon reaching lakeshore, a 2 mi. botanical path known as the Oliver Matthews Trail circles the lake. From the lake in a clockwise direction, the trail goes east to the top of a ridge for some outstanding views before it begins its descent, passing a small pond and ending back at the beginning of the loop.

Miller Lake was deepened and dammed to provide irrigation water to the Thompson Creek Ditch. It is stocked with trout. The lake is quite noted for its botanical interest. Rhododendrons are in bloom usually around June first.

HISTORY: "MILLER LAKE: Named for Walter Miller, a 19th century Applegate Valley rancher who made his annual hunting camp at the lake." (USFS quote)

58

STURGIS FORK TRAIL #903. (See map 25)

TRAIL BEGINS:	-End of Forest Road 1020/600.	ELEV.	5040'
TRAIL ENDS:	-Boundary Trail 1207.	ELEV.	5600'
DISTANCE:	-1.7 miles, moderate for hiker/horse.		
	Difficult for mountain and motor bikes.		
SEASON:	-Usually snow-free July through September.		
CONNECTING TR.	-Boundary National Recreation Trail 1207.		
BRING MAPS:	-Applegate Ranger Dist.-Rogue River Ntl. Forest.		

ACCESS: From the town of Ruch, Oregon, travel west on Hwy.
238 for 7 miles to the town of Applegate. Cross
the bridge and turn left onto Thompson Creek Road which later becomes Forest Route 10. Continue southwest on Thompson Creek Road,
12 miles to the junction with Forest Road 1020. Continue south
and west on Rd. 1020, 8.1 mi. to the junction with Road 1020/600.
Turn right onto Road 600 and go about 1/2 mile to the trailhead.

FEATURES: The trail criss-crosses streams of the Sturgis Fork
thru a virgin stand of timber within Craggy Moun-
tain Scenic Area and joins the Boundary National Recreation Trail
1207. This is an easy access to Lake Mtn. Trail 1206 that leads
to Oregon Caves National Monument. Treatment of water is important due to cattle grazing.

HISTORY: "STURGIS FORK: Named for Albert Sturgis, a local
miner who, during the early 20th century, develop-
ed several large hydraulic mines, including one on Forest Creek,
southwest of Jacksonville." (USFS quote)

STEVE FORK TRAIL #905. (See map 25)

TRAIL BEGINS:	-Forest Road 1030 near milepost 11.	ELEV. 4400
TRAIL ENDS:	-Fir Glade Trail 955.	ELEV. 5200
DISTANCE:	-3.0 miles. Moderate, hiker/horse.	
SEASON:	-Usually snow-free July to October.	
CONNECTING TR.	-Fir Glade Trail 955.	
BRING MAPS:	-USFS Applegate Ranger Dist. -Rogue River N.F.	
	-USFS Red Buttes Wilderness brochure.	

ACCESS: From the town of Ruch, Oregon, travel south on Up-
               per Applegate Road, and go 18.8 miles to Carberry
Creek Rd.(County Route 777). Turn right onto Route 777 and follow
mileposts to mile 6.9 at the junction with Steve Fork Road 1030
Go left onto Road 1030 and continue 11.1 miles to a parking area
and trailhead on the right. From the trailhead, it is about 1 mi
to the Steve Fork and Sucker Creek Gap Trail junction. The Steve
Fork Trail bears left at this location.

FEATURES: The trail traverses the upper Steve Fork Valley
               swings to the east, crosses a ridge and joins the
Fir Glade Trail 955, about one mile southwest of Fir Glade. Turn
right (south) onto 955 if continuing to Azalea Lake. MOTOR VEHI-
CLES ARE NOT ALLOWED.

HISTORY: "STEVE PEAK, FORK: Named for Stephen Oster, a sol-
               itary prospector of the area during the 1860s and
1870s. Sometimes mapped as Steve's Fork, and shown on some ca.
1900 maps as Steamboat Creek." (USFS quote)

SUCKER CREEK GAP TRAIL #906. (See map 25)

TRAIL BEGINS:	-Near milepost 11, Road 1030.	ELEV.	4400'
TRAIL ENDS:	-Boundary Ntl. Recreation Trail 1207.	ELEV.	5200'
DISTANCE:	-2.0 miles. Moderate.		
USE:	-Hiker, horse. MOTORIZED VEHICLES NOT ALLOWED.		
SEASON:	-Usually snow-free July to October.		
CONNECTING TR:	-Boundary National Recreation Trail 1207.		
BRING MAPS:	-USFS Applegate Ranger District-Rogue River N.F.		
	-USFS Red Buttes Wilderness brochure.		

ACCESS: From the town of Ruch, Oregon, travel south on Up-
          per Applegate Road and go 18.8 miles to Carberry
Creek Road (County Route 777). Turn right and follow mileposts on
777 to mile 6.9 at the junction with Steve Fork Road 1030.   Turn
left onto 1030 and continue 11.1 mi. to the Steve Fork Trailhead.
Follow the Steve Fork Trail about 1 mile upstream to the signed
junction with the Sucker Creek Gap Trail. Keep to the right for
the beginning of the Sucker Creek Gap Trail.

FEATURES: This Rogue River National Forest trail ends at the
          Boundary/National Recreation Trail 1207 at Sucker
Creek Gap. Directly across the Boundary Trail, what appears to be
a continuation of Sucker Creek Gap Trail 906 is Sucker Cr. Trail
1237 dropping about 3 miles through the Siskiyou National Forest
to Road 4616/098.

From Sucker Creek Gap, the Boundary Trail leads south about 5 mi.
to Tannen Lakes, or north about 12 mi. to Sugarloaf Mtn.

HISTORY: "SUCKER CREEK GAP: The name 'Sucker Creek' result-
          ed when large numbers of inexperienced men flocked
to the placer deposits of that stream,a tributary of the Illinois
River. Actually, Sucker Creek proved to pay quite well during the
1860's and 1870s." (USFS quote)

WHISKEY PEAK LOOKOUT TRAIL #910.   (See map 25)

TRAIL BEGINS:	-Forest Road 1035/350.	ELEV. 6000'
TRAIL ENDS:	-Whiskey Peak Lookout.	ELEV. 6497'
DISTANCE:	-1/2 mile. Moderate, hiker only.	
SEASON:	-Usually snow-free July to October.	
BRING MAPS:	-USFS Applegate Ranger Dist. Rogue Riv. Ntl. For.	

ACCESS: From the town of Ruch, Oregon, travel south on Upper Applegate Road and go 18.8 miles to Carberry Creek Rd.(County Route 777). Turn right onto Route 777 and follow the mileposts 4.5 miles to Forest Road 1035. Turn left onto 1035 and travel 10.8 miles to the junction with Forest Road 1035/350. Turn right onto 350 and continue 2.3 miles to the trailhead near Whiskey Springs. The trail begins on a blocked Road 1035/356.

FEATURES: The trail to the lookout is maintained for hikers only.   Views of the surrounding mountain tops are terrific! The lookout building is no longer being used.

HISTORY: "WHISKEY PEAK, CREEK: Named in the 19th Century when a group of inebriated hunters camped at the base of the steep-walled peak and one extremely drunk member of the party began running away, screaming that the mountain 'was falling over on them.'"   (USFS quote)

62

BALDY PEAK TRAIL SYSTEM. (See map on following page)
Mule Mtn./Mule Tie/Mule Creek/Charlie Buck-Baldy Peak Trails.

USE: -Hiker/horse/mountain and motor bikes. DIFFICULT.
SEASON: -Year-round except for occasional winter snows.
BRING MAPS: -USFS Applegate Ranger District-Rogue River N.F.

ACCESS TO LOWER END, MULE MTN./MULE CREEK TRAILS ELEV. 1760'
From the town of Ruch, go south on Upper Applegate Road to milepost 12. MULE MTN. TR. climbs about 1/2 mile to a junction where
MULE MTN. TIE TRAIL leads 1.0 mile right to MULE CR. TRAIL 920,or
climbs left 3.5 mi. to junction of Charlie Buck/Baldy Peak Trails.

ACCESS TO LOWER END, CHARLIE BUCK/BALDY PEAK TRAIL 918.
From Ruch,follow Upper Applegate Road just beyond milepost 9 and
turn left onto Forest Route 20. Go 1.25 mi. on 20 and turn right
onto Road 941. After 1/4 mile turn left onto Road 940 and go 1.0
mile to a parking place near a gravel pile just before Road 940
makes a sharp, uphill bend. ELEV. 2560'. From here, ROAD 940 is
undrivable! (Steep, narrow, rockfall, no turn-around).

When reaching the ridge, hike around another sharp turn, and look
on the right for the lower end of CHARLIE BUCK/BALDY PEAK TR. 928

ACCESS TO UPPER END; MULE MTN., MULE CREEK, CHARLIE BUCK/BALDY
PEAK TRAILS.
From the junction of Upper Applegate Road and Forest Route 20, go
3.6 mi. and turn onto Road 2010. Follow 2010 and go 4.8 miles to
Road 2010-300 (closed to vehicles,please do not block gate). Fol-
low Road 300 about 1.0 mi. to a road triangle from where Road 329
leads downhill left (west), about 1/4 mile to the UPPER TRAILHEAD
of MULE CREEK TRAIL 920, ELEV.4000'. There may be no signs, look
RIGHT for the trail as it heads 6 mi.down the canyon to Mule Mtn.
Tie Trail, Mule Mtn. Trail and Upper Applegate Road.

From the above triangle, Rd. 300 continues north, 200 feet to Rd.
330. Just before a gate on 330, ELEV.4000', MULE MTN. TR. begins
as a short Jeep track and climbs 2 mi. to the base of Baldy Peak
at a junction (ELEV.4240') WHERE MULE MTN. TRAIL SLOPES DOWNHILL
LEFT, 4.0 Mi. TO UPPER APPLEGATE ROAD. FROM THE ABOVE JUNCTION,
CHARLIE BUCK/BALDY PEAK TRAIL STAYS HIGH FOR AWHILE BEFORE DROP-
PING 1.5 MI. NORTH TO RD.940.

FEATURES: Trails can be combined for making LOOP or SHUTTLE trips
For example, a loop starting from Upper Applegate Road,up on MULE
CREEK TRAIL 920 and down MULE MTN. TRAIL 919 would be almost 12.0
miles, rated strenuous for hikers.   Shuttle trips starting from
the upper elevations would be considerably easier.

From the upper elevations, there are wide-open views of the Mule
Creek or Rock Gulch canyons, and of the surrounding area. The re-
moteness of the trails lead to a very memorable experience!

Mule Mountain, Mule Tie, Mule Creek and Charlie Buck/Baldy Peak
Trails are maintained by "Lutheran Evergreens".

Middle Fork Trail 950, A beautiful trail
but a little difficult in places in the
upper portion of the trail.

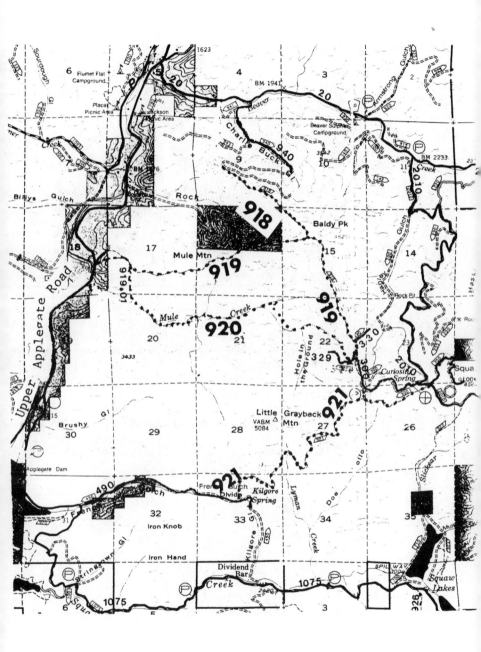

LITTLE GRAYBACK TRAIL #921. (See map 26)

TRAIL BEGINS:	-French Gulch Road. ELEV. 3200'
TRAIL ENDS:	-Forest Road 2010 near milepost 5. ELEV. 4240'
DISTANCE:	-5.4 miles, difficult.
USE:	-Hiker/horse/mountain bike/motor bike.
SEASON:	-Snow-free most of year, access roads may be hazardous during winter. Look for poison oak.
BRING MAPS:	-USFS Applegate Ranger District -Rogue River N.F.

LOWER ACCESS: From the town of Ruch, Oregon, follow mileposts on Upper Applegate Road to mile 14.9 and turn east across Applegate Dam onto Squaw Creek Road. Follow this road 1.5 miles then turn left onto French Gulch Road, past a row of mailboxes. Continue 2.1 miles to where the road reaches its crest at a logging road junction. The trailhead is on the left. (FRENCH GULCH ROAD HAS A VERY ROCKY SURFACE, AND COULD BE UNDRIVABLE FOR SMALLER CARS.)

UPPER ACCESS: From the town of Ruch, travel 9.2 miles on Upper Applegate Rd. to the junction with Forest Route 20 (Beaver Creek Road). Follow Route 20 for 3.6 miles and turn right onto Forest Road 2010. Continue on Road 2010 for 5.1 miles and look on the right for Forest Road 2010-340.Take Road 340, 0.3 mi. west to a parking area and trailhead.

FEATURES: This trail climbs along the south slopes of Little Grayback Mountain, with open views of Squaw Lakes directly below, Elliott Ridge and of the Siskiyou Mtns.

LITTLE SQUAW TRAIL #923.   (See map 26)

TRAIL BEGINS:	-Squaw Lakes parking area. ELEV.3200'
TRAIL ENDS:	-Mulligan Bay on Big Squaw Lake.
DISTANCE:	-1.0 mile.
DIFFICULTY:	-Easy. **USE:** Hiker/mountain bike.
SEASON:	-All year.
BRING MAPS:	-USFS Applegate Ranger Dist.Rogue River Ntl.Forest.

ACCESS: From the town of Ruch, Oregon, follow mileposts on
Upper Applegate Road to mile 14.9 then turn left
across the dam. Keep right at a junction 1.5 miles further.Squaw
Creek Road becomes Forest Road 1075, and the Squaw Lakes parking
area is just beyond milepost 8, uphill to the right.

From the parking area, the trail follows a maintenance road for
1/8 mile to Big Squaw Lake. Immediately after reaching the lake,
continue east 100 yards further to a road junction. Turn right
and follow this road for another 1/4 mi. to Little Squaw Lake.The
trail crosses a foot bridge below the outlet of the lake,and then
climbs a short distance before entering a mixed conifer and hard-
wood forest.   Interpretative signs identify trees and vegetation
along the trail.

The trail ends at Mulligan Bay on Big Squaw Lake. For those wish-
ing to extend the hike, continue north on the lakeshore road that
circles Big Squaw Lake.   Visitors ending their hike at Mulligan
Bay can return to the parking area by following the maintenance
road west for 1/2 mile. CARRY WATER.

This outing provides the visitor with opportunities for picnicking, swimming, and fishing for rainbow and cutthroat trout.

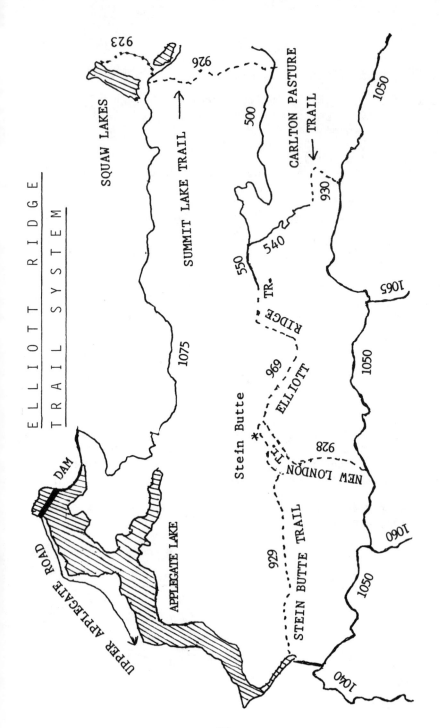

ELLIOTT RIDGE
TRAIL SYSTEM

SQUAW LAKES

923

926

500

CARLTON PASTURE
TRAIL

1050

SUMMIT LAKE TRAIL

930

540

550

1065

TR.

RIDGE

969

ELLIOTT

1050

Stein Butte

*

928

NEW LONDON

DAM

929

1060

APPLEGATE LAKE

STEIN BUTTE TRAIL

1050

UPPER APPLEGATE ROAD

1040

SUMMIT LAKE TRAIL #926.   (See map 26)

TRAIL BEGINS:	-Squaw Lakes parking area.	ELEV.	3040'
TRAIL ENDS:	-Elliott Creek Ridge.	ELEV.	4720'
DISTANCE:	-3.0 miles. Difficult.		
USE:	-Hiker/horse/mountain bike/motor bike.		
SEASON:	-All year except for occasional winter snows.		
BRING MAPS:	-USFS Applegate Ranger Dist.-Rogue River N.F.		

ACCESS: Follow directions to Little Squaw Trail. The Sum-
               mit Lake Trail begins as an old logging track from
the Squaw Lakes parking area, and leads uphill to the south.

FEATURES: Streams have washed out the logging track in three
               places. Hike approximately 1 mi. just beyond the
third washout and look for blazes on another track leading uphill
left. Follow this track 300 ft. to a meadow and keep left on the
blazed trail to Summit Lake. (You can also reach the meadow by
staying on the logging track 350' further to its end and turning
left a few hundred feet.) The trail climbs steeply before reaching Road 1075-580.   Do not cross the road-keep right and drop a
short distance to Summit Lake.

Summit Lake is small and shallow and is surrounded by old growth
ponderosa pines. It lies just below Elliott Creek Ridge.   Paths
lead up to the ridge for some good views of the surrounding area.

Summit Lake, Carlton Pasture, Elliott Ridge, New London and Stein
Butte Trails comprise a trail system maintained by "Motorcycle
Riders Association."

NEW LONDON TRAIL #928.   (Map 26)
(Formerly the eastern portion of Stein Butte Trail #929)

TRAIL BEGINS:	-Forest Road 1050.	ELEV. 2160'
TRAIL ENDS:	-Jnc. Stein Butte & Elliott Ridge Tr.	ELEV. 4000'
DISTANCE:	-2.6 miles, plus 5.0 miles on Stein Butte Trail if using a shuttle arrangement to Seattle Bar.	
DIFFICULTY:	-Difficult. Steep, sharp switchbacks.	
SEASON:	-All year except for occasional winter snows.	
CONNECTING TR.	-Stein Butte Trail 929, Elliott Ridge Trail 969.	
USE:	-Hiker, horse, mountain and motor bikes.	
BRING MAPS:	-USFS Applegate Ranger Dist.- Rogue River N.F.	

ACCESS: From the town of Ruch, Oregon, follow mileposts on
                  Upper Applegate Road 18.8 miles to Carberry Creek
Road. Turn left (southeast) to the California-Oregon border near
milepost 20 at the signed junction of Forest Roads 1040 and 1050.
Turn left on 1050 and travel 2.7 mi.to the trailhead on the left.
Parking is available directly across the road.

The 2.6 mile New London Trail meanders steeply, passing two mine
adits and ends at a saddle just east of Stein Butte at the junction with the Stein Butte and Elliott Ridge Trails.   Stein Butte
Trail is on the left (west) leading 0.5 mi. to a ridge from where
a side trail leads uphill left to Stein Butte.   The Stein Butte
Trail continues about 4.5 miles to its Seattle Bar Trailhead at
Applegate Lake.

ELLIOTT RIDGE TR. #969 leads right (east) from the above saddle,
1.7 mi. to Road 550. A road system from this point makes connec-
tions with CARLTON PASTURE TRAIL #930 and SUMMIT LAKE TR. #926.
CARRY WATER ON ALL OF THE ABOVE TRAILS!

For a car shuttle using the above trails, cars could be placed
at the appropriate lower trailheads.

New London, Stein Butte, Elliott Ridge, Summit Lake and Carlton
Pasture Trails are maintained by "Motorcycle Riders Assn."

CARLTON PASTURE TRAIL #930.   (See map 26)

TRAIL BEGINS:	-Forest Road 1050.	ELEV. 2640'
TRAIL ENDS:	-Forest Road 1075/540.	ELEV. 3680'
DISTANCE:	-1.6 miles. DIFFICULT.	
SEASON:	-All year except for occasional winter snows.	
USE:	-Hiker, horse, mountain and motor bikes.	
BRING MAPS:	-USFS Applegate Ranger Dist.- Rogue River N.F.	

ACCESS: From the town of Ruch, Oregon, follow mileposts on
               Upper Applegate Road, 18.8 miles to Carberry Creek
Road.   Turn left (southeast) to the California-Oregon border near
milepost 20 at the signed junction of Forest Roads 1040 and 1050.
Turn left on 1050 and travel 6.6 mi.to CARLTON PASTURE TRAIL #930
trailhead on the left.

The 1.6 mile Carlton Pasture Trail climbs steeply, about 1/2 mile
to the base of Carlton Pasture, and then heads west about 1.0 mi.
to Forest Road 1075/540. To reach Elliott Ridge, follow Road 540
0.5 mile to Road 550. TURNING LEFT(West) onto Road 550 leads 0.5
mi. to ELLIOTT RIDGE TRAIL #969 that leads 1.7 mi.to the junction
with STEIN BUTTE TRAIL #929 and NEW LONDON TRAIL #928.

From the above junction of Roads 540 and 550,TURNING RIGHT (east)
onto Road 550 leads 0.5 mile to Road 500.   Keep RIGHT onto Road
500 and go about 2.5 miles. Look on the left (downhill north)for
Summit Lake and SUMMIT LAKE TRAIL #926.

For a car shuttle using the above trails, cars could be placed
at the appropriate lower trailheads. This trail is maintained by
the Motorcycle Riders Association.

MIDDLE FORK TRAIL #950 (A National Recreation Trail) (See map 25)

TRAIL BEGINS:	-Forest Road 1035, northern Calif. ELEV. 2640'
TRAIL ENDS:	-Forest Road 1040/600. ELEV. 4200'
DISTANCE:	-Lower section 3 miles, upper section 3.1 miles.
USE:	-Hiker/horse. Difficult for horses upper 3 miles.
SEASON:	-May through October.
CONNECTING TR:	-Frog Pond Trail 953.
BRING MAPS:	-USFS Applegate Ranger Dist.-Rogue River Ntl. For.
	-USFS "Red Buttes Wilderness" brochure.
	-USFS Recreation Opportunity Guide-Middle Fork Tr.

ACCESS: From the town of Ruch, Oregon, follow mileposts on Upper Applegate Road to mile 18.8 at Carberry Creek Road. Turn left and continue 1.3 miles to the junction with Forest Road 1040 and 1050. Turn onto Road 1040 and drive the following distances:

LOWER TRAILHEAD-5 miles to junction with Rd. 1035. Turn right onto Road 1035 and go 0.2 mi. to the trailhead on the left.

MIDDLE TRAILHEAD: Continue 7.0 mi. on Road 1040 to where Middle Fork Trail crosses the road and continues upstream from the Frog Pond Trailhead.

UPPER TRAILHEAD: Continue 2.0 miles on Road 1040 to the junction with Road 1040/600. Turn left onto Road 600 and go 1/8 mile to a new trailhead on the left.

FEATURES: The lower end of the trail begins as a rough road that very soon breaks into a trail on the right. It follows the Middle Fork of the Applegate River and passes two old mining cabin sites along the way (ca.1930). The trail continues its climb and crosses Road 1040 at the Frog Pond Trailhead.It then continues 3.1 mi. to the Upper Trailhead. There is an abundance of autumn color from the vine maples, alder, yew, dogwood, huckleberry and other surrounding plants.

The upper section of this trail is not recommended for horse use at this time due to narrow tread and rocky creek crossings. Check with Star Ranger District for updated information.

FROG POND TRAIL #953. (See map 25)

TRAIL BEGINS:	-LOWER END: Forest Road 1040.	ELEV. 3440'
TRAIL ENDS:	-UPPER END: Forest Road 1040.	ELEV. 3880'
DISTANCE:	-5.4 miles, steep grades.	HIGHPOINT ELEV. 5200'
DIFFICULTY:	-Moderate for hikers/difficult for horses and they are not recommended.	
SEASON:	-Early July through October.	
CONNECTING TR:	-Middle Fork Trail 950. NO MOTORIZED VEHICLES.	
BRING MAPS:	-USFS Applegate Ranger Dist.-Rogue River N.F.	
	-USFS "Red Buttes Wilderness" brochure.	

ACCESS: From the town of Ruch, Oregon, follow mileposts on
                 Upper Applegate Road 18.8 miles to Carberry Creek
Road. Turn left and continue 1.3 miles to the junction with Forest Roads 1050 and 1040. Keep right onto 1040 and go 9.7 miles to
the lower trailhead or 2 miles more to the upper trailhead.

FEATURES: From the lower end, the trail begins along a faint
                 track soon becoming a good trail.   Near the top
end of the loop the trail may become obscure. Follow the blazes,
stakes, and green "X" trail signs. At one point the trail passes
a small pond into a larger meadow and becomes difficult to follow. Follow cairns in the center of the meadow and head for the
uprooted tree on the far side. The trail becomes easy to follow
then climbs steadily to the north with views of the Red Buttes.
After reaching a crest, the trail descends sharply to the southwest shore of Frog Pond and then passes an old cabin that uses a
cluster of cedar trees as its mainstay. The cabin was built by
John Knox McCloy in about 1900. The trail drops sharply about 1
mile to the upper trailhead on Road 1040.

FIR GLADE TRAIL #955. (A ROUTE TO AZALEA LAKE)   (See map 25)

TRAIL BEGINS: -Forest Road 1040/800.   ELEV. 5200'
TRAIL ENDS: -Azalea Lake.   ELEV. 5400'
DISTANCE: -5.8 miles.   HIGH POINT ELEV. 6000'
SEASON: -Usually open late June through October.
USE: -Hiker/horse MODERATE GRADE, NO ORV'S.
BRING MAPS: -USFS Applegate Ranger Dist.-Rogue River N.F.
              -USFS "Red Buttes Wilderness" brochure.
CONNECTING TR.-Steve Fork Trail 905, Phantom Meadows Trail 955A,
              Butte Fork Trail 957.

ACCESS: From the town of Ruch, Oregon, follow mileposts on
                 Upper Applegate Road, 18.8 miles to Carberry Creek
Road (County Route 777).Turn right on Route 777, and follow mileposts to mile 6.9 at the junction with Steve Fork Road 1030.   Go
4.8 mi. on Road 1030 to the junction of Forest Road 400 (Low Gap
Road). Turn left onto Road 400 and travel 4.2 miles, just beyond
the ridge crest, to the junction of Forest Roads 700 and 1040. Go
straight ahead on Road 1040 for 0.1 mi. to the junction with Forest Road 800 on the right. NOTE: ROAD 800 MAY BE UNDRIVABLE FOR
SOME PASSENGER CARS, but it is only 0.4 mi. to the Hinkle Lake
junction.   Keep left at this junction and go 0.1 mi. to the   Fir
Glade Trailhead.

FEATURES: This trail affords open views of the Middle Fork
                 drainage, Buck Peak, Figurehead Mountain and Klam-
ath Mountains. Not far from the trailhead, the route follows an
old road for a short distance. Look left to where the trail continues to Fir Glade, a large open meadow with a collapsed shelter.   On the near edge of the meadow, look left for the continuation of the trail. 1 mile further, pass the junction with the
Steve Fork and Phantom Meadows Trails then continue to the crest
of the divide between Rogue River and Klamath Ntl. Forests.   The
trail switchbacks to a saddle N.W. of Figurehead Mountain before
dropping down to Azalea Lake. At Azalea Lake,hikers camp is north
of the lake and stock camp east of the lake. "No camping in the
day-use area between the perimeter trail and the lake. LIMIT PER
GROUP 8 persons,12 stock. Bring pellets/grain for stock" (USFS)

BUTTE FORK TRAIL #957.   (See map 25)

TRAIL BEGINS: -From Horse Camp Trail 958,or from SHOO FLY TRAIL-
                HEAD on Forest Road 1040.
TRAIL ENDS: -Azalea Lake.
DISTANCE: -10 miles to Azalea Lake via the Horse Camp
                Trail, or 8 miles from the Shoo Fly Trailhead.
SEASON: -June through October. USE: hiker/horse only.
CONNECTING TR. -Horse Camp Trail #958, Shoo Fly Trail #954, Fort
                Goff Trail #956, Fir Glade Trail #955.
BRING MAPS: -USFS "Red Buttes Wilderness" brochure.
                -USFS Applegate Ranger Dist. -Rogue River N.F.

ACCESS: From the town of Ruch, Oregon, follow mileposts
                on Upper Applegate Road, 18.8 miles to Carberry
Creek Road. Turn left and go 1.3 mile to the signed junction of
Forest Roads 1040 and 1050. Turn right onto Road 1040 and go 3.6
miles to Cook and Green Campground on the left(signs may be miss-
ing). Turning left onto the camp road leads 1/4 mile to the Horse
Camp Trailhead. Take the Horse Camp Trail about 0.5 mile to the
Butte Fork Trail on the right.

SHOO FLY TRAILHEAD is 4 mi. further on Road 1040 near milepost 9.
The trail drops 0.7 mile to the Butte Fork Trail. Turn right and
continue about 7.5 miles upstream to Azalea Lake.

FEATURES: From its junction with Horse Camp Trail,the Butte
                Fork Trail passes below the Butte Fork Slide be-
fore dropping to Echo Canyon and the Butte Fork of the Applegate
River. In another 0.5 miles,you reach a bridge taking you to the
north bank of the river with a good view of Hello Canyon. Follow
the trail about 0.5 mile to the lower end of the Shoo Fly Trail.

Butte Fork Trail continues upstream,passing an old Forest Service
toolhouse and a marked grave of persons killed in a 1945 airplane
crash, before reaching Cedar Basin and the junction of Fort Goff
Trail 956. Azalea Lake is one mile west of Cedar Basin.

BUTTE FORK TRAIL HAS BEEN ADOPTED BY THE "SOUTHERN OREGON CHAPTER
OF MISTER LONGEARS".

HORSE CAMP TRAIL #958. (See map 26)

<u>TRAIL BEGINS:</u>	-Forest Road 1040. <u>ELEV.</u> 2400'
<u>TRAIL ENDS:</u>	-Pacific Crest National Scenic Trail. <u>ELEV.</u> 5900'
<u>DISTANCE:</u>	-3.9 miles, very steep grades. CARRY WATER.
<u>SEASON:</u>	-June through October. <u>USE:</u> hikers/horses.
<u>CONNECTING TR:</u>	-Butte Fork Trail 957.
	-Pacific Crest National Scenic Trail.
<u>BRING MAPS:</u>	-USFS Applegate Ranger Dist. -Rogue River N.F.
	-USFS "Red Buttes Wilderness" brochure.
	-USFS Recreation Opportunity Guide-Horse Camp Tr.

<u>ACCESS:</u>   From the town of Ruch, Oregon, follow mileposts on Upper Applegate Road, 18.8 miles to Carberry Creek Road. Turn left and go <u>1.3 miles</u> to the junction of Roads 1050 and 1040. Turn right onto Road 1040 and go <u>3.6 miles</u> to the former Cook and Green Campground on the left. Signs may be missing. Turning left onto the camp roads leads 1/4 mile to the Horse Camp Trailhead.

<u>FEATURES:</u>   Horse Camp Trail is popular with backpackers as an access to the Pacific Crest National Scenic Trail. About 3500 ft. of elevation is gained in only four miles, rating the trail one of the steepest in the Siskiyou Mountains.

In about 0.5 mi. KEEP LEFT at the new Butte Fork Trail junction. It is 1.0 mile further to Horse Camp and a nearby spring. WATER TREATMENT IS RECOMMENDED. The trail continues another 1.5 miles to a high mountain meadow before reaching the Echo Lake junction. The trail to the right leads to Echo Lake nestled in a small cirque basin below Red Buttes. To reach the Pacific Crest National Scenic Trail, keep left at the above junction and go 0.5 miles.

A 15 mile loop is possible by using the Horse Camp, Pacific Crest and Cook and Green Trails. <u>MOTORIZED VEHICLES ARE NOT ALLOWED ON THE PACIFIC CREST TRAIL OR IN THE RED BUTTES WILDERNESS.</u>

<u>HISTORY:</u>   "Horse Camp: Named by John Knox McCloy in the early 20th century." (USFS quote)

COOK AND GREEN TRAIL #959. (See map 26)

TRAIL BEGINS:	-(Lower Trailhead) Forest Road 1040. ELEV. 2280'
TRAIL ENDS:	-(Upper Trailhead) Cook and Green Pass ELEV. 4765'
	Forest Road 1055.(Road directions in Chapter 14).
DISTANCE:	-About 8.2 miles.
DIFFICULTY:	-Moderate for hikers and horses, Difficult for
	mountain and motor bikes.
SEASON:	-Usually snow-free June through October.
CONNECTING TR:	-Pacific Crest National Scenic Trail.
BRING MAPS:	-USFS Applegate Ranger Dist.-Rogue River Ntl. For.
	-USFS Recreation Opportunity Guide-this trail.
	-USFS Pacific Crest Trail-Oreg. Southern Portion.

ACCESS: (LOWER TRAILHEAD).   From Ruch, Oregon, turn left
                 onto Upper Applegate Road and continue 18.8 miles
to the junction with Carberry Creek Road.   Turn left and go 1.3
miles to the junction of Forest Roads 1050 and 1040.   Turn right
onto Road 1040 and go 2.8 mi. to the trailhead on the left. WATCH
SOON AFTER 1996 WHEN THIS TRAILHEAD MAY BE CONSOLIDATED WITH THE
HORSE CAMP TRAILHEAD. (CHECK WITH STAR RANGER STATION).

FEATURES: The trail passes through a sizable stand of the
                 rare Brewer spruce trees recognizable by its four
to eight foot long, string-like branchlets hanging down from its
limbs.   Noble and white fir are also seen at higher elevations.
No-See-Em Camp is reached just before crossing Cook and Green Cr.
The trail then climbs along the west side of Bear Gulch and pass-
es a small spring just before reaching Cook and Green Pass.   See
Chapter 14 for road directions to Cook and Green Pass. MOTORIZED
VEHICLES NOT ALLOWED ON THE PCNST OR IN RED BUTTES WILDERNESS.
WATER TREATMENT IS RECOMMENDED.

HISTORY: "COOK AND GREEN CREEK, PASS, CAMPGROUND: Robert
                 Cook and the two Green brothers were partners in
several mining ventures in this vicinity during the 1870s and
1880s; the name undoubtedly resulted from their activities."
"NO-SEE-EM CAMP: Probably named by early day Forest Service
employees, for the clouds of small gnats (no-see-ums) which ha-
rass campers during the spring and summer months." (USFS quotes)

TIN CUP TRAIL #961. (See map 26)

TRAIL BEGINS:	-End of Forest Road 1060/600.	ELEV. 5240'
TRAIL ENDS:	-Siskiyou crest.	ELEV. 6000'
DISTANCE:	-1.6 miles, moderate grades. USE: hiker/horse.	
SEASON:	-Usually snow-free July through October.	
CONNECTING TR.	-Pacific Crest National Scenic Trail.	
BRING MAPS:	-USFS Applegate Ranger Dist.- Rogue River N.F.	

ACCESS: From the town of Ruch, Oregon, follow mileposts on
                 Upper Applegate Road, 18.8 miles to Carberry Creek
Road. Turn left (southeast) to the California-Oregon border near
milepost 20 at the signed junction of Forest Roads 1040 and 1050.
Turn left on 1050 and travel 1.6 miles to the junction with Forest Road 1060.   Turn right onto 1060 and continue 3.5 mi. to a
hairpin turn leading back to the north. (The old Blue Ledge Copper Mine is located on the right, southwest of this turn.)   Continue northeast on 1060, gaining Nabob Ridge in about 2 miles at
the junction with Forest Road 1060/600. Turn right onto Road 600
for about 1.5 miles to its end. The Tin Cup Trail then continues
up the ridge from this point.

FEATURES: This short trail connects with the Pacific Crest
                 National Scenic Trail near Lowdens' Cabin and
                 Slaughterhouse Flat. MOTORIZED VEHICLES ARE NOT
ALLOWED ON THE PCNST OR IN RED BUTTES WILDERNESS.

HISTORY: "JOHN LOWDEN settled at the mouth of Seiad Creek in
                 1860 and operated a ferry across the Klamath River
for   several years.   He and his two sons mined, raised wheat and
began a small dairy.   Their beef cattle ranged on the high meadows of the Siskiyou crest during the summers."

"SLAUGHTERHOUSE FLAT may have been the site of an early hog butch-
ering operation   providing   meat for the sudden influx of miners
during the 1850s." (USFS quotes)

CHAPTER 6 - SKY LAKES WILDERNESS

Sky Lakes Wilderness is a land of lakes, rocky ridges and timber-ed slopes, and was designated by Congress in 1984. Its 113,590 acres straddles southern Oregon's Cascade Range from Crater Lake National Park southward to Highway 140. It is approx. six miles wide and twenty seven miles long, with elevations ranging from 3800 feet in the canyon of the Middle Fork of the Rogue River to a lofty 9495 feet at the top of Mt. McLoughlin.

More than 200 pools of water, from small ponds to lakes of 30-40 acres, dot the landscape. Fourmile Lake, near the southern end of the area, exceeds 900 acres. The lake basins can sometimes be crowded with other campers, but the wilderness has thousands of acres of forest and scenic ridges where the visitor can find solitude.

SPECIAL RULES are enforced to protect the Wilderness resource:

1) Campsites must be at least 100 ft. from lakeshores and 50 ft. from streams.

2) Graze and tether horses and pack animals at least 200 feet from lakes or ponds and 50 feet from streams. Avoid tying animals directly to trees and do not picket. Use a "high-line" stretched between two trees.

3) Stay out of specially marked areas being revegetated.

4) Visitors should travel in groups no larger than 8 people and twelve animals throughout Sky Lakes Wilderness.

5) Bicycles, motorbikes, hang gliders, carts, wagons and other forms of mechanized transport are not allowed (disabled per-sons in wheelchairs permitted).

6. Bring adequate food (pellets or grain, not hay) for your animals because feed is scarce in the Wilderness, use nosebag.

(continued on next page)

SPECIAL RULES CONTINUED:

7. Refrain from operating loud radios or other audio devices.
   Discharging of firearms within or near occupied areas or
   across lakes is prohibited.

8. Grazing is not allowed before August 1, unless otherwise
   posted at trailhead bulletin boards.

THE WILDERNESS CONTAINS TWO LAKE BASINS WHERE FURTHER RESTRIC-
TIONS APPLY (SEVEN LAKES BASIN and BLUE CANYON BASIN).

A. In sensitive areas of these two basins, groups with pack/
   saddle animals must camp only within designated "horse camp"
   sites. These sites are marked with signs; sensitive areas and
   horse camp locations are shown on maps posted at trailheads.

B. In the two basins, grazing is permitted only in designated
   meadows and only after August 1 (unless otherwise posted at
   trailhead bulletin boards).

Be sure to check the trailhead bulletin board for current rules
and other information pertaining to the Sky Lakes Wilderness.
The complete management regulations enforced in the area may be
reviewed in the Forest Supervisor or District Ranger offices.

A SKY LAKES WILDERNESS MAP, and other very detailed information,
can be obtained from:

Forest Supervisor, Rogue River National Forest, 333 W. 8th St.,
Medford, OR 97501.
-District Ranger, P.O. Box 227, Butte Falls, OR 97522.

Forest Supervisor, Winema National Forest, 2819 Dahlia St.,
Klamath Falls, OR 97601.
-Klamath District Ranger, 1936 California Ave., Klamath Falls, OR
 97601.

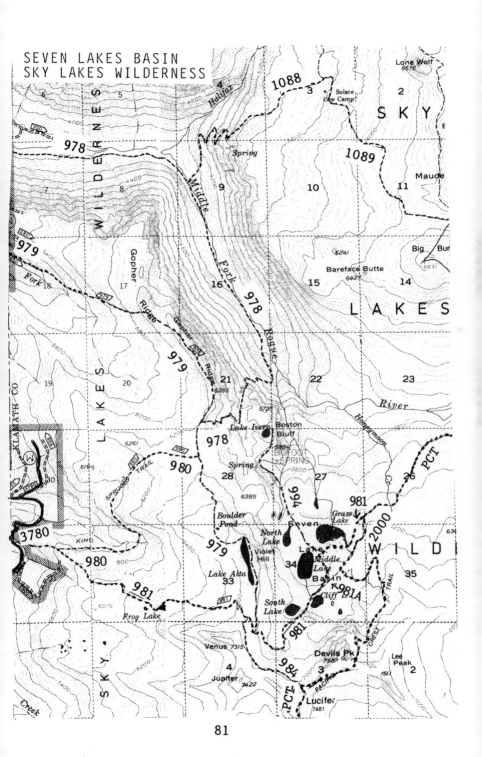

SEVEN LAKES BASIN
SKY LAKES WILDERNESS

MIDDLE FORK TRAIL #978.   (See map 11)

TRAIL BEGINS:	-Middle Fork Trailhead Road 3790. ELEV. 3500'
TRAIL ENDS:	-Alta Lake Trail junction. ELEV. 6200'
DISTANCE:	-8.5 miles, moderate/difficult. Hiker/horse.
SEASON:	-Lower segment of trail usually open by May 15.
	-Upper segment of trail, July-October.
CONNECTING TR.	-Halifax Tr. 1088 AFTER DIFFICULT RIVER CROSSING.
	-Alta Lake Trail 979.
BRING MAPS:	-Butte Falls Ranger Dist.-Rogue River Ntl.Forest.
	USFS Sky Lakes Area-Rogue River/Winema Ntl. For.
	USFS Rec. Opportunity Guide, Middle Fork Trail.

ACCESS: From the town of Butte Falls, Oreg., travel east
                  out of town 1.0 mile to County Route 992,leading
north to the town of Prospect. Turn onto this route and follow it
8.7 miles to Forest Route 34. Turn east and continue 8.2 miles to
Forest Route 37. Turn left on 37 and continue 5.2 miles to Forest
Road 3790. Travel 3 miles east on 3790 to the trailhead.

FEATURES: For the first six miles, the trail follows along
                  the south bank of the river. There are a number
of camp spots, though not obvious from the trail. The junction
with Halifax Tr. is reached after the first 3.5 miles. The Middle
Fork Trail then climbs steeply out of the canyon to the junction
with Alta Lake Trail on Gopher Ridge. A 30 mile loop is possible
by linking the Alta Lake, Devils Peak, Pacific Crest, McKie Camp
and Halifax Trails.   There is no bridge crossing the Rogue River
connecting Halifax and Middle Fork Trails.   Hikers can cross on
downed logs. Horses may ford the river.

The USFS advises that there is no horse feed in the canyon, and
that water is available not far from the trail along most of its
length.   Visitors should recognize that water in wilderness and
backcountry areas may not be safe to drink. Water is not tested.
(Excerpts USFS Recreation Opportunity Guide)

See beginning of **Chapter 6** for historical notes and regulations.

ALTA LAKE TRAIL #979. (See map 11)

TRAIL BEGINS:	-Forest Road 3785.	ELEV. 4800'
TRAIL ENDS:	-Seven Lakes Trail junction.	ELEV. 6800'
DISTANCE:	-6.2 miles, moderate to difficult.	
SEASON:	-Usually snow-free July to October.Preferred use: hikers. No horse feed at Alta Lake.	
CONNECTING TR.	-Middle Fork Trail 978, King Spruce Trail 980 and Seven Lakes Trail 981.	
BRING MAPS:	-Butte Falls Ranger Dist.-Rogue River Ntl. Forest. -USFS Rec. Opportunity Guide-Alta Lake Trail. -USFS Sky Lakes Area-Rogue River/Winema Ntl. For.	

ACCESS: From the town of Butte Falls, Oreg., travel east
                  one mile to County Route 992 leading north to the
town of Prospect. Turn onto this road and follow it 8.7 miles to
Forest Route 34. Turn right onto 34 and go 8.2 miles to the junction with Forest Route 37. Keep left onto 37 and travel 2.2 miles
to the junction with Forest Road 3785. Turn onto Road 3785 and
go 3.5 miles to the Alta Lake Trailhead. Parking is limited to
roadside turnouts with space for horse trailer turn-around.

FEATURES: This trail gets little use. It begins at Wallowa
                  Creek and climbs to the open parklands on the
south slope of Gopher Ridge. The trail junctions with the Middle
Fork and King Spruce Trails, then ends at Seven Lakes Trail 981.
Camp sites are on high ground both east and west of Alta Lake. A
9.1 mile loop uses the upper section of the Alta Lake Trail, the
Seven Lakes Trail 981 and King Spruce Trail 980. Water is available at Alta Lake and seasonally at Boulder Pond, but should be
treated. Alta Lake has no horsefeed. See beginning of Chapter 6
for Sky Lakes Wilderness regulations and historical notes.

HISTORY: "ALTA LAKE: One of the lakes in the Seven Lakes
                  Basin, probably named by early Forest Svc. per-
sonnel because of its location on the slopes of a bluff, several
hundred feet higher than the other six lakes." (USFS quote)

KING SPRUCE TRAIL #980. (See map 11)

TRAIL BEGINS: -Near Seven Lakes Trailhead, Road 3780. ELEV. 5600'
TRAIL ENDS: -Junction with Alta Lake Trail. ELEV. 6350'
DISTANCE: -2.8 miles, moderate, preferred use: Hikers.
SEASON: -Usually snow-free July to October.
CONNECTING TR.-Alta Lake Trail 979, Seven Lakes Trail 981.
BRING MAPS: -Butte Falls Ranger Dist.-Rogue River Ntl. Forest.
-USFS Sky Lakes Area-Rogue River/Winema Ntl. For.

ACCESS: From the town of Butte Falls, travel east one mile
to County Route 992, leading north to the town of
Prospect. Turn onto this route and follow it 8.7 miles to Forest
Route 34. Turn onto 34 and go 8.2 miles to Forest Route 37. Keep
left onto 37, and travel 0.4 miles to Forest Road 3780. Turn onto
3780 and go 3.6 miles to the Seven Lakes Trailhead. There is
ample parking/turnaround space at the trailhead. Water not available. The lower end of the KING SPRUCE TRAIL is reached by hiking
along the Seven Lakes Trail, 0.5 mile from its trailhead.

FEATURES: The 2.8 mi. King Spruce Tr. passes the site of the
old King Spruce Camp before climbing to the junction with the Alta Lake Trail 979. TURNING LEFT at this junction
leads to the Middle Fork Trail in less than 1 mile, or 3.6 miles
to the Alta Lake lower trailhead.

TURNING RIGHT from King Spruce Trail leads 2.5 miles, past Alta
Lake, to the Seven Lakes Trail. See beginning of Chapter 6 for
Sky Lakes Wilderness regulations and history.

It is a good idea to keep
Raingear in your pack

SEVEN LAKES TRAIL #981. (See map 11 and 12)

TRAIL BEGINS:	-Forest Road 3780. ELEV. 5000'
TRAIL ENDS:	-Pacific Crest National Scenic Trail, ELEV. 6200'
DISTANCE:	-6.1 miles, moderate to difficult. Hiker/horse.
SEASON:	-Usually snow-free July to October.
CONNECTING TR.	-King Spruce Trail 980, Alta Lake Trail 979, Devils Peak Trail 984, Lake Ivern Trail 994, and Pacific Crest Trail.
BRING MAPS:	-USFS Butte Falls Ranger Dist., Rogue River N.F.
	-USFS Rec. Opportunity Guide, Seven Lakes Trail.
	-USFS Sky Lakes Area-Rogue River/Winema Ntl. For.

ACCESS: From the town of Butte Falls, travel east 1 mile
                   to County Route 992,leading north to the town of
                   Prospect.Turn onto this route and travel 8.7 mi.
to Forest Route 34. Turn east on 34 and travel 8.2 miles to the
junction with Forest Route 37 and keep left for 0.4 mi. to Forest
Road 3780. Follow 3780, 3.6 miles to the trailhead. Parking and
turnaround space is ample. Water is not available.

FEATURES: Seven Lakes Trail passes the lower King Spruce
                   Trailhead in the first 0.5 mile before climbing
1700 feet to a saddle at a junction with Alta Lake and Devils Pk.
Trails.   Seven Lakes Trail then drops into Seven Lakes Basin and
the junction with Lake Ivern Trail 994, before ending on the Pacific Crest Trail.

For a cross-wilderness experience, follow the PCT 2.5 miles northeast to the junction with Sevenmile Trail 3703 that travels northeast to its trailhead in Winema National Forest.

A 9.1 mile loop uses Trail 981, the upper end of Alta Lake Trail
979 and King Spruce Trail 980. The Seven Lakes Trail may be dusty due to overuse. Cliff Lake may be overcrowded. CARRY WATER,
as lake water in the area is not recommended for drinking without
treatment. Mosquitos are bad from June to mid-August.

Please see beginning of Chapter 6 for historical information and
for a mention of wilderness regulations.

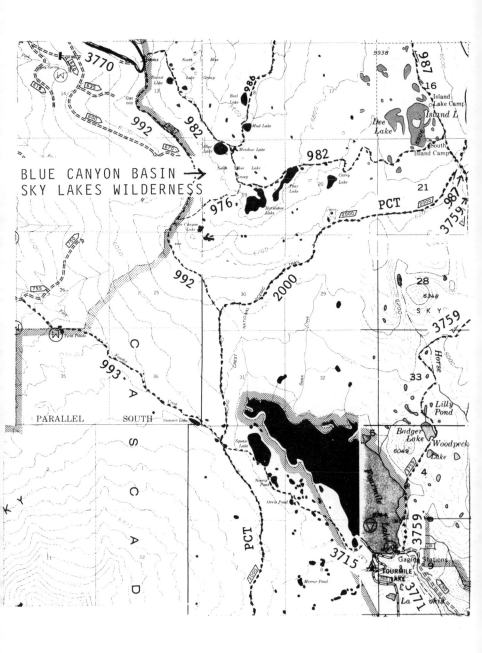

BLUE CANYON BASIN →
SKY LAKES WILDERNESS

BLUE CANYON TRAIL #982.(See maps 11 and 16)

TRAIL BEGINS:	-Road 3770 at Saddle Camp.	ELEV. 6200'
TRAIL ENDS:	-Junction with Red Lake Trail 987.	ELEV. 6000'
DISTANCE:	-5.1 miles, easy to moderate.	USE: hiker/horse.
SEASON:	-Usually snow-free June to October, trailhead often not accessible by car until the end of June or the first of July. Mosquitos are numerous until about August 15.	
CONNECTING TR.	-Cat Hill Way Tr.992, Meadow Lake Tr. 976, South Fork Tr. 986 (formerly 988), Red Lake Tr. 987.	
BRING MAPS:	-USFS Butte Falls Ranger Dist., Rogue River N.F. -USFS Sky Lakes Area, Rogue Riv.-Winema Ntl. For. -USFS Rec. Opportunity Guide-Blue Canyon Trail.	

ACCESS: From White City, OR., follow mileposts on State Hwy. 140, 28.6 miles to the junction with County Route 821.Continue north on 821,8.8 mi. just beyond milepost 26 to a junction where Route 37 leads right(east). Follow mileposts on 37, 10.9 miles to the junction with Road 3770 on the right. Follow 3770, 6 miles to the trailhead. Parking and turn-around space is adequate.

FEATURES: Trail 982 passes Blue, Meadow, Horseshoe, Pear and Island Lakes. The trail may be dusty from overuse, and the surrounding lakes may be overcrowded. There is no horsefeed in the Blue Canyon Area. A 5.6 mile day loop hike is possible by using the Cat Hill Way Trail 992 (trailhead just a few hundred feet down from the Blue Canyon Trailhead), Meadow Lake Trail 976 and the Blue Canyon Trail. A longer 12.5 mile loop uses the Cat Hill Way, the Pacific Crest and Blue Canyon Trail.

Please see beginning of Chapter 6 for Sky Lakes Wilderness regulations and history notes.

SOUTH FORK TRAIL #986 (Formerly #988). (See maps 11 and 16)

TRAIL BEGINS:	-Forest Road 37/720.	ELEV.	4000'
TRAIL ENDS:	-Junction with Blue Canyon Trail.	ELEV.	5700'
DISTANCE:	-5.1 miles, moderate to difficult.		
SEASON:	-Usually snow-free June to October. Mosquitos bad until mid-August. USE: Recommended, hiker only.		
CONNECTING TR:	-Blue Canyon Trail 982.		
BRING MAPS:	-Rogue River Ntl. Forest-Butte Falls Ranger Dist. -USFS Sky Lakes Area-Rogue River/Winema Ntl. For. -USFS Rec. Opportunity Guide-South Fork Trail.		

ACCESS: From White City OR.,   follow mileposts on State
Hwy. 140, 28.6 miles to the junction with County
Route 821.Turn north on 821 and go 8.8 miles(just beyond Milepost
26) to where Forest Route 37 leads right (east). Follow   mileposts on 37, 13.3 miles to the junction with Forest Road 37/720
on the right. Turn and continue on 720, 1 mile to the end of the
road at the South Fork Trailhead.

ALTERNATE ALL PAVEMENT ROUTE: From Butte Falls, travel east one
mi.to County Route 992, that leads north to the town of Prospect.
Turn onto this route and go 8.7 miles to the junction with Forest
Route 34.   Turn right onto 34 and go 8.2 miles to the junction
with Forest Route 37. Turn right onto 37 and go 5.7 miles to the
junction with Road 720. Turn left and follow 720 one mile to the
trailhead at the end of the road.

FEATURES: This trail is recommended for hiker use only. It
passes Beal, Mud and Meadow Lakes before termina-
ting at Blue Lake and Blue Canyon Trail 982. If using a car shuttle, the hike could be made easier by hiking from the Blue Canyon
Trailhead to Blue Lake, and taking the South Fork Trail down to
Forest Road 37/720. Water is plentiful along the trail, but like
all wilderness water, should be treated before drinking. (See the
beginning of Chapter 6 for historical notes and a mention of Wilderness regulations).

CAT HILL WAY TRAIL #992. (See maps 11 and 16)

TRAIL BEGINS:	-Road 3770 at Saddle Camp.	ELEV. 6200'
TRAIL ENDS:	-Junction with Pacific Crest Trail.	ELEV. 6160'
DISTANCE:	-3.4 miles, moderate. Preferred use: hikers.	
SEASON:	-Usually snow-free June to October, trailhead often not accessible by car until the end of June or first of July. Mosquitos are numerous until mid August.	
CONNECTING TR.	-Blue Canyon 982, Meadow Lake 976 and Pacific Crest Trails.	
BRING MAPS:	-USFS Butte Falls Ranger Dist., Rogue River N.F.	
	-USFS Sky Lakes Area-Rogue River/Winema Ntl. For.	

ACCESS: From White City, OR., follow mileposts on State Hwy. 140, 28.6 miles to the junction with County Route 821. Continue north on 821, 8.8 miles just beyond milepost 26, to where Forest Route 37 leads right (east). Follow mileposts on 37, 10.9 miles to the junction with Road 3770 on the right. Follow 3770, 6 miles to the trailhead. Parking and turn-around space is adequate.

FEATURES: To reach the Cat Hill Way Trail, hike a few hundred feet down from the Blue Canyon Trailhead. Look for a trailhead sign on the right.

A 5.6 mile day loop hike is possible by using the Cat Hill Way Trail 992, Meadow Lake Trail 976 and Blue Canyon Trail 982. A longer 12.5 mile loop uses the Cat Hill way, Pacific Crest and Blue Canyon Trails.

The Cat Hill Way Trail is maintained by the Rogue Chapter of the Sierra Club. Please see beginning of Chapter 6 for Sky Lakes Wilderness regulations and historical notes.

<u>TOM AND JERRY TRAIL #1084.</u> (See map 6)

<u>TRAIL BEGINS:</u> -Forest Road 3795/600.   <u>ELEV.</u> 5000'
<u>TRAIL ENDS:</u> -McKie Shelter.   <u>ELEV.</u> 5500'
<u>DISTANCE:</u> -5 miles, moderate, hiker/horse, June to October.
<u>CONNECTING TR:</u> -Mudjekeewis Trail 1085 and McKie Camp Tr. 1089.
<u>BRING MAPS:</u>   -USFS Butte Falls Ranger Dist., Rogue River N.F.
            -USFS Sky Lakes Area-Rogue River/Winema Ntl. For.
            -USFS Rec. Opportunity Guide, Tom and Jerry Trail.

<u>ACCESS:</u>   From the town of Prospect, Oregon, travel east on
               County Route 992,leading toward Butte Falls for
2.5 miles to Forest Route 37. Turn onto 37 and continue east, 2.8
miles to Road 3795. Turn left onto 3795 and continue 5.7 miles to
the junction with Forest Road 3795/600. Turn right onto 600 and
go 0.6 mile to the trailhead. Parking and turn-around space is
adequate.

<u>FEATURES:</u>   After 1.5 miles, you reach the junction with the
               5.1 mile Mudjekeewis Trail 1085 (that skirts the
south edge of Kerby Peak with views of the Middle Fork Canyon before re-joining the Tom and Jerry Trail at Mckie Shelter).   KEEP
LEFT AT THE 1.5 MILE JUNCTION to reach McKie Shelter via the Tom
and Jerry Trail. Water is usually available on the first portion
of the trail and at McKie Camp.   Horse feed is plentiful in the
McKie vicinity. Returning (westbound) on the Tom and Jerry Trail,
a saddle is reached in about 1.5 miles.   Just west of the saddle
look for the trail as it leads southwest. <u>BEWARE OF A TREE BLAZE</u>
<u>ON AN OLD ABANDONED TRAIL THAT LEADS NORTHWEST.</u> The Tom and Jerry
Trail is maintained by the Oregon Hunters' Assn., and Mudjekeewis
Trail by the Jackson County Horsemans' Assn.

If making a 11.5 mile loop with the Tom and Jerry and the Mudjekeewis Trails, stay along the west edge of the meadow at McKie
Camp. See beginning of Chapter 6 for Sky Lakes Wilderness information and regulations.

<u>HISTORY:</u> "McKIE SHELTER: (now collapsed), is an old trail camp
           location. The shelter was built between 1934 and 1936
and was named after a sheepherder, Tom McKie." (USFS quote)

RED BLANKET TRAIL #1090. (See map 6 and 7)

TRAIL BEGINS:	-End of Road 6205.	ELEV. 3900'
TRAIL ENDS:	-Stuart Falls Trail 1078.	ELEV. 5400'
DISTANCE:	-3.9 miles, moderate grades.	USE: hiker/horse.
SEASON:	-Usually snow-free June to October. Closed to all use from the end of elk hunting season until April 1 for protection of winter range.	
CONNECTING TR:	-Lucky Camp Tr. 1083, and Stuart Falls Tr. 1078.	
BRING MAPS:	-USFS Butte Falls Ranger Dist., Rogue River N.F.	
	-USFS Sky Lakes Area-Rogue River/Winema Ntl. For.	

ACCESS: From the town of Prospect, Oregon, drive east on County Route 992, leading toward Butte Falls,1.1 mile to the junction with Red Blanket Road. Follow Red Blanket Road 0.3 mile and turn left onto Forest Road 6205. Continue on 6205, about 12 miles to the trailhead at the end of the road.

FEATURES: The Red Blanket Trail begins near the southwest corner of Crater Lake National Park. After 1/4 mile, look for the large concrete corner post on the left. The trail follows along Red Blanket Creek and reaches the Lucky Camp Trail 1083 in approx. three miles. Keeping to the left at this junction brings you to Stuart Falls Trail 1078 in about one mile. To reach Stuart Falls, keep left for about 1/2 mile. This is a popular access route to Sky Lakes Wilderness and Crater Lake National Park. See beginning of Chapter 6 for Sky Lakes Wilderness information and regulations.

HISTORY: "RED BLANKET CREEK, MOUNTAIN: Said to have been named in about 1865 after a white man purchased a large parcel of land from a group of Indians for one red blanket." (USFS quote)

SKY LAKES TRAIL #3762 and connecting trails. (See map 12)

TRAIL BEGINS:	-PCNST South of Deer Lake. ELEV. 5900'
TRAIL ENDS:	-Snow Lakes Trail #3739, Nannie Creek Tr. #3707.
DISTANCE:	-6.0 miles, moderate grades. USE: hiker/horse.
SEASON:	-June through October.
BRING MAPS:	-USFS Sky Lakes Wilderness.
	-USFS Pacific Crest National Scenic Trail-Oregon Central Portion.
	-USFS Recreation Opportunity Guide (this trail).
	-USFS Winema National Forest.

ACCESS: The Sky Lakes Trail,once called the Skyline Trail,
                   parallels the Pacific Crest through the Sky Lakes
Basin. This intra-wilderness trail departs from the Pacific Crest
Trail south of Deer Lake, and passes the trailhead access trails
of Cold Springs, South Rock Creek, Cherry Creek and Nannie Creek.
This route ends at the junction with Snow Lakes Tr. on the north,
which is not maintained for stock users.

TRAIL LOG-MILEAGE READINGS ARE APPROXIMATE.

Mile 0.6	Deer Lake.
Mile 0.9	Junction (Right) COLD SPRINGS TRAIL #3710.
Mile 1.3	Junction (Left) South end of ISHERWOOD LOOP TR. #3729.
Mile 1.5	Junction (Right) SOUTH ROCK CREEK TRAIL #3709, just past Heavenly Twin Lakes.
Mile 2.0	Junction (Left) North end of ISHERWOOD LOOP TR. #3729.
Mile 4.0	Junction (Right) CHERRY CREEK TRAIL #3708.
Mile 4.1	Junction (Right) (North end of Trapper Lake) South end DONNA LAKE LOOP TR. #3734-NOT MAINTAINED FOR STOCK USE.
Mile 4.4	Junction (Left) Between Lakes Margurette and Trapper, DIVIDE TRAIL #3717, 2.9 miles,elevation gain 600',maintained for stock users,connects to Pacific Crest Trail.
Mile 4.7	Junction (Right) North end-DONNA LAKE LOOP TRAIL #3734.
Mile 5.6	Martin Lake.
Mile 6.0	Junction (Right) NANNIE CREEK TRAIL #3707. SNOW LAKES TRAIL #3739 begins from this junction,a 2.3 mile steep climb to re-join the Pacific Crest Trail.Not maintained for stock users. Elevation gain 800'.

Please see beginning of Chapter 6 for Sky Lakes Wilderness information and regulations.

SEVENMILE TRAIL #3703.   (See map 12)

TRAIL BEGINS:	-Sevenmile Trailhead Forest Road 3334,ELEV. 5600'
TRAIL ENDS:	-Pacific Crest Trail. ELEV. 5825'
DISTANCE:	-1.9 miles, easy grades. USE: hiker/horse.
SEASON:	-June through October.
CONNECTING TR.	-Pacific Crest National Scenic Trail (PCNST).
BRING MAPS:	-USFS Sky Lakes Area-Rogue River/Winema Ntl. For.
	-USFS Winema National Forest.
	-USFS Pacific Crest Trail-Oregon Southern Portion

ACCESS: This description begins from State Hwy. 140 just
               east   of   milepost 43 (43.6 miles   east of White
City).   Turn north onto Westside Road (County Route 531), and go
16.9 miles to the junction with Forest Route 33. Follow Route 33,
2.8 miles to a 3-way junction,then go northwest on Road 3334, 5.7
miles to the trailhead at the end of the road.

FEATURES: This 2 mile trail provides a quick and easy ac-
               cess to the Pacific Crest National Scenic Trail.
From the PCNST,   options exist for a side-trip to Ranger Springs,
an entry into Seven Lakes Basin near Devils Peak and Cliff Lake,
or numerous other possibilities.

Ranger Springs is one of the headwater springs that feed the Middle Fork of the Rogue River.   To get there, take Sevenmile Trail
3703 to the junction with the Pacific Crest Trail. Turn right and
go 1/4 mile north to a junction on the left leading another mile
to the springs.

See beginning of Chapter 6 for Sky Lakes Wilderness information
and regulations.

NANNIE CREEK TRAIL #3707. (See map 12)

TRAIL BEGINS:	-End of Forest Road 3484.	ELEV. 6000'
TRAIL ENDS:	-Jnc. Snow Lakes & Sky Lakes Trails.	ELEV. 6000'
DISTANCE:	-4.3 miles, strenuous.	HIGH POINT 6520'
USE:	-Hikers/horses.	
SEASON:	-June through October, mosquitos till mid-August.	
BRING MAPS:	-USFS Winema National Forest.	
	-USFS Sky Lakes Area-Winema/Rogue River Ntl. For.	

ACCESS: This description begins from State Hwy. 140 just east of milepost 43 (43.6 mi. from White City). Turn north onto Westside Road (County Route 531), and go 12.1 mi. to the junction with Forest Road 3484 on the left.   Travel north and west on 3484, 4.5 mi. to the trailhead (end of the road).

FEATURES: From the trailhead, the trail climbs up a steep slope and follows the rocky contours,through the heavily forested slopes of Lather Mtn.(Elev. 6917') to the southwest. After coursing across a relatively level basin, the trail passes the southern shore of Puck Lakes and up through towering mixed conifer groves. The trail reaches the junction of the Snow Lakes and Sky Lakes Trails about 0.3 mile south of the Snow Lakes group.

See the page describing SKY LAKES TRAIL 3762, and the map showing how it connects with other lakes in Sky Lakes Basin.

Sky Lakes Wilderness information and regulations are noted at the beginning of Chapter 6.

SNOW LAKES TRAIL #3739.   (See map 12)

TRAIL BEGINS:	-Junction of Sky Lakes Trail #3762.
	and Nannie Creek Trail #3707. ELEV. 5800'
TRAIL ENDS:	-Pacific Crest National Scenic Trail ELEV. 6600'
DISTANCE:	-2.3 miles, moderate. USE: hiker/horse.
SEASON:	-Summer season: July-Oct.
BRING MAPS:	-USFS Sky Lakes Wilderness.
	-USFS Pacific Crest National Scenic Trail-Oregon Central Portion.
	-USFS Recreation Opportunity Guide.
	-USFS Winema National Forest.

ACCESS: The Snow Lakes Trail is an intra-wilderness trail
               connecting Sky Lakes Trail and Pacific Crest Tr.
It has a rather steep section that is not maintained for stock
use. This trail departs from the northern end of Sky Lakes Trail
at the junction with Nannie Creek Trail #3707.

FEATURES: The Snow Lakes Trail begins at elevation 5800',
                 as it departs from Sky Lakes Trail.The route ini-
tially climbs gradually along the northern slopes of Sky Lakes
Basin, crossing flower-splashed meadows.   The trail then climbs
steeply up the rock outcrops and windswept ridges offering breath
taking vistas to the south and east. Gaining nearly 1000 feet in
elevation in just under 1 mile, the trail joins the Pacific Crest
Trail on the backbone of the Cascade Mountain Range.   The rugged
scenery and magnificent views along this trail are a vivid remind
er of our responsibility to practice minimum impact visitation so
the primitive wilderness environment may remain.   (USFS INFO)

See the page describing SKY LAKES TRAIL 3762, and the map showing
how it connects to other lakes. in Sky Lakes Basin. Sky Lakes Wilderness information and regulations are listed in Chapter 6.

CHERRY CREEK NATIONAL RECREATION TRAIL #3708. (See map 12)

TRAIL BEGINS: -Forest Road 3450.   ELEV. 4672'
TRAIL ENDS: -Sky Lakes Trail 3762.   ELEV. 6000'
DISTANCE: -5.3 miles, strenuous.   USE: hiker/horse.
SEASON: -Usually snow-free June to October. Mosquitos
                   bad until mid-August.
BRING MAPS: -USFS Winema National Forest.
                  -Sky Lakes Area-Winema/Rogue River Ntl. Forests.

ACCESS: FROM WHITE CITY, Oregon, follow mileposts east
                  on State Hwy. 140, 43.6 miles to the junction of
Westside Road (County Route 531). FROM ASHLAND, take Dead Indian
Memorial Road (Jackson County 722, Klamath County 533), 36 miles
to the junction with State Highway 140. Turn right (east) on 140
and go 6 miles to Westside Road.

Follow Westside Road 11 miles to the junction with Road 3450 (on
the left). Turn west onto Road 3450 and go 1.6 mile to the trailhead at the end of the road.   Trailhead parking and turn-around
space is limited.

FEATURES: Although strenuous, this trail is a good access
                  route to the Sky Lakes Wilderness. The Cherry
Creek drainage, a U-shaped canyon formed by glaciation, is being
proposed as a Research Natural Area. The USFS encourages "horseback riders to dismount and walk their horses through the (creek)
crossings and wet boggy areas."

See the page describing SKY LAKES TRAIL 3762, and the map showing
how it connects to other lakes in Sky Lakes Basin.

Cherry Creek Trail became a part of the National Recreation Trail
System in 1979. Sky Lakes Wilderness information and regulations
are noted at the beginning of Chapter 6.

DIVIDE TRAIL 3717. (See map 12)

TRAIL BEGINS:	-Sky Lakes Trail #3762. ELEV. 6000'
TRAIL ENDS:	-Pacific Crest National Scenic Trail. ELEV. 7000'
DISTANCE:	-2.9 miles, moderate grades. USE: hiker/horse.
SEASON:	-June through October.
BRING MAPS:	-USFS Sky Lakes Wilderness.
	-USFS Pacific Crest National Scenic Trail-Oregon Central Portion.
	-USFS Recreation Opportunity Guide (this trail).
	-USFS Winema National Forest.

ACCESS: The Divide Trail is an intra wilderness trail con-
            necting Sky Lakes Trail and the Pacific Crest Tr.
Although the trail is steep, it is maintained for stock use.   It
departs from Sky Lakes Trail between Margurette Lake and Trapper
Lake, and climbs to the west to join the Pacific Crest Trail.

FEATURES: The Divide Trail begins at an elevation of 6000'
            as it departs from the Sky Lakes Trail. The route
climbs gradually along the southwestern shores of Lake Margurette
crossing flower-splashed meadows,then climbs steeply up the rock
outcrops and wind swept ridges of Luther Mountain.The trail gains
1000 feet in elevation in just under 3 miles. The rugged scenery
and magnificent vistas along this trail are a vivid reminder of
our responsibility to practice minimum impact visitation so the
primitive wilderness environment may remain. (USFS info)

See the page describing SKY LAKES TRAIL 3762, and the map showing
how it connects to other lakes in Sky Lakes Basin.

Please see beginning of Chapter 6 for Sky Lakes Wilderness information and regulations.

SOUTH ROCK CREEK TRAIL #3709. (See map 12)

<u>TRAIL BEGINS:</u>	-Cold Springs Trail, Forest Road 3651,<u>ELEV.</u> 5800'
<u>TRAIL ENDS:</u>	-Sky Lakes Trail 3762. <u>ELEV.</u> 6000'
	(At Heavenly Twin Lakes).
<u>DISTANCE:</u>	-1.6 mile.
<u>USE:</u>	-Hiker/horse.
<u>SEASON:</u>	-Usually snow-free June to October.
<u>CONNECTING TR:</u>	-Cold Springs Trail 3710, Sky Lakes Trail 3762.
<u>BRING MAPS:</u>	-USFS Winema National Forest.
	-USFS Rec. Opportunity Guides, Winema Ntl. For.
	-Sky Lakes Area-Rogue River/Winema Ntl. Forests.

<u>ACCESS:</u>   <u>FROM WHITE CITY</u>, Oregon, follow mileposts east
on State Hwy. 140, 40.9 miles to the junction of
Lost Creek Road 3651. If driving <u>FROM ASHLAND</u>, take Dead Indian
Memorial Road (Jackson County 722, Klamath County 533) to State
Highway 140,and turn right 3.1 miles to Road 3651.

Turn onto Road 3651 and go 10.5 miles to the COLD SPRINGS TRAIL-
HEAD at the end of the road.

After about 0.7 mi. along the Cold Springs Trail, the SOUTH ROCK
CREEK Trail begins on the right and continues about 1.6 mile to
the Sky Lakes Trail near Heavenly Twin Lakes. From here, a loop
trip back to Cold Springs Campground is possible by taking a left
turn (southwest) on the Sky Lakes Trail and going 1.0 mile to the
junction with Cold Springs Trail 3710 on the left. Follow Cold
Springs Trail,2.7 miles southeast to the campground on Road 3651.

See the page describing SKY LAKES TRAIL 3762, and the map showing
how it connects to other trails in Sky Lakes Basin.

Mosquitos are bad, especially at Cold Springs Campground, usually
until mid-August.   Sky Lakes Wilderness information and regulations are noted at the beginning of Chapter 6.

COLD SPRINGS TRAIL #3710.   (See map 12)

<u>TRAIL BEGINS:</u>	-Cold Springs Camp, Forest Road 3651. <u>ELEV.</u> 5800'
<u>TRAIL ENDS:</u>	-Sky Lakes Trail 3762. <u>ELEV.</u> 6000'
	(Near Lake Notasha).
<u>DISTANCE:</u>	-2.7 mile.
<u>USE:</u>	-Hiker/horse.
<u>SEASON:</u>	-Usually snow-free June to October.
	Mosquitos bad till about mid-August.
<u>CONNECTING TR.</u>	-South Rock Creek Trail 3709 and Sky Lakes Trail
	3762.
<u>BRING MAPS:</u>	-USFS Winema National Forest.
	-USFS Rec. Opportunity Guides, Winema Ntl. For.
	-Sky Lakes Area-Rogue River/Winema Ntl. Forests.

<u>ACCESS:</u>   <u>FROM WHITE CITY,</u> Oregon, follow mileposts east
              on State Hwy. 140, 40.9 miles to the junction of
Lost Creek Road 3651.   If driving <u>FROM ASHLAND,</u> take Dead Indian
Memorial Road (Jackson County 722, Klamath County 533) to State
Highway 140 and turn right for 3.1 miles to Road 3651.

Turn onto Road 3651 and go 10.5 miles to COLD SPRINGS TRAILHEAD
at the end of the road.

After about 0.7 mile on the Cold Springs Trail, keep left at the
junction with the South Rock Creek Trail and continue on the Cold
Springs Trail to the Sky Lakes Trail near Lake Notasha.

<u>FEATURES:</u>   This is a short and easy access to Dwarf Lakes-
              Sky Lakes Basin.   A loop trip back to Cold Spr.
Campground is possible by turning right (northeast) onto the Sky
Lakes Trail and go one mile to the junction with South Rock Creek
Trail 3709 on the right just beyond Heavenly Twin Lakes.   Follow
3709 southeast 1.6 miles to its junction with Cold Springs Trail,
turn left and go 0.7 miles back to Cold Springs Camp.

See the page describing SKY LAKES TRAIL 3762, and the map showing
how it connects to other lakes in Sky Lakes Basin.

Sky Lakes Wilderness information and regulations are noted at the
beginning of Chapter 6.

TWIN PONDS TRAIL #3715, Winema National Forest.   (See map 16)

TRAIL BEGINS:	-Fourmile Lake Campground. ELEV. 5700'
TRAIL ENDS:	-Pacific Crest National Scenic Trail. ELEV. 5900'
DISTANCE:	-2.5 miles.
SEASON:	-June to October. USE: hiker/horse.
CONNECTING TR.	-Pacific Crest Trail, Twin Ponds Trail #993.
BRING MAPS:	-Sky Lakes Area-Rogue River/Winema Ntl. Forests.
	-USFS Recreation Opportunity Guides.

ACCESS: FOURMILE LAKE.   From White City, follow mile-
               posts on Hwy. 140, 35.7 miles to the junction of
Road 3661. Go 5.6 miles north on 3661 to a road junction at Four-
mile Lake. Turn left and go 0.1 mile to a spur leading left to a
PARKING FACILITY FOR ALL TRAILS. 400ft. south of a trailhead sign,
KEEP RIGHT at a junction where Twin Ponds Tr.leads toward the PCT.

FEATURES: In the vicinity of Fourmile Lake, Trail #3715 is
                 often swampy or partly submerged. After pass-
ing Squaw Lake, it joins the Pacific Crest Trail about 2.5 miles
northwest of the trailhead.

TWIN PONDS TRAIL #993,managed by the Rogue River National Forest,
continues northwestward for 3.5 miles down Fourbit Creek. Summit
Lake is reached within the first 0.5 mi., Twin Ponds 2.0 mile beyond, and 1.0 mile further to the lower trailhead on Road 3760.
These waters sometimes dry-up in late summer.

Trail 993 has a very rocky surface in places but is much easier
to follow than in previous years. In a couple of places, it is
still suggested to look carefully for rock cairns and tree blazes.

ACCESS TO LOWER TRAILHEAD, TRAIL #993.   From White City OR,
follow mileposts on Hwy. 140, 28.6 mi. to County Route 821. Turn
north onto 821 and go 8.8 mi. to where Forest Route 37 turns east.
Follow Route 37, 1.5 mi. to Road 3760 on the right. Go 4.4 miles
on 3760 to the trailhead at the end of the road.

Trails #3715 and 993 follow the route of the 1864 Fort Klamath-
Jacksonville Military Wagon Road. Sky Lakes Wilderness information and regulations are listed at the beginning of Chapter 6.

MT. McLOUGHLIN

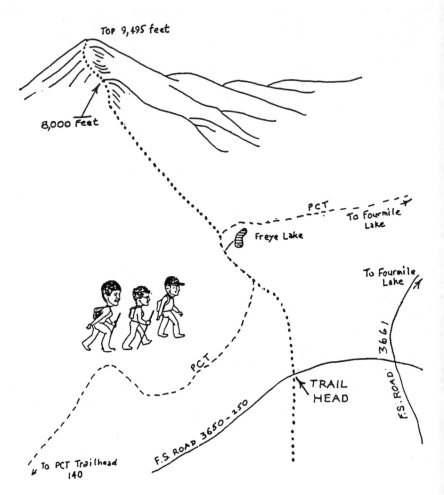

Top 9,495 feet

8,000 Feet

PCT

To Fourmile Lake

Freye Lake

To Fourmile Lake

3661

F.S. ROAD

PCT

TRAIL HEAD

F.S. ROAD 3650-250

To PCT Trailhead 140

Mt. McLOUGHLIN TRAIL #3716. (See Map 16)

TRAIL BEGINS:	-Trailhead, Forest Road 3650.	ELEV. 5580'
TRAIL ENDS:	-Mt. McLoughlin summit.	ELEV. 9495'
DISTANCE:	-About 4.9 miles, strenuous-time up 4 to 5 hours.	
SEASON:	-July thru September.	
CONNECTING TR.	-Pacific Crest National Scenic Trail.	
BRING MAPS:	-USFS Sky Lakes Area-Rogue River/Winema Ntl. For.	
	-USFS Winema National Forest.	
	-USFS "Mt. McLoughlin" information leaflets.	
	-USGS Mount McLoughlin, 7.5 minute series.	

ACCESS: From White City, Oregon, follow mileposts east
on State Hwy. 140, 35.7 miles to the junction of
Forest Road 3661. Turn left and follow mileposts on 3661, 2.9
miles to the junction with Road 3650. Turn left on 3650 and continue 0.3 mi. to the trailhead and parking area.

ROUTE: The Mt. McLoughlin Trail meets the Pacific Crest
(PCNST) Trail in about 1 mile. Turn right (N.W.)
and follow the PCNST, 1/2 mile to where the Mt. McLoughlin Trail
continues its northwesterly ascent to the summit. The trail is
not maintained beyond the tree line. ON THE WAY UP, NOTICE THAT
THE ROUTE PARALLELS A RIDGE THAT SLOPES IN AN EAST TO WEST DIREC-
TION.

ON THE RETURN TRIP.....KEEP THE SAME RELATIONSHIP WITH THE RIDGE!
INFORMAL PATHS CAN BE MISLEADING! NOTE THAT THE RIDGE RUNS MORE
EAST THAN IT DOES SOUTH.   THERE IS NO TRAIL OUT FROM THE SOUTH
SLOPES OF THE MOUNTAIN OTHER THAN THE PACIFIC CREST TRAIL! WATCH
ALSO FOR THE JUNCTIONS WITH THE PACIFIC CREST TRAIL. The McLough-
lin Trail follows the Pacific Crest Trail southeast for 1/2 mile
and turns southeast to the Road 3650 Trailhead.

From the summit; Mt. Shasta, the Klamath Basin,Rogue River Valley,
Crater Lake Rim and points into Central Oregon come into view. A
fire lookout building was once located at the summit.

103

PRECAUTIONS: (Quotes from USFS -HIKING THE McLOUGHLIN TRAIL)
"Remember.....Every year someone gets lost hiking Mt. McLoughlin.
This could be prevented by following three basic rules: 1). Never
travel alone. 2). Stay with your group.   3). Stay on the trail.
Allow plenty of time for your climb (average 8 hours round trip).
Travel only during the daylight hours and don't attempt to travel
during unsettled weather or when storms are forecast. Wilderness
areas challenge your skills in traversing using map and compass."

"BE AWARE OF THE SYMPTOMS OF HYPOTHERMIA. Hypothermia is a rapid
and progressive mental and physical collapse, resulting from low-
ering the inner temperature of the body.   Left untreated, hypothermia can result in death.   Briefly, the symptoms to watch for
are: uncontrollable shivering; vague, slow speech; memory lapses;
immobile or fumbling hands; frequent stumbling; drowsiness and
apparent exhaustion. The best treatment is to eliminate exposure.
Get the victim out of the wind and rain. Strip off all wet clothing and put him in a sleeping bag with another person........also
stripped.   Keep the victim awake and give warm drinks.   If possible, build a warming fire."

BRING DRINKING WATER: THERE IS NO WATER ALONG THE SUMMIT TRAIL.
FOOD: "High energy foods such as nuts, raisins, hard candy,
fruit, fruit juices and grain products are excellent choices."
CLOTHING AND EQUIPMENT: "Vibram-soled hiking boots, extra wool
socks, light/warm clothing (preferably wool) that can be layered,
raingear, gloves, and hat. EQUIPMENT: MAP AND COMPASS, FIRST AID
KIT with matches, moleskin or tape for blisters, goggles or sun-
glasses, suntan cream and a flashlight for emergencies.

NOTE: The Mt. McLoughlin trail can also be accessed by hiking
the Pacific Crest Tr. about 4 mi. north from its Hwy. 140 Trailhead, located between mileposts 32 and 33 on State Highway 140.
Sky Lakes Wilderness information and regulations are noted at the
beginning of Chapter 6.

BADGER LAKE TRAIL #3759   (See Maps 16,17)

TRAIL BEGINS:	-Fourmile Lake Campground.	ELEV. 5750'
TRAIL ENDS:	-Jnc. Red Lake Trail and unmaintained	
	Lost Creek Trail.	ELEV. 5950'
DISTANCE:	-Woodpecker Lake 1.3 mile, Badger Lake 1.6 mile,	
	Long Lake 3.6 Mile. Easy grades. Hiker/horse.	
SEASON:	-July to October, mosquitos until mid-August.	
CONNECTING TR.	-Rye Spur 3771, Red Lake 987, unmaintained Lost	
	Creek 3712.	
BRING MAPS:	-USFS Sky Lakes Area-Rogue River/Winema Ntl. For.	
	-USFS Winema National Forest.	

ACCESS: From White City, follow mileposts on State Highway 140, 35.7 miles to the junction with Forest
Road 3661. Turn north onto 3661 and go 5.6 miles to the junction
at Fourmile Lake.

A PARKING AREA FOR ALL TRAILS can be reached by turning left for
0.1 mile, then left again to the parking area.   A sign indicates
the Twin Ponds, Pacific Crest, and Badger Lake Trails. 400' south
of this sign is a junction leading left to Rye Spur Trail.   When
reaching the Rye Spur Trail, turn left (north) and cross the Cascade Canal to the BADGER LAKE TRAILHEAD.

FEATURES: This is an easy access route into Sky Lakes Wil-
derness leading north to Woodpecker,Badger,Lilly
Pond, and Long Lakes before ending at the junction with Red Lake
Trail 987 and unmaintained Lost Creek Trail 3712.

Traveling southward on the Pacific Crest Trail to the Twin Ponds
Trail and back to Four Mile Lake Campground makes for an adven-
turous day trip, total loop distance about 13 miles.

Sky Lakes Wilderness information and regulations are noted at the
beginning of Chapter 6.

CHAPTER 7 - MOUNTAIN LAKES WILDERNESS

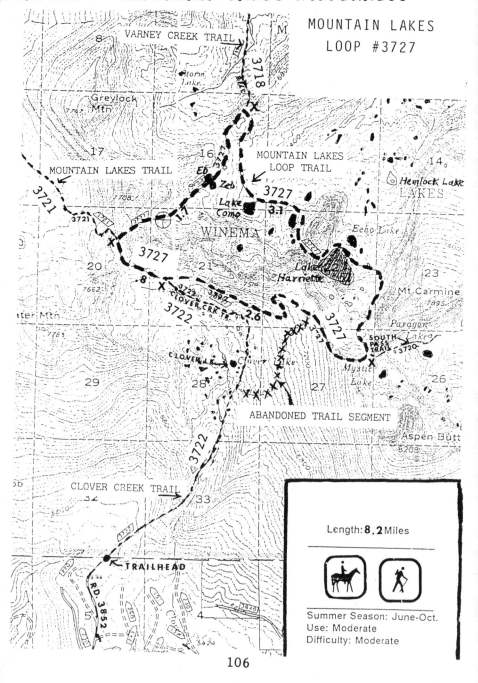

MOUNTAIN LAKES
LOOP #3727

Length: **8.2** Miles

Summer Season: June-Oct.
Use: Moderate
Difficulty: Moderate

MOUNTAIN LAKES WILDERNESS AREA. (See map 17)

HISTORY: "In 1930 Mountain Lakes was established as one of the first three primitive areas in the Pacific Northwest Region. In 1940 the original 13,444 acres was increased to 23,071 acres and the name was changed to the Mountain Lakes Wild Area. The Mountain Lakes became a part of the National Wilderness System in 1964." (Quote: USFS Winema National Forest)

FEATURES: Most of the area is above 6000 ft. elevation. The "hub" of the maintained trail system is the Mountain Lakes Loop Trail that circles the old volcanic caldera rim in the heart of the wilderness. It is accessed by the Varney Creek Trail 3718 from the north, Mountain Lakes Trail 3721 from the west and Clover Creek Trail 3722 from the south. Eb and Zeb Lakes, Lake Como, Lake Harriette and Clover Lake are just a few of the highlights on the loop trail. Aspen Butte (elevation 8208') is the highest point in the wilderness.

REGULATIONS. "To protect the wilderness resource, the following regulations are enforced:

1. Hiking and camping group size is limited to 10 people and/or stock in any combination.
2. Hikers must camp at least 100 feet from lakeshores, streams and springs.
3. Pack and saddle stock should stay at least 200 feet away from all water sources,except when traveling on established trails.
4. Campers with pack and saddle stock must camp at least 200 feet from lakeshores, streams and springs.
5. Bicycles, motorbikes, and other mechanized equipment are not allowed within the wilderness area. Please contact the Klamath Ranger District Office for information on areas designated for these and other recreation opportunities."
   (Quote: Winema National Forest-Klamath Ranger District)

VARNEY CREEK TRAIL #3718.   (See map 17)

TRAIL BEGINS:	–End of Forest Road 3664.	ELEV. 5600'
TRAIL ENDS:	–Mountain Lakes Loop Trail 3727.	ELEV. 6630'
DISTANCE:	–4.4 miles, moderate. USE: hikers/horses.	
SEASON:	–Usually snow-free June through October, carry insect repellant during early summer months.	
BRING MAPS:	–USFS Recreation Opportunity Guide, Varney Cr. Tr.	
	–USFS Mountain Lakes Wilderness.	
	–USFS Winema National Forest.	

ACCESS: The Varney Creek Trailhead is located at the end
of Forest Road 3664, and can be reached from two
points on STATE HIGHWAY 140:

NEAR MILEPOST 43 (mile 43.3). Turn south on Forest Road 3610 and
continue 1.7 miles to the junction with Forest Road 3667. Turn
left and continue 3.0 miles to Forest Road 3664. Turn right and
continue 2 miles to the trailhead at the end of the road.

NEAR MILEPOST 48.   Turn south onto Forest Road 3667 and continue
1.8 miles to Forest Road 3664. Turn left and continue 2 miles to
the trailhead at the end of the road.

FEATURES: Trail 3718 maintains a steady uphill grade as it
               follows Varney Cr. into the wilderness area. The
"hub" of the maintained trail system is the Mountain Lakes Loop
Trail 3727, forming a 8.2 mile loop around the old caldera rim
in the heart of the wilderness.   This loop trail can also be ac-
cessed by Mountain Lakes Trail 3721 from the west and Clover Cr.
Trail 3722 from the south.   THE SOUTH END OF THE LOOP TRAIL HAS
BEEN REROUTED THROUGH MAP SECTIONS 21 and 22 AT THE 7000' LEVEL
AND NO LONGER DROPS DOWN TO CLOVER LAKE.   THE CLOVER CREEK TRAIL
HAS BEEN EXTENDED NORTHWEST OF CLOVER LAKE TO JOIN THE LOOP TRAIL
REROUTE.   THE SECTION OF THE OLD LOOP TRAIL LEADING EAST   FROM
CLOVER LAKE TO THE LOOP TRAIL HAS BEEN ABANDONED. See beginning
of Chapter 7 for information and wilderness regulations.

MOUNTAIN LAKES TRAIL #3721.   (See map 17)

TRAIL BEGINS:	-Forest Road 3660.	ELEV. 5200'
TRAIL ENDS:	-Mountain Lakes Loop Trail 3727,	ELEV. 7400'
DISTANCE:	-5.1 miles. USE: hiker/horse. Moderate. HIKERS	

DISTANCE: -5.1 miles. USE: hiker/horse. Moderate. HIKERS
              can also access the trail from Rainbow Bay Pic-
              nic Area, across from the restrooms.
SEASON: -Usually snow-free June through October.
BRING MAPS: -USFS Winema National Forest Recreation Map/Guide.
              -USFS Mountain Lakes Wilderness map.

ACCESS: Follow mileposts (numbering from WHITE CITY) on
              State Hwy. 140 to mile 37.7 at the junction with
Dead Indian Memorial Road (Klamath County Rte. 533). If using the
UPPER ACCESS where parking is limited and there is no turn-around
facility, turn right onto Dead Indian Memorial Road and go 0.1 mi.
to Road 3610.   Turn left onto Road 3610, and go 0.8 mile to Road
3660.   The trailhead is 0.8 mile up Road 3660.

Using   the LOWER, Lake of the Woods facility where horses are not
allowed: across from the restrooms at the Rainbow Bay Picnic Area
follow the Family Loop(Mtn.Lake) Trail a short distance, crossing
the Sunset Trail and Road 3704. A junction is soon reached at the
beginning of the Family Trail Loops, and where MOUNTAIN LAKES TR.
turns right to cross Dead Indian Memorial Rd. and on to the upper
Mountain Lakes Trail access on Road 3660.

FEATURES: The trail climbs up Seldom Creek through tranquil
              meadows and along volcanic outcrops. The scenery
gradually changes to higher elevation mountain hemlock/subalpine
fir communities before ending at Mountain Lakes Loop Trail #3727.

Mountain Lakes Loop Trail makes an 8.2 mile loop around the old
caldera rim in the heart of the wilderness.The loop trail is also
accessed by Varney Creek Trail 3718 from the north and Clover Cr.
Trail 3722 from the south.   THE SOUTH END OF THE LOOP TRAIL HAS
BEEN REROUTED   THROUGH MAP SECTIONS 21 and 22 AT THE 7000' LEVEL,
AND NO LONGER DROPS TO CLOVER CREEK TRAIL   SOUTH OF CLOVER LAKE.
THE CLOVER CREEK TRAIL HAS BEEN EXTENDED NORTHWEST OF CLOVER LAKE
TO JOIN THE LOOP TRAIL REROUTE.   See beginning of Chapter 7 for
Mountain Lakes historical notes and regulations.

CLOVER CREEK TRAIL #3722. (See map 17)

TRAIL BEGINS:	-End of Forest Road 3852.	ELEV.	5600'
TRAIL ENDS:	-Mountain Lakes Loop Trail 3727.	ELEV.	7000'
DISTANCE:	-About 3.4 miles. Moderate grades.		
SEASON:	-Usually snow-free June-Oct. Hiker/horse.		
BRING MAPS:	-USFS Mountain Lakes Wilderness.		
	-USFS Winema National Forest.		
	-USFS Recreation Opportunity Guide, Clover Creek Trail 3722.		

ACCESS: From Interstate Hwy. 5, Ashland-Klamath Falls Exit 14, travel 0.6 mi. east on State Highway 66 to the junction with Dead Indian Memorial Road(Jackson County Route 722, Klamath County 533). Turn left and follow this road 28.3 miles to the junction with Clover Creek Road (Klamath County Route 603). Travel southeast on Clover Creek Road, 5.8 miles to the junction with Forest Road 3852 on the left. Turn onto Road 3852 and go 3.3 miles to the trailhead at the end of the road.

FEATURES: It is 2.3 miles up the trail to an older,abandoned section of the Mountain Lakes Loop Trail heading east. The Clover Creek Trail has been extended from this point, passing Clover Lake and junctions WITH A RELOCATED SECTION OF THE MOUNTAIN LAKES LOOP TRAIL 1.1 MILE FURTHER THROUGH MAP SECTIONS 20 and 21, elevation 7000'.

Mountain Lakes Loop Trail 3727 is an 8.2 mile loop around an old caldera rim in the heart of the wilderness and can also be accessed via Mountain Lakes Trail 3721 from the west, and Varney Creek Trail 3718 from the north.

See beginning of Chapter 7 for Mountain Lakes historical notes and regulations.

<u>MOUNTAIN LAKES LOOP TRAIL #3727.</u> (See map 17)

<u>DISTANCE:</u>   -8.2 miles,moderate grade. <u>USE:</u> hiker/horse.
<u>SEASON:</u>   -June to October.
<u>CONNECTING TR.</u> -Mountain Lakes #3721; Varney Creek #3718, Clover
                 Creek #3722.
<u>BRING MAPS:</u>   -USFS Recreation Opportunity Guide-Trail #3727.
                 -USFS Mountain Lakes Wilderness.
                 -USFS Winema National Forest.

<u>ACCESS:</u>   This trail can be accessed by entering the wil-
                derness from any of the 3 Mountain Lakes Trail-
heads; Varney Creek, Clover Creek, and Mountain Lakes(See text).

<u>FEATURES:</u>   "Following this trail clockwise FROM THE JUNCTION
                OF THE LOOP TRAIL WITH MOUNTAIN LAKES TRAIL, the
Loop Trail climbs gently through a pass north of Whiteface Peak
and descends into the caldera between crystal blue Lake Eb & Lake
Zeb.   Past the junction with Varney Creek Trail, the Loop Trail
passes along gentle slopes north of Lake Como and many small wilderness lakes. The trail then climbs a short steep pass to skirt
the windblown waters of Lake Harriette, the largest lake in the
Mountain Lakes Wilderness. From Harriette, the trail meanders up
the lower slopes of Mt.Carmine before steeply climbing the southern caldera rim. Views of the wilderness lakes and peaks, as well
as vast southern vistas, are spectacular from this vantage point.
The section of trail from here to the Clover Creek Trail has been
relocated and is easily found. The new route switchbacks down a
rugged rock scree, then follows this land feature to the west,
where the trail completes the circuit at the Mountain Lakes Trail
junction. The wet meadows, stream banks, and lakeshores which the
traveller discovers in this high elevation setting are both beautiful and extremely fragile microenvironments which require the
practice of minimum trace visitation in order to survive"
                                                      (USFS Quote)
See beginning of Chapter 7 for Mountain Lakes historical notes
and regulations.

CHAPTER 8 - FISH LAKE - LAKE OF THE WOODS

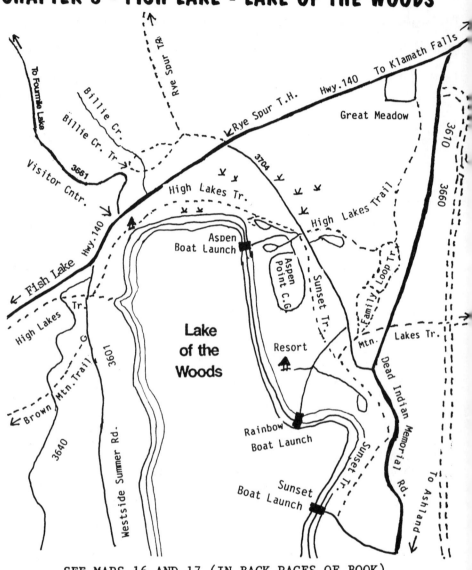

SEE MAPS 16 AND 17 (IN BACK PAGES OF BOOK)

HIGH LAKES TRAIL #6200.-Scheduled Completion, summer 1996.

TRAIL BEGINS:	-WEST TRAILHEAD-Fish Lake,Hwy.140 near Milepost 30.
	-EAST TRAILHEAD-Great Meadow- 140 near Milepost 37.
DISTANCE:	-9.0 mile, easy. USE: hiker/jogger/mtn. bikes,
	motorized wheelchairs,no other motorized vehicles.
SEASON:	-June through October. Winter skiing, snowmobiles.
CONNECTING TR.	-Family Loop,Sunset,Pacific Crest,Fish Lake Trails.
BRING MAPS:	-Info from Rogue River-Winema Ntl. Forest Offices.

ACCESS POINTS ALONG HIGHWAY 140,MILEPOSTS NUMBER FROM WHITE CITY.
-Mile 30.4: FISH LAKE TRAILHEAD, along Fish Lake Access Road.
-MILE 35.4 ROAD 3601 JUNCTION. Turn right and go 0.1 mile to
Road 3640. Follow Road 3640, 0.3 mile to a HIGH LAKES TRAILHEAD.
-Mile 36.4: ROAD 3704 JUNCTION. Turn right onto Road 3704 and go
0.6 mile to the entrance of Aspen Point Campground. Drive to the
end of the first campground loop on the right, HIGH LAKES TRAIL-
HEAD is located near the restrooms.
-Mile 36.4: ROAD 3704 JUNCTION leading 1.0 mile to the Resort
turnoff. Turn right and go 0.1 mile to the RAINBOW BAY PICNIC
AREA. Across from the restrooms, the Family Loop Trail uses the
Mtn. Lakes Trail to a junction where the Family Loops keep LEFT
to join a portion of HIGH LAKES TRAIL in less than 1.0 mile.
-Mile 37.5: GREAT MEADOW TRAILHEAD. The trail begins just beyond
the restrooms, crossing a spillway before skirting the far end
of the meadow, on its way to the west terminus at Fish Lake.

FROM ASHLAND,   Follow Dead Indian Memorial Road (Jackson County
Route 722,Klamath County 533),36 miles to State Highway 140. Turn
left onto Hwy. 140, GREAT MEADOW is immediately to the left. Hwy.
140 leads west to Fish Lake and other access points of the trail.

FEATURES: The High Lakes Trail travels through 2.5 miles of lava
flows and groves of aspen and fir. You can also experience views
of Mt. McLoughlin and Pelican Butte. Interpretive signs indicate
geological, wildlife and botanical features. A map at the beginning of Chapter 8 shows loops and connection opportunities with
other trails. The trail crosses the Pacific Crest Trail (closed
to mechanized vehicles),to co-locate with FISH LAKE TR. #1013 for
one mile before the Fish Lake Trail departs left to Fish Lake,and
High Lakes Trail keeps right to end north of Fish Lake Resort.SEE
MAPS 16-17 (Back of Book).

<u>SUNSET TRAIL #6202.</u> (See map beginning of Chapter 8)

<u>TRAIL BEGINS:</u>   -Sunset Campground, Lake of the Woods,milepost 34,
                     Dead Indian Memorial Road(Klamath County Rte.533).
<u>TRAIL ENDS:</u>   -Aspen Point Campground, Lake of the Woods.
<u>DISTANCE:</u>   -About 2 miles.   <u>USE:</u> bikers/hikers.
<u>SEASON:</u>   -Usually snow-free June through October.
<u>CONNECTING TR.</u> -Family Loop, Mtn. Lakes and Highlakes Trails.
<u>BRING MAPS:</u>   -Info from Rogue River-Winema Ntl. Forest Offices.

<u>FROM ASHLAND,</u> Follow Dead Indian Memorial Road (Jackson County
Route 722,Klamath County 533),34 miles to SUNSET CAMPGROUND. Turn
left to the boat launch parking area.
<u>RAINBOW BAY PICNIC AREA.</u> Continue 1.0 mile on Dead Indian Memo-
rial Road to Road 3704. Turn onto 3704 and go 0.3 mi. to the
Resort turnoff. Take the turnoff 0.1 mi. to RAINBOW BAY PICNIC
AREA and turn left past the restrooms to Sunset Tr.(end of road).
<u>ASPEN POINT CAMPGROUND</u> turnoff is located 0.4 miles further along
Road 3704.

<u>FROM WHITE CITY,</u> Follow State Highway 140, 36.4 miles to Road
3704 on the right. Take Road 3704, 0.6 miles to ASPEN POINT
CAMPGROUND turnoff and 0.4 miles further to the Resort turnoff
leading to RAINBOW BAY PICNIC AREA. To reach SUNSET CAMPGROUND,
continue 0.3 mile further on Road 3704 to Dead Indian Memorial
Road and turn right to milepost 34.Turn right to boat dock area.

<u>FEATURES:</u> Sunset Trail begins from the SUNSET BOAT LAUNCH par-
king lot and continues 1.0 mile northwest along the Lake of the
Woods shoreline to the parking spaces at RAINBOW BAY PICNIC AREA.
Go straight across the parking spaces, and look immediately left
for the trail leading about 0.5 mile to the junction with <u>Family
Loop Trail,</u>and about 0.5 miles further to ASPEN POINT CAMPGROUND
where Sunset Trail terminates at the <u>HIGHLAKES TRAIL.</u>

<u>NOTE:</u> Family Loop Trail uses the <u>Mtn. Lakes Trail</u> to a junction
where the family loops begin left to join a portion of <u>Highlakes
Trail</u> in less than one mile.

A map at the beginning of Chapter 8 shows the many loop and connection opportunities with other trails.

RYE SPUR TRAIL #3771.   (See maps 16 and 17)

TRAIL BEGINS:	-Fourmile Lake Campground.	ELEV. 5750'
TRAIL ENDS:	-State Hwy. 140, near milepost 36.	ELEV. 5000'
DISTANCE:	-6.1 miles, SEASON: July-October.	
USE:	-Hikers, horses. Motor bikes allowed, but beginning riders may find lower 1.5 mi. too steep.	
BRING MAPS:	-USFS Winema Ntl. Forest/Rec. Opportunity Guide.	

ACCESS: From White City,OR,follow mileposts on State Highway 140, 35.7 mile to the jnc. with Road 3661. UPPER TRAILHEAD: Turn left (north) onto 3661 and go 5.6 miles to the signed PARKING AREA FOR ALL TRAILS, at Fourmile Lake Campground.   South of a trail sign, a trail leads east, crossing Road 3661, to the jnc. with Rye Spur Trail, just below the dam at the southeast end of the lake.   Turn right (south) to continue toward the lower trailhead.

LOWER TRAILHEAD: From the above junction of Highway 140 and Road 3661, continue east on Hwy.140, 0.4 mile,just beyond milepost 36, and turn left (north) onto a road track paralleling Hwy.140. Make an immediate right turn leading toward RYE SPUR TRAILHEAD.The one mile BILLIE CREEK NATURE TRAIL, for hikers and horses only,is located 1000ft. up the trail and loops through stands of ponderosa pine, white fir and other coniferous trees. It crosses Billie Cr. in two locations. Decayed logs from past logging activities provide food and cover for wildlife. After passing Billie Creek Tr., Rye Spur Trail continues about 6 mi. to Fourmile Lake Campground.

HIKERS would benefit mostly by hiking 3.4 mi.from the upper trailhead to the viewpoint and return. From the viewpoint, there are views of Pelican Butte,Mountain Lakes Wilderness and of the fault systems below, leading north into Sky Lakes Wilderness and south into California.You could also return to the campground by hiking beyond the viewpoint to the Cascade Canal and turning left(northeast) along the canal road. Total loop distance is 9.0 miles.

South of the Cascade Canal, Rye Spur Trail continues,crossing Rd. 3633, and 0.9 more miles to the junction with BILLIE CREEK NATURE TRAIL, for hikers and horses only. Keep left and go about 1000ft. to Rye Spur lower trailhead. Rye Spur Trail,a portion of the former Oregon Skyline Trail, is maintained by "Desert Trail Riders" of Klamath Falls.

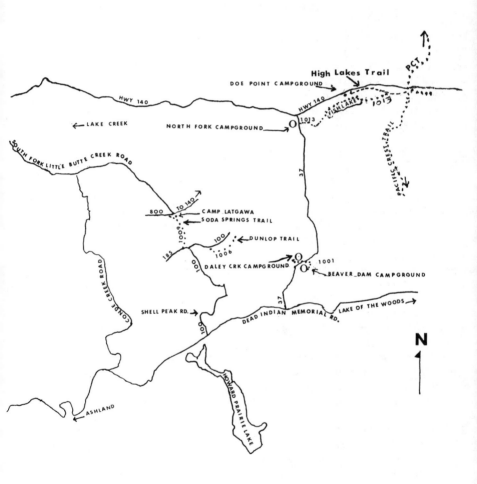

FISH LAKE TRAIL #1013.   (See map 16)

TRAIL BEGINS:	-North Fork Campground, Forest Route 37-ELEV. 4560'
TRAIL ENDS:	-Pacific Crest National Scenic Trail. ELEV. 4950'
DISTANCE:	-5 miles (one way), EASY, MAY-OCTOBER.
USE:	-Hikers/mountain bikes. Bikes not allowed on PCT!
CONNECTING TR.	-Pacific Crest and High Lakes Trails.
BRING MAPS:	-USFS Ashland Ranger Dist.-Rogue River Ntl. Forest.
	-USFS Pacific Crest Trail-Oregon Southern Portion.
	-USFS Recreation Opportunity Guide-(this trail).

ACCESS: From Interstate Hwy. 5, Ashland-Klamath Falls Exit
                14, travel 0.6 mile east on State Hwy. 66 to the
junction with Dead Indian Memorial Road (County Route 722). Turn
left onto this road and go 22 miles to the junction with Forest
Route 37 (Big Elk Road). Turn left onto Route 37 and go 7 miles
to NORTH FORK CAMPGROUND. The western end of the FISH LAKE TRAIL
is across Route 37 from the campground.
TO BEGIN AT DOE POINT OR FISH LAKE CAMPGROUNDS, continue 1.0 mile
north on Route 37 to Highway 140. Turn right and go 2.0 miles to
the Fish Lake turnoff. Turn right and follow signs. Parking is at
either of the day use picnic areas.
TO BEGIN AT THE PCNST SUMMIT TRAILHEAD: continue 2 miles east on
Highway 140 just beyond milepost 32, to the trailhead entrance on
the left. Hike the PCNST south (crossing Hwy. 140) and go 0.5 mi
to the junction with Fish Lake and High Lakes Trails that are co-
located for one mile west before Fish Lake Tr. keeps left to Fish
Lake and beyond to terminate at Forest Route 37.

FEATURES: From the trailhead at North Fork Campground, the
                trail follows the North Fork of Little Butte Creek
and after 0.5 mi., a side trail leads right to Fish Lake Dam. The
main trail turns left and follows the north shore of Fish Lake.
The picnic areas at DOE POINT and FISH LAKE campgrounds are good
midpoints to begin a hike either direction on the trail. Continuing through these campgrounds, the trail leads past Fish Lake Resort, skirts the end of the lake and heads east through a forest
with large openings of basalt lava. Fish Lake Trail reaches the
High Lakes Trail and the two trails co-locate for one mile east,
to where Fish Lake Trail terminates. PACK/SADDLE STOCK NOT PER-
MITTED IN DEVELOPED RECREATION SITES AT FISH LAKE. SEE THE LATEST
USFS RECREATION GUIDES FOR DETAILS OF A NEARBY TETHERING AREA.

PACIFIC CREST NATIONAL SCENIC TRAIL-HWY. 140 TO FOREST ROAD 700.
(See maps 16 and 23)

TRAIL BEGINS: -PCNST parking area off Hwy. 140.   ELEV. 5100'
TRAIL ENDS: -Forest Road 700.   ELEV. 5200'
DISTANCE: -10.6 miles (one way) MODERATE.
SEASON: -June through October.
CONNECTING TR:-Fish Lake, High Lakes, Brown Mountain Trails.
BRING MAPS: -USFS Pacific Crest Trail-Oregon Southern Portion.
              -USFS Ashland Ranger Dist.-Rogue River Ntl. Forest.
              -USFS Recreation Opportunity Guide.

FEATURES: CARRY WATER-...There are no sources along the way!
              Beginning from the Pacific Crest Trailhead on Hwy.
              140,a 0.2 mile access trail leads to the PCNST. At
this junction, turn left (SOUTH) and follow the trail along the
Cascade Canal for 0.5 mile to Hwy.140. The trail crosses the Hwy.
and continues 0.5 miles to the junction with High Lakes Trail and
Fish Lake Trail 1013 that are co-located for one mile before Fish
Lake Trail keeps LEFT (south) on its way to Fish Lake Resort and
High Lakes Trail keeps RIGHT (north) to end north of the resort.

Continuing south, the trail begins a 5.0 mile traverse over Brown
Mountain lava flows (on a cinder trail surface), gaining 800 ft.
in elevation. Once leaving the lava flows, the trail enters a
dense conifer forest. Solomon's seal, prince's pine, and huckle-
berries blanket the forest floor. A small campsite is reached
just prior to the junction with the Brown Mountain Trail. (8.6
mile point). From this junction, the trail continues south another 2 miles to Forest Road 700. This is the ending point for
this hike.

Along this section of trail, there are good views of Brown Mtn.,
Robinson Butte and Mt. McLoughlin. (Excerpts USFS Recreation Opportunity Guide)

Some folks may wish to extend the trip to the trailhead on Dead
Indian Memorial Road, 1.9 trail miles further south. Just 800 ft.
south of Road 700, a short side-trail leaves the PCNST to the
SOUTH BROWN MOUNTAIN SHELTER. A WATER PUMP HAS BEEN INSTALLED AT
THIS LOCATION.

118

-Continued

HWY.140 ACCESS   From Ashland Interstate 5 Exit 14, drive east on
                 Highway 66, 0.6 mile to Dead Indian Memorial Road
(Jackson County Route 722, Klamath County 533).   Turn onto this
road and go 22 miles to the junction with Forest Route 37. Turn
left onto Route 37 and proceed 8 miles to the junction with Highway 140. Turn right onto 140 and go 4.2 miles to Forest Rd. 3650.
Turn left onto Rd. 3650 and an immediate left onto Road 010 leading to the Pacific Crest Summit Trailhead. A short 0.2 mi. access
trail leads to the Pacific Crest Trail.

RD. 700 ACCESS   From Ashland Interstate 5 Exit 14, drive east on
                 Highway 66, 0.6 mile to Dead Indian Memorial Road
(Jackson County Route 722, Klamath County 533).   Turn onto this
road and go 26.5 miles to Forest Road 3720. Turn left onto 3720
and go 2 miles to Road 700. Turn right onto 700 and continue 0.4
miles to where the PCNST crosses the road.   Parking is available
between the Road 500 spur and the trail.

DEAD INDIAN MEMORIAL ROAD ACCESS: From Ashland Interstate 5 Exit
14,drive east on Highway 66, 0.6 mile to Dead Indian Memorial Rd.
(Jackson County Route 722, Klamath County 533).   Travel left onto
this road, 27.2 miles to the Pacific Crest Trail parking area, at
Pederson Snow Park.

SHUTTLE ARRANGEMENTS:
Driving distance between Pederson Park-PCT Trailhead and the PCT
Summit Trailhead on Hwy. 140 is 15.1 miles, (north on Dead Indian
Memorial Rd. to Hwy. 140 and turning west 5.1 mi. to the PCT Sum-
mit Trailhead).

Driving distance from the Road 700 PCT crossing-to the PCT Summit
Trailhead on Hwy. 140 is 12.8 miles,by returning 0.4 miles to Rd.
3720. Turn right and go 2 miles to Road 3705.   Turn right again
and go 4 miles to Route 37. Turn right onto 37 and go 2.2 miles
to Hwy. 140. Turn right and go 4.2 miles to Road 3650 (PCT Trailhead) on the left.

BROWN MTN. TRAIL #1005-ROGUE RIV. NTL. FOREST SECTION. (Map 16)

TRAIL BEGINS:	-Forest Road 3705.	ELEV. 4850'
TRAIL ENDS:	-Forest Road 3640.	ELEV. 5650'
DISTANCE:	-5.3 miles (one way), moderate.	
SEASON:	-Mid May to October.	
USE:	-Hikers, horses, mountain bikes when trail sur- faces are dry.	
CONNECTING TR.	-Pacific Crest National Scenic Trail #2000. -Brown Mtn. Trail 3724 (Winema Ntl. Forest).	
BRING MAPS:	-USFS Ashland Ranger Dist.-Rogue River Ntl. Forest. -USFS Pacific Crest Trail-Oregon Southern Portion. -USFS Rec. Opportunity Guide-Brown Mountain Trail.	

ACCESS: FOREST ROAD 3705 TRAILHEAD. From Interstate Hwy.
5 Ashland-Klamath Falls Exit 14,go 0.6 mile east
on State Hwy. 66 to the junction with Dead Indian Memorial Road
(County Route 722). Turn left onto this road and travel 22 miles
to the junction with Forest Route 37 (Big Elk Road). Turn left
onto Route 37 and go 6.0 miles to Forest Road 3705. Turn right on
3705 and continue 3.0 miles to the trailhead.

FOREST ROAD 3640 TRAILHEAD. From the above Road 3705 Trailhead,
continue southeast on Road 3705 for 1.0 mile to the junction with
Forest Road 3720. Turn left onto Road 3720 and continue for 1.5
miles to the junction with Road 700. Turn left onto Road 700 and
travel 3 miles to Road 3640. Turn left onto Road 3640 and proceed
1.5 miles to the trailhead.

FEATURES: From the Rd. 3705 Trailhead, the Brown Mtn. Trail
                crosses Road 500 in 1.5 miles. At 2.5 miles you
cross Road 560 and at 2.9 miles you cross the Pacific Crest National Scenic Trail. At 5.2 miles the trail forks; TAKE THE TRAIL
TO THE RIGHT 0.1 MI. TO THE RD. 3640 TRAILHEAD. The trail to the
left is Brown Mtn. Trail 3724 (Winema Ntl. Forest section) that
continues 2.5 miles to Lake of the Woods.

BROWN MTN. TRAIL #3724 WINEMA NTL. FOREST SECTION. (Maps 16 & 17)
(See preceding page for continuation in Rogue River Ntl. Forest).

TRAIL BEGINS: -Forest Road 3640 Trailhead.   ELEV. 5640'
TRAIL ENDS: -Forest Road 3601 Trailhead.   ELEV. 4960'
DISTANCE: -2.5 miles.
SEASON: -June-October.
USE: -Hiker/horse.
CONNECTING TR. -Brown Mtn. Trail 3705- Rogue River Ntl. Forest.
BRING MAPS: -USFS Winema National Forest.

ACCESS: Take State Highway 140 to summer home Road 3601,
                located at the west end of Lake Of The Woods near
milepost 35. Turn south on Road 3601 and go 0.1 mile to the junction with Forest Road 3640 and:

Keep left on Road 3601 and go 0.4 mi. to the LOWER TRAILHEAD near
Camp McLoughlin, OR.....

Turn right onto Rd. 3640 and go 3 miles to the UPPER TRAILHEAD on
the right side of the road.

DUNLOP TRAIL #1006. Moderate, May-Oct., hiker only beyond meadow.
SODA SPRINGS TRAIL #1009.Moderate, yearlong from Soda Springs.
BRING MAPS: -USFS Recreation Opportunity Guides.
               -Rogue River Ntl. Forest- Ashland Ranger District.
               (See maps 15-16 back of this book).

ACCESS to UPPER TRAILHEADS-SHELL PEAK ROAD-FOREST ROAD 2500-100.
From Interstate Hwy. 5 Ashland-Klamath Falls Exit 14, go 0.6 mile
east on State Hwy. 66 to the junction with Dead Indian Memorial
Road (County Route 722) and travel 18.5 miles to Shell Peak Road
on the left. Follow Shell Peak Road 5.6 miles to the junction of
Road 2500-185 and turn left 250 ft. to SODA SPRINGS TRAILHEAD.

SODA SPRINGS TRAIL #1009 begins at ELEVATION 4060'dropping steeply 2.5 miles to the lower trailhead on Forest Road 3730-800 ELEV-
ATION 2740'. The trail begins through heavy timber and soon comes
to a site of a clearcut that affords a wide view of the surround
ing area before re-entering the forest. A grove of oak and maple
is reached at the lower elevations,soon to be followed by a rocky
ledge with more good views. Descending further, you come to the
junction with the trail leading right to Latgawa Church Camp. But
turn left to the soda springs, cross a foot bridge, and continue
to the lower trailhead on Road 3730-800.See next page for access.

The DUNLOP TRAILHEAD is reached by going 0.9 mile further on ROAD
2500-100 at a road gate just before MILEPOST 7, ELEVATION 3700'.
Trail distance is 1.5 miles one way,that takes you past beautiful
meadows, an interesting old homestead site,and some of the grand-
est ponderosa pines that you will ever see. The trail ends in the
canyon of the South Fork of Little Butte Creek where fishing for
small cutthroat trout is usually very good. ELEVATION 2400'.

Sierra Club volunteers and Forest Service trail crews rebuilt the
Dunlop Trail in 1990. Soda Springs Trail was rebuilt in 1992 by
Forest Service crews and the Northwest Youth Corps.

"The Dunlop Ranch was said to have been settled by a bootlegger
referred to as 'ol' man Dunlop-in the 1920's.   During the 1930's
a family named Nickerson'got by' raising goats, whose hides were
used for car upholstery and convertible tops.   The site has been
abandoned since the late 1930's."

122

-Continued

ACCESS TO SODA SPRINGS LOWER TRAILHEAD. (See map 14 and 15)
FROM ASHLAND: Follow Dead Indian Memorial Road (County Route 722)
just before milepost 14 and turn left onto Conde Creek Road.   Go
11.3 mi. to the junction with South Fork Little Butte Creek Road.
Turn right and go about 3.7 miles to the junction with Road 3730-
800 and turn right 0.5 miles to the Soda Springs lower trailhead.
FROM MEDFORD: Follow Hwy. 62, 6 mi. to the junction with Highway
140.   Turn right onto 140 and go 12.3 miles to the community of
Lake Creek. Follow South Fork Little Butte Creek Road 13 miles to
the junction with Road 3730-800. Turn right and go 0.5 mi. to the
Soda Springs lower trailhead.
FROM THE LOWER TRAILHEAD, Soda Springs Trail follows Dead Indian
Creek a short distance to Soda Springs.   Cross the footbridge to
the junction with the trail to Latgawa Church Camp.Turn right for
the steep uphill climb to the upper trailhead on Road 2500-185.
(Elevation gain 1320').

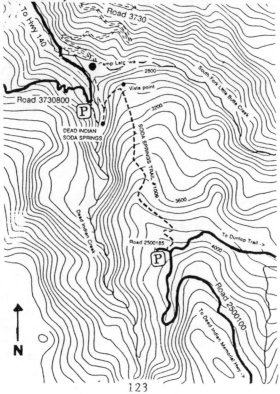

BEAVER DAM TRAIL #1001, hiker only.
2.1 mi.,easy, May-Oct. Elev. 4500'.

Beaver Dam Trail is between two dif-
ferent types of habitat; streamside
and forest. The setting is the confluence of three small creeks which
drain the southern Dead Indian Plateau. Beaver Dam Creek, Daley Creek
and Deadwood Creek flow through an
area of grassy banks, willows, false
hellbore and beaver ponds. The trail
connects Beaver Dam and Daley Creek
Campgrounds, forming a partial loop.

TREES: Douglas fir, white pine. Pacific yew is poisonous, eating fo-
liage or seeds contained in bright
red berries can result in death.

WILDFLOWERS: bleeding heart,calypso
orchid and trillium.

BIRDS: CAVITY NESTERS:pileated woodpecker, red-breasted nuthatch. ALSO,
watch and listen for the belted king-
fisher who makes his livlihood cap-
turing small fish.

BEAVERS may be spotted in early morning or evening. Gnawed branches and
several active dams are visible from
the trail.

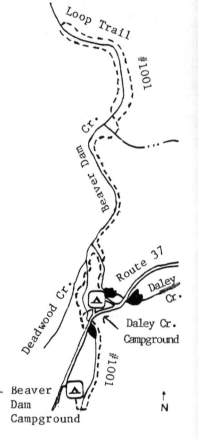

ACCESS: From Ashland Interstate 5, Exit 14, drive east on Hwy.66,
0.6 mi. to Dead Indian Memorial Road (County 722). Turn left onto
this road and go 22 mi. to the junction of Forest Route 37. Turn
left onto Route 37 and go 1.5 miles to Beaver Dam and Daley Creek
Campgrounds. You can begin in either campground. (Excerpts: Rogue
River National Forest, Ashland Ranger District, Recreation Opportunity Guide)

CHAPTER 9 - BUTTE FALLS AREA

WHISKEY SPRINGS INTERPRETIVE TRAIL.   (See map 16)

TRAIL BEGINS/ENDS: WHISKEY SPRINGS CAMPGROUND PICNIC AREA.
DISTANCE: -1.0 mile.   ELEV. 3200'
DIFFICULTY: -Easy, wheelchair accessible.
SEASON: -June thru October. USE: hikers only.
BRING MAPS: -Butte Falls Ranger Dist.-Rogue River Ntl. Forest.

ACCESS: From Butte Falls: Go 10 miles east on the Butte
                Falls-Fish Lake Hwy.(County Route 821)to Whiskey
                Springs Campground.

From Ashland: Go 0.6 mile east on Hwy. 66, turn left onto Dead
Indian Memorial Road (County Route 722), and continue 22 miles to
the junction with Forest Route 37. Follow Route 37, 8 mi. to Hwy.
140. Turn right and go 1/4 mi. to County Route 821 that continues
north 9.3 miles to Whiskey Springs Campground.

FROM WHITE CITY: Follow mileposts on Highway 140, 28.6 miles and
turn north onto County Route 821. Follow 821, 9.3 mi. to Whiskey
Springs Campground.

FEATURES: The one mile loop trail starts at the picnic area and
leads through a forested area before arriving at a viewing plat-
form that overlooks a marshland created by beavers.   Wood Ducks,
frogs,and other wildlife habitats may be seen along the way.   Interpretive signs are frequently located throughout the area.

ALSO: NEARBY SKY LAKES WILDERNESS AREA TRAILS: (See Chapter 6)
                Middle Fork Trailhead....p.82
                Alta Lake Trailhead......p.83
                Seven Lakes Trailhead....p.85
                Blue Canyon Trailhead....p.86
                South Fork Trailhead.....p.88

                                        -continued

SOUTH FORK ROGUE RIVER TRAILS

SOUTH FORK TRAILS

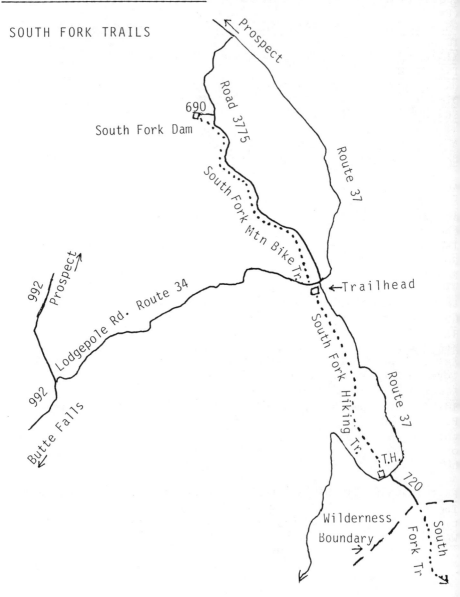

SOUTH FORK HIKER TRAIL-SOUTH FORK MTN. BIKE TRAIL #988. (Map 11)
(Previously referred to as the LOWER SOUTH FORK TRAIL)

TRAIL BEGINS: -Upper Trailhead-(Hiker) Route 37.   ELEV. 4400'
MID-POINT: -Middle Trailhead-Forest Route 34.   ELEV. 4000'
TRAIL ENDS: -Lower Trailhead- (Mtn. bike) Rd. 3775/690 near
              South Fork Dam.   ELEV. 3400'
DISTANCE: -HIKER SECTION, 5.3 mi., MTN.BIKE SECTION 6.8 mi.
SEASON: -Spring, summer, fall. Mosquitos can be very bad in
              late spring and early summer. They should be vir-
              tually absent by the first of July.
BRING MAPS: -Butte Falls Ranger Dist.-Rogue River Ntl. Forest.

ACCESS: From Butte Falls, Oregon, travel east one mile to
               the County road leading north to the town of Pros-
pect. Turn onto this road and go 8.7 mi. to the junction of Forest Route 34. Turn right onto 34 and go 8.1 miles. The MID-POINT
TRAILHEAD is on the right just before reaching the junction with
Forest Route 37 and Rd.3775. South of this trailhead is the South
Fork Hiking Trail and north is the South Fork Mtn. Bike Trail.You
may hike on the bike tr., BUT PLEASE -NO BIKES ON HIKING SECTION!

UPPER (HIKER) TRAILHEAD: Continue on Route 34 to the junction of
Route 37. Turn right (south) onto 37 and go 5.6 mi. to the trailhead on the right. This HIKER ONLY trail proceeds 5.3 miles along
the river,downstream to the parking area on Forest Route 34.

LOWER (MTN. BIKE-HIKER) TRAIL.   From the mid-point trailhead on
Route 34, take Forest Road 3775 for 5.2 mi. to the junction with
Forest Road 3775/690. Turn left onto Road 690 and go 0.5 mile to
the end of the road. The trailhead is on the left. This portion
of trail follows 6.8 miles upstream, back to the Route 34 trailhead.

FEATURES: Parking and turn-around is adequate at the trailheads.
The trails follow the river along its entire length. A car shut-
tle would be most helpful when doing these trail sections. CARRY
WATER!

127

CHAPTER 10 - PROSPECT AREA

MILL CREEK FALLS. (See map 5)

TRAILS BEGIN: —Mill Creek viewpoint parking area, 1 mile south of Prospect; and from the State Park at the south town limits of Prospect.

DIFFICULTY: —Easy. USE: hikers only.

SEASON: —All year except for occasional winter snows.

ACCESS: From Medford, take Crater Lake Highway (Hwy. 62) to the community of Cascade Gorge (milepost 38). Mill Creek Drive junctions on the right (east). Follow mileposts on Mill Creek Drive, 5.4 miles to the Mill Creek viewpoint parking area on the right. A large sign-map is erected here; giving directions to the Avenue of the Giant Boulders, and viewpoints of Barr Creek Falls and Mill Creek Falls. The trail to these points begins from the south end of the parking area. While hiking these trails note the signs that are posted to alert visitors:

"DANGER: POWER DAM SPILLWAY UPSTREAM. WATCH OUT FOR ANY FAST RISE OF WATER AT ANY TIME AND WITHOUT WARNING. BE SURE THAT YOU CAN REACH SHORE SAFELY."

There are no restrooms along the trails, but they are provided at the State Park, 1 mile further north on Mill Creek Drive.

AN OREGON STATE PARK, with restrooms, is located one mile further north on Mill Creek Drive, just at the south town limits of Prospect. THE TRAIL TO PEARSONY FALLS begins here. Metal posts indicate the names of the various trees. After about one mile, the trail descends to the Rogue River bed, sometimes dry due to water diversion from a power company dam upstream. DANGER SIGNS WARN THAT WATER COULD SUDDENLY BE RELEASED FROM THE DAM, and should be taken seriously.

These trails were designed for public use by BOISE CASCADE TIMBER AND WOOD PRODUCTS GROUP.

MAMMOTH PINES NATURE TRAIL.   (See map 5)

TRAIL BEGINS/ENDS: -State Highway 62 between mileposts 50 and 51.
DISTANCE: -1/4 mile loop, easy.
SEASON: -June through October.
BRING MAP: -USFS Prospect Ranger Dist.-Rogue River N.F.
                   -USFS brochure-Mammoth Pines Nature Trail.

ACCESS: From the town of Prospect, take State Highway
                   62 to milepost 50.   Road 6200/060 is 0.6 mile
further.   Turn left onto Road 060 that leads to a parking area.

FEATURES: An information board is located at this park-
                   ing area.   Brochures may be available from a
receptacle at this point.   The short loop trail travels through a
mixed conifer forest.   Each "station" is numbered and is keyed to
the brochure as follows:
1. Snowbrush   11. Thimbleberry
2. Western Hemlock   12. Mountain Ash
3. California Hazel   13. The Continuing Story of
4. Mammoth Sugar Pine   Succession
5. Douglas Fir   14. Bracken Fern
6. Grand Fir   15. Pacific Yew
7. Ponderosa Pine   16. The End and the Beginning
8. Oregon Grape   17. Sugar Pine
9. Mixed Coniferous Forest   18. Pacific Dogwood
10. Serviceberry   19. Golden Chinquapin
                                 20. Scouler's Willow

HISTORY: In October 1979, Douglas fir trees infected by lamin-
               ated root rot were felled by a windstorm.   This dis-
ease weakens the root system, and eventually kills the tree.   In
May 1981, the trees were removed for visitor safety.   Laminated
root rot is spread from tree to tree through the root system, and
future generations of trees can become re-infected.   The area has
been replanted with ponderosa pines, and other species resistant
to laminated root rot.

Upper Rogue Trails

UPPER ROGUE RIVER TRAIL #1034-CRATER RIM VIEWPOINT TO HAMAKER
MEADOWS.   Segment 1   (See map 2)

DISTANCE: -9.3 miles, easy to moderate. USE: hikers only.
SEASON: -June to October. Wildflowers until mid-August.
CONNECTING TR.-Boundary Springs Trail 1057.
BRING MAPS: -Prospect Ranger District-Rogue River Ntl. Forest.
                 -USFS Rec. Opportunity Guide-Upper Rogue River Tr.

ACCESS TO CRATER RIM VIEWPOINT, ELEV. 5174'.
Just north of the Union Creek Resort, at the junction with State
Hwys. 62 and 230, follow mileposts northeast on 230, 18.6 miles
to the viewpoint parking area and trailhead. Hike 0.6 mile to the
junction with Boundary Springs Trail 1057, that begins a 7.2 mile
hike to the Pacific Crest Trail. KEEP RIGHT at this junction onto Trail 1034, which reaches Hamaker Campground in 9.3 miles.

FEATURES: Starting from Crater Rim Viewpoint, the trail tra-
                vels downstream.   After 1/2 mile, it drops to the
river's edge, crosses a small creek before climbing to 200 foot
cliffs of compacted pumice.   The next two miles offer impressive
sights, Ruth Falls can be heard below but is hard to see.   Rough
Rider Falls is 2 miles further. Another waterfall is located 1.5
miles downstream. The trail leaves the river and winds 2.5 miles
through the woods, crosses Forest Road 6530 and then returns to
the river's edge at Hamaker Campground on Forest Road 900.   THIS
IS 1 OF 7 SEGMENTS OF THE 48 MILE UPPER ROGUE RIVER TRAIL.

ACCESS TO HAMAKER CAMPGROUND, see next page.

HISTORY: "The Upper Rogue River Trail is a National Recre-
                ational Trail.   Some segments of the trail were
built by the Civilian Conservation Corps as access routes for
recreation and fire supression purposes. The construction of the
rest of the trail began in 1975 as a Volunteer Bicentennial com-
memorative project, and was completed in late 1977.   Long range
plans envision the Upper Rogue Trail extending from the Pacific
Crest Trail to the Pacific Coast." (USFS quote)

UPPER ROGUE RIVER TRAIL #1034....HAMAKER CAMPGROUND TO NEW TRAIL-
HEAD FOREST ROAD 6530/070. Segment 2 (See map 2)

DISTANCE: -About 7.5 miles, easy to moderate.
SEASON: -June through October. USE: hiker/horse. Motor
                   vehicles not allowed.
BRING MAPS: -Prospect Ranger District-Rogue River Ntl. Forest.
                   -USFS Rec. Opportunity Guide-Upper Rogue River Tr.

ACCESS: HAMAKER CAMPGROUND, ELEV. 4000'.
                   From the junction of State Hwys. 62 and 230, fol-
low mileposts northeast on 230, 12.1 miles to the junction with
Forest Road 6530. Turn right onto Road 6530 and go 0.6 mi. to the
junction with Forest Road 6530/900.   Turn right onto 900, and go
0.8 mi. to Hamaker Campground at the end of the road. Trail 1034
heading north is along the left side of the road just before you
reach the Rogue River bridge.

FEATURES: From Hamaker Campground, Trail 1034 begins right
                   (south) just after crossing the bridge. It first
leads away from the river and rejoins it two miles later near the
confluence of Muir Creek and the Rogue River.   The trail follows
through grassy meadows, crosses Hurryon Creek, then rejoins Rogue
River near Highway Falls. Beyond Highway Falls, the trail climbs
to the top of a pumice cliff with views of the Rogue River below.
After descending to the river bank and then crossing National Cr.
on a footlog, the trail meets Forest Road 6530.   Hike across the
bridge and make a left turn to continue south along the west bank
of the river.   About 1/4 mile further, look for an access trail
leading to a NEW (1989) trailhead/parking area on Road 6530/070,
replacing the Foster Creek Trailhead on Hwy. 62 that was difficult to reach.
THIS IS ONE OF 7 SEGMENTS OF THE 48 MILE UPPER ROGUE RIVER TRAIL.

ACCESS TO FOREST ROAD 6530/070 TRAILHEAD, see next page.

UPPER ROGUE RIVER TRAIL #1034-ROAD 6530/070 TRAILHEAD TO BIG BEND
Segment 3 (See maps 2,5,and 6)

DISTANCE: -About 9.5 miles, easy to moderate.
SEASON: -June through October. USE: hiker/horse. Motorized
                 vehicles not allowed.
BRING MAPS: -Prospect Ranger District-Rogue River Ntl. Forest.
                 -USFS Rec. Opportunity Guide-Upper Rogue River Tr.

ACCESS: FOREST ROAD 6530/070 TRAILHEAD.
                 North of the Union Creek Resort, at the junction
of State Hwys. 62 and 230, follow mileposts on 230 to milepost 6
at the County line.Turn right onto Forest Road 6530 and go 0.7 mi.
to the junction with Road 070 on the right. Turn right and go 0.1
mile to the trailhead and parking area.   This new trailhead was
built in 1989 by Gregory Forest Products and USFS to replace the
old, difficult to reach, Foster Creek Trailhead.

FEATURES: An access trail leads to the Upper Rogue River
                 Trail. Turn right to continue south and after a
short distance the trail climbs away from the river, crosses Hwy.
230 two miles south, and continues 0.5 mile to the former Foster
Creek Trailhead.

Hiking south from Foster Creek,it is necessary to wade the creek.
In about 1 mile downstream, the trail leaves the Rogue River and
climbs a pumice cliff. It then continues through a series of wet
marshy areas. 5 miles downstream, on the south side of a footbridge, Trail 1034 passes the abandoned 0.5 mile trail that went
to the Brown's Cabin Trailhead. Continuing south along the river,
the trail climbs and traverses a pumice bluff. It then follows
the river's edge as it winds around Big Bend and terminates on
Forest Road 6510, 3/4 mile north of its junction with Hwy. 230.

THIS IS ONE OF 7 SEGMENTS OF THE 48 MILE UPPER ROGUE RIVER TRAIL.

ACCESS TO BIG BEND, see next page.

UPPER ROGUE RIVER TRAIL #1034-BIG BEND TO NATURAL BRIDGE CAMP-
GROUND AND VIEWPOINT. Segment 4 (See map 5)

DISTANCE: -7 miles, moderate grades, must ford Flat Creek.
SEASON: -June through October.
USE: -Hiker only.
CONNECTING TR.   -Rogue Gorge Trail 1034A.
BRING MAPS: -Prospect Ranger District-Rogue River Ntl. Forest.
                   -USFS Rec. Opportunity Guide-Upper Rogue River Tr.

ACCESS: BIG BEND TRAILHEAD, ELEV. 3500'.
                   North of the Union Creek Resort, at the junction
with State Hwys. 62 and 230, continue 0.9 mi. northeast on 230 to
the junction with Forest Road 6510. Turn left across Rogue River
bridge, and continue 3/4 mile to the crossing of the Upper Rogue
River Trail. Hiking north leads 7 miles to Foster Creek. Hiking
south leads 6 miles toward Natural Bridge Campground.

FEATURES: From Big Bend Trailhead, the trail climbs a rocky
                   embankment, and traverses a steep slope overlook-
ing the Rogue River. Fish Mountain to the north, becomes visible
through a brief opening in the trees.   Further south, after frequent switchbacks, a steep forested slope overlooks Farewell Bend
Campground across the river. The trail then momentarily descends
to river level to view the water raging through the long, narrow
chute of a collapsed lava tube. South of Union Creek Campground,
the trail returns to a calm river and crosses Flat Creek, 4 miles
further south.   The river regains its turbulent nature and Trail
1034 then reaches the first of 2 footbridges crossing to the east
bank of the river, at the junction with Rogue Gorge Trail 1034A,
1/4 mile north of Natural Bridge Campground.   Traveling one mile
further along the west bank, leads one mile to the Natural Bridge
Viewpoint facility and footbridge. This area is 0.5 mile west of
Hwy. 62 accessible by Forest Road #300.

THIS IS ONE OF 7 SEGMENTS OF THE 47 MILE UPPER ROGUE RIVER TRAIL.

ACCESS TO NATURAL BRIDGE CAMP/VIEWPOINT FACILITY (See next page)

UPPER ROGUE RIVER TRAIL #1034-NATURAL BRIDGE CAMPGROUND/VIEWPOINT
TO WOODRUFF BRIDGE. Segment 5 (See map 5)

DISTANCE: -3.5 miles, easy. USE: hikers only.
SEASON: -June through October.
CONNECTING TR.   -None.
BRING MAPS: -Prospect Ranger District-Rogue River Ntl. Forest.
                 -USFS Rec. Opportunity Guide-Upper Rogue River Tr.

ACCESS: NATURAL BRIDGE CAMPGROUND, ELEV. 3200'.
                 From the town of Prospect, follow mileposts north
on State Highway 62 to mile 54.8 at the junction with Forest Road
300. Turn left and go 1/2 mile to Natural Bridge Viewpoint parking lot. Follow a paved path to a footbridge. Do not cross the
footbridge if you are going toward Woodruff Bridge. Crossing the
bridge leads to the Natural Bridge Viewpoint facility interpretative stations, and then on further north to other segments of the
Upper Rogue River Trail.

FEATURES: From the above footbridge, continue downstream on
                 the east bank of the river, over a rough tread of
mossy lava rock which becomes slippery in wet weather. The trail
later climbs to view the river as it makes a sharp bend and rages
through a narrow chute of a collapsed lava tube.   This rapids is
known as Knob Falls.

Several old skid roads are encountered, as trail 1034 approaches
Woodruff Bridge developed picnic area.   The U.S. Forest Service
advises, "The pools and river can be dangerous due to cold water
and a forceful current." THIS IS ONE OF 7 SEGMENTS OF THE 48 MI.
UPPER ROGUE RIVER TRAIL.

ACCESS TO WOODRUFF BRIDGE, see next page.

135

UPPER ROGUE RIVER TRAIL #1034-WOODRUFF BRIDGE TO RIVER BRIDGE
CAMPGROUND. Segment 6 (See map 5)

DISTANCE: -4.6 miles, easy, some moderate pitches. The
                 tread is rocky on the southern end.
SEASON: -June through October. USE: hikers only.
CONNECTING TR. -None.
BRING MAPS: -Prospect Ranger District-Rogue River Ntl. Forest.
                 -USFS Rec. Opportunity Guide-Upper Rogue River Tr.

ACCESS: WOODRUFF BRIDGE, ELEV. 3000'.
                 From the town of Prospect, follow mileposts north
on State Highway 62 to mi. 51.3 at the junction with Forest Route
68. Turn left onto 68 and travel northwest 1.8 miles to Woodruff
Bridge. Trailhead signs are on the east bank of the river indicating NORTH, 3.5 miles to Natural Bridge Campground; and SOUTH,
4.6 miles to River Bridge Campground.

FEATURES: From Woodruff Bridge Picnic Area, the trail heads
                 downstream along the east bank of the river, and
after about 1.5 miles, approaches the dark-colored cliffs of Takelma Gorge. The river drops through a series of rapids and turns
sharply to enter the gorge itself. The narrow channel continues
for nearly 1.25 miles. The tread on this section of the trail is
quite rocky and the grades become steeper.

Below Takelma Gorge, the trail goes past the Upper Rogue Baptist
Church Camp, and then continues 1.4 miles to River Bridge Campground on Road 6210. (Excerpts USFS Recreation Opportunity Guide)

THIS IS ONE OF 7 SEGMENTS OF THE 48 MILE UPPER ROGUE RIVER TRAIL.

ACCESS TO RIVER BRIDGE CAMPGROUND, see next page.

UPPER ROGUE RIVER TRAIL #1034-RIVER BRIDGE CAMPGROUND TO PROSPECT
Segment 7 (See map 5)

DISTANCE: -6.5 miles, easy.   USE: hikers only.
SEASON: -June through October.
CONNECTING TR: -None.
BRING MAPS: -Prospect Ranger District-Rogue River Ntl. Forest.
                       -USFS Rec. Opportunity Guide-Upper Rogue River Tr.

ACCESS: RIVER BRIDGE CAMPGROUND, ELEV. 2800'.
                       From the town of Prospect, follow mileposts north
on State Highway 62 to mile 49.2 at the junction with Forest Road
6210.   Turn left and continue 1 mile to the trail crossing at the
near (east) end of the bridge.   Trail signs are on the east bank
of the river and indicate 4.6 miles north to Woodruff Bridge, and
6.5 miles south to Prospect.

PROSPECT TRAILHEAD, southern terminus of the trail, ELEV. 2598'.
On State Hwy. 62, travel to the northern edge of Prospect,0.1 mi.
north of milepost 45.   Turn left (west) onto the narrow dirt access road leading 1/2 mile to a picnic area and a power company
reservoir.   Follow the road leading north along the east bank of
the river to the Upper Rogue River Trailhead.   River Bridge Campground is 6.5 miles north.

FEATURES: From River Bridge Campground, the trail continues
                       south along the east bank of the river, crosses a
sandy beach, then enters a forest of tall sugar pines.   Views of
the river occur where the trail nears the edge of 20 foot bluffs
bordering the river channel.   The last four miles of trail leaves
the river, and the backwaters of the reservoir later become visible as the trail returns to the river bank.   The trail joins and
follows an old road to the reservoir and a picnic area near Prospect. A 1/2 mile access road connects to Hwy. 62 from the dam.

THIS IS ONE OF 7 SEGMENTS OF THE 48 MILE UPPER ROGUE RIVER TRAIL.

ROGUE GORGE TRAIL #1034A   (See map 5)

TRAIL BEGINS:	-Rogue Gorge Viewpoint, Highway 62. ELEV. 3363'
	-Also accessed from Farewell Bend Campground.
TRAIL ENDS:	-Near Natural Bridge Campground. ELEV. 3200'
DISTANCE:	-3.5 miles, easy grade. USE: hiker only.
SEASON:	-June through October-wildflowers through August.
CONNECTING TR.	-Union Creek Trail 1035.
	-Upper Rogue River Trail 1034.
BRING MAPS:	-Prospect Ranger Dist.-Rogue River Ntl. Forest.

ACCESS: ROGUE GORGE VIEWPOINT, ELEV. 3363'.   From Union
                Creek Resort,travel northeast on Highway 62, 0.3
mile to the Rogue Gorge viewpoint on the left. This viewpoint is
also reached from Farewell Bend Campground.Trail 1034A runs south
to Natural Bridge Campground on the east bank of the Rogue River.

NATURAL BRIDGE CAMPGROUND, ELEV. 3200'.   From the town of Prospect, follow mileposts north on State Hwy. 62 to mile 54.8 at the
junction with Forest Road 300. Turn left onto 300 and go 0.5 mi.
to the campground. Trail 1034A runs north along the east bank of
the Rogue River.

FEATURES: From the Rogue Gorge Viewpoint, the trail reach-
                es Union Creek Campground in 0.5 mile. 1.5 miles
further, a footbridge crosses to the west bank to join the Upper
Rogue River Trail 1034. Continuing south on the east bank of the
river leads 1/4 mile to Natural Bridge Campground.

The views of the Rogue River as it winds its way through the narrow channel of basalt lava, are very impressive.   Autumnal color
may be enjoyed from mid-September through mid-October.

UNION CREEK TRAIL #1035. (See maps 5 and 6)

TRAIL BEGINS: -Union Creek Campground.   ELEV. 3240'
TRAIL ENDS: -Forest Road 6200/610.   ELEV. 3730'
                  Some maps and signs may show this as Road 700.
                 -4.4 miles, easy. USE: hiker/fishermen/camping.
SEASON: -June through October.
CONNECTING TR.   -Rogue Gorge Trail 1034A.
BRING MAPS: -Prospect Ranger District-Rogue River Ntl. Forest.
                 -USFS Rec. Opportunity Guide -Union Creek Trail.

ACCESS: FROM UNION CREEK CAMPGROUND: At the confluence
                 of Union Creek and the Rogue River, cross a foot-
bridge over Union Creek and follow the trail east to a point just
south of the Union Creek Resort on State Hwy. 62.

The trail crosses Hwy. 62, just south of the resort and then continues east along the north bank of the creek with a good view of
Union Falls in about 3 miles. The upper trailhead is 1 mile further.

By road, the UPPER TRAILHEAD is reached by travelling 1.3 miles
northeast of Union Creek Resort to the junction of State Highways
230 and 62. Continue northeast on 62, 2 miles to the junction of
Forest Road 6200/600. (Some maps/signs may show the upper trailhead on Forest Road 700.)   Turn right onto Road 600 and continue
0.2 mi. to the junction with Forest Road 6200/610. Turn left onto 610 and go 0.1 mi. to the trailhead on the right.

HISTORY: "UNION CREEK, PEAK: Named in 1862 (the Civil War
                 had begun the year before) by 'patriotic' pros-
pectors Chauncy Nye and Hiram G. Abbott. (Pro-confederate feel-
ings, however, ran high among a large segment of the Jackson
County population.)"   (USFS quote)

<u>SPHAGNUM BOG TRAIL #1038.</u> (See map 2)

<u>TRAIL BEGINS:</u>	-Forest Road 6535 near milepost 5.	<u>ELEV.</u> 5360'
<u>TRAIL ENDS:</u>	-West Boundary Crater Lake Ntl. Park.	<u>ELEV.</u> 5572'
<u>DISTANCE:</u>	-1.1 mile. Easy grades. <u>USE:</u> hiker/horse.	
<u>SEASON:</u>	-Usually snow-free July through September.	
<u>CONNECTING TR:</u>	-Crater Springs Trail, Crater Lake Ntl. Park.	
<u>BRING MAPS:</u>	-USFS Prospect Ranger Dist. Rogue River Ntl.Forest.	
	-CRATER LAKE map/brochure-National Park Service.	
	-USGS Crater Lake West, 7.5' series, 1985.	

<u>ACCESS:</u>   Just north of Union Creek Resort from the junction
with State Highways 62 and 230, follow Hwy. 230 to
milepost 6 at the junction with Forest Road 6530. Turn RIGHT onto
Road 6530 and go 1.3 miles to the <u>second junction with loop Road</u>
<u>6535.</u> Follow Road 6535, 5.5 miles (just beyond milepost 5) to the
trailhead on the left. This trailhead was constructed in 1995 to
provide adequate parking and turn-around space for stock trailers
and other vehicles.

The trail begins its climb to a road gate at the upper end of Rd.
6535/660. The trail continues beyond the gate,1/2 mi. to the West
Boundary of Crater Lake Park, at the junction with <u>Crater Springs</u>
<u>Trail.</u> A sign reads; Sphagnum Bog 1.7 mi., PCT 4.7 mi., Boundary
Springs 7.9 mi.

<u>Crater Springs Trail</u> continues 1.2 mi. to the junction with Oasis
Butte Trail on the left, that leads 6.7 miles to Boundary Springs.
Keep right at the above junction and follow Crater Springs Trail,
0.5 mile south to <u>Crater Springs,</u> where a short spur leads south
to unmarked routes to <u>SPHAGNUM BOG.</u> Crater Springs Trail continues east from this spur to Pacific Crest Trail.

<u>FEATURES:</u> It is possible to continue south along unmarked routes
to Sphagnum Bog, thru wet meadows filled with bog dwelling plants.
Care should be taken not to trample the fragile plant life or to
accidently step into deep, cold water pools.   Water is available
at Crater Springs. Camping is not allowed within a 0.5 mile rad-
ius of Sphagnum Bog. <u>SEE BEGINNING OF CHAPTER 11 FOR CRATER LAKE</u>
<u>PARK BACKCOUNTRY USE REGULATIONS.</u>

MINNEHAHA TRAIL #1039.   (See map 2)

TRAIL BEGINS:	-Forest Road 6530/800.	ELEV.	3825'
TRAIL ENDS:	-Soda Springs.	ELEV.	4400'
DISTANCE:	-3.1 miles,easy. USE hiker,horse,mtn.& motorbikes.		
SEASON:	-Usually snow-free June through October.		
BRING MAPS:	-Prospect Ranger Dist. -Rogue River Ntl. Forest.		

ACCESS: From the Union Creek Resort, travel northeast on
                 Crater Lake Hwy. 62, 1.3 miles to the junction
with State Hwy. 230.   Follow mileposts on 230, 12.1 miles to the
junction with Forest Road 6530. Turn right onto 6530 and go 1.0
mile to Road 800. Turn right onto Road 800 and go 0.1 mi. to the
Minnehaha Trailhead on the left, near the old Minnehaha Camp.

FEATURES: The route begins as an old road that diminishes
                 to a trail, then follows Minnehaha Creek to Soda
Springs. Along the way, the trail passes at the edge of a large,
grassy meadow from where there are good views of Minnehaha Creek
with its beautiful waterfalls.

HISTORY: "MINNEHAHA CREEK, CAMP: The date of this name is
                 unknown; probably post-1900. The term is an In-
dian name from the eastern United States, made famous in Long-
fellow's poem 'Song of Hiawatha'."   (USFS quote)

141

SHERWOOD CREEK TRAIL #1041. (See map 2)

TRAIL BEGINS:	-State Hwy. 230 near milepost 15.	ELEV. 4634'
TRAIL ENDS:	-Three Lakes Camp, Road 3703.	ELEV. 6000'
DISTANCE:	-4.5 miles, MORE DIFFICULT, stream crossings.	
SEASON:	-June thru Oct. Snow often till Aug. on Road 3703.	
USE:	Hiker/horse.	
CONNECTING TR.	-Beaver Meadows Trail (Abandoned)	
BRING MAPS:	-USFS Rec. Opportunity Guide-Sherwood Creek Trail.	
	-Prospect Ranger District-Rogue River Ntl. Forest.	

ACCESS: LOWER END OF TRAIL: Just north of the Union Creek
               Resort, at the junction of State Highways 62 and
230, go northeast on Hwy. 230, 0.2 mile beyond milepost 15. Turn
left to a parking area and trailhead.

UPPER END OF TRAIL: Continue east on Hwy. 230 following mileposts
to mile 20.6 at the junction with Three Lakes Road 3703. Turn
left onto 3703 and go about 5.7 miles to the junction with Forest
Road 3703/400 at the far (west) end of Three Lakes Camp.   Turn
left onto 3703/400 for 0.2 mile to the parking area at the west
end of the lake. Follow blazes along an old road,0.8 mile to the
beginning of the trail.

FEATURES: FROM THE LOWER TRAILHEAD: The trail rises through
                a series of small meadows and high elevation for-
ests. Stream crossings can be difficult even in late summer. In
a few places the trail may be hard to follow when it passes thru
meadows and stream crossings, as cattle trails can look like the
main trail. Watch carefully for blazes and trail signs and note
your route for the return trip. TRAIL LOG IS AS FOLLOWS:
.25 mile: Junction with ABANDONED Beaver Meadows loop trail,keep
          left.
1.25 mile: Junction with upper end of the Beaver Meadows Trail.
          Keep left.
1.5 mile SHERWOOD MEADOW: CAUTION:About half way along the west
          edge of the meadow, look for trail signs on trees.What
looks like the continuation of the trail is an informal trail to
a forest road. FROM SIGNS,THE TRAIL LEADS AT RIGHT ANGLES ACROSS
THE MEADOW. LOOK FOR A ROCK DUCK AT THE FAR END OF THE MEADOW.The
trail continues about 3 miles to Three Lakes Camp.

MUIR CREEK TRAIL #1042.   (See map 2)

<u>TRAIL BEGINS:</u>	-State Hwy. 230 near milepost 10.	<u>ELEV.</u> 3825'
<u>TRAIL ENDS:</u>	-Buck Canyon Trail 1046.	<u>ELEV.</u> 4100'
<u>DISTANCE:</u>	-3.9 miles, easy. <u>USE:</u> hiker/horse.	
<u>SEASON:</u>	-June through October.	
<u>CONNECTING TR.</u>	-Buck Canyon Trail 1046.	
<u>BRING MAPS:</u>	-Prospect Ranger Dist. -Rogue River Ntl. Forest.	
	-USFS Rec. Opportunity Guide-Muir Creek Trail.	

<u>ACCESS:</u>   Just north of the Union Creek Resort, at the in-
                tersection of State Highways 62 and 230, follow
mileposts on 230, 10.4 miles just before crossing the bridge at
Muir Creek.   Muir Creek Trailhead is on the left (west) side of
the road at the site of a horse unloading ramp and hitching rail.

<u>FEATURES:</u>   Muir Creek Trail winds along the west bank of
                the creek, passing Muir Creek Falls in about 2.5
miles, and ends at Buck Canyon Trail 1046. Turning RIGHT onto
Trail 1046 leads 0.5 mile to Forest Road 6560. This is a popular
trail for fishermen.

I Think We Should Have Checked
The Map Sooner.

BUCK CANYON TRAILS

1046   Buck Canyon   1046B Wiley Camp Trail
1046A Hummingbird   1044   Meadow Creek Tr.
       Meadows trail.
1047   Hole In The Ground Trail.

BUCK CANYON TRAIL #1046   (See map 2)

TRAIL BEGINS:	-Forest Road 6560.	ELEV. 4160'
TRAIL ENDS:	-Hole In The Ground Camp.	ELEV. 5300'
DISTANCE:	-10.7 mi. plus 3 miles of access trails. High-point ELEV. about 6000 feet. USE: hiker/horse.	
	-Usually snow-free June through October.	
CONNECTING TR.	-Muir Creek Trail 1042.	
	-Hummingbird Meadows Trail 1046A. (Access #2)	
	-Wiley Camp Trail 1046B. (Access #3)	
	-Meadow Creek Trail 1044. (Access #4)	
	-Hole In The Ground Trail 1047. (Access #5)	
BRING MAPS:	-Prospect Ranger Dist. -Rogue River Ntl. Forest.	
	-USFS Rec. Opportunity Guide-Buck Canyon Trail.	

ACCESS #1 BUCK CANYON TRAILHEAD, ELEV. 4160'.   MORE DIFFICULT.
From the junction of Highways 62 and 230 just north of Union Cr.
Resort,follow mileposts northeast on Highway 230 to mile 12.1, at
the junction with Road 6560 on the left. Follow Road 6560,one mi.
and turn left onto Road 6560-190. Follow this road 0.5 mi. to the
trailhead.

ACCESS #2 HUMMINGBIRD MEADOWS TRAIL 1046A, ELEV. 4000'. EASIEST.
Near milepost 12 on State Hwy. 230 at the junction with Forest
Road 6560, turn and continue northwest on 6560, 1.8 miles to Road
6560/400. Follow Road 400, 1.2 miles to the trailhead at the end
of the road.   This 1/2 mile access trail passes through Hummingbird Meadows and then fords Muir Creek.   There is no bridge, the
crossing may be difficult early in the season. The junction with
the Buck Canyon Trail is just beyond. ELEV. about 4400'.

Good hikers always leave a
trail cleaner than they
find it.

ACCESS #3 WILEY CAMP TRAIL 1046B, ELEV. 5200'.   Near milepost 12
on State Hwy. 230 at the junction with Forest Road 6560, turn and
travel northwest on Road 6560, 4 miles to the Rogue-Umpqua Divide
where the road number changes to Forest Route 37.   Continue on 37
for 1/2 mile to Forest Road 3700/800.   Turn left and follow Road
800, 2.3 mi. to the junction with Forest Road 3700/870. Turn left
and follow 870, 2.5 mi. to the trailhead on the left side of the
road.   The 1 mile Wiley Camp Trail descends from the Rogue-Umpqua
Divide,and crosses Muir Creek. Wiley Camp is located at the southeast side of the creek.   This trail, rated DIFFICULT, joins Buck
Canyon Trail at appx. ELEV. 4800'.

ACCESS #4 MEADOW CREEK TRAIL 1044, ELEV. 4900'.   Follow mileposts
on State Highway 230 to mile 9.2 at the second junction with loop
Road 6540.   Turn left onto 6540 and go 3 miles to the junction of
Road 6540/700.   Turn right onto 700 and go about 1.0 mi. WATCHING
CAREFULLY ON THE LEFT for the trailhead sign.   This steep 1 mile
trail passes Bear Camp in about 0.5 mi. through a series of mead-
ows before joining the Buck Canyon Trail.ELEV. about 5360'. Rated
DIFFICULT.

ACCESS #5 HOLE-IN-THE-GROUND TRAIL 1047, ELEV. 5200'.   From State
Highway 230, near milepost 9 (mile 9.2), at the northern turnoff
for loop Road 6540, turn left on Road 6540 and continue 4.5 miles
(at milepost 6) to the junction with Forest Road 6540/500.   Turn
right onto Road 500, and continue 1.5 mi. to the trailhead at the
end of the road. The trail leads 0.5 mi. across Log Cr. and joins
Buck Canyon Trail and Rogue Umpqua Divide Trail 1470 at the edge
of a small meadow. Hole in the Ground Camp is east of the meadow
just inside the trees. ELEV. about 5600'. Rated DIFFICULT.

BUCK CANYON TRAIL #1046, page 3. (See map 2)

FEATURES: The views along the way, north to south direction, include Buckneck Mtn., the knob of Devil's Slide, the
Rogue-Umpqua Divide, the Foster Creek and Rogue River drainages,
Mt. McLoughlin, Mt. Shasta, Buck Canyon Rim, Fish Mountain, Mt.
Thielsen, the Crater Lake Rim and Union Peak. In early June when
wildflowers are at their best, numerous hummingbirds feed on red
horsemint at Hummingbird Meadow.

The Buck Canyon Trail ends at Hole In The Ground, a marshy meadow
that at one time was a shallow, glacial lake at the head of Foster Creek. While passing through the high elevation meadows and
glacial valleys, there is sometimes confusion between recreation
trails and stock trails, created by summer grazing. Watch carefully for tree blazes and signs.

Most of the Buck Canyon Trail System lies within the Rogue-Umpqua
Divide Wilderness Area. It is advised to obtain maps and Recreation Opportunity Guides from the Prospect, or Tiller Ranger Stations, before attempting any of these trails. "HORSE/PACK SADDLE
users are encouraged to enter via ACCESS # 1, the main Buck Canyon Trailhead." (Quote: USFS Recreation Opportunity Guide)

The Rogue-Umpqua Divide Wilderness was created by the Oregon Wilderness Act of 1984. Wilderness regulations include:

PACK OUT ALL LITTER, especially foil packaging that doesn't burn.
BURY HUMAN WASTE 6 to 8 inches deep 200' or more from open water.
CAMPFIRES only in safe spots, keep small. Best to carry stoves.
CAMP IN TENT SITES, no drainage ditches, leave area as found.
MOTORIZED and MECHANICAL EQUIPMENT- prohibited in wilderness.

NATIONAL CREEK FALLS TRAIL #1053. (See map 2)

TRAIL BEGINS:	-Forest Road 6530/300.	ELEV. 4000'
TRAIL ENDS:	-National Creek Falls.	ELEV. 3760'
DISTANCE:	-0.4 mile, moderate, USE: hiker only.	
SEASON:	-June through October.	
BRING MAPS:	-Prospect Ranger Dist.-Rogue River Ntl. Forest.	
	-USFS Rec. Opportunity Guide-National Creek Falls.	

ACCESS: Just north of the Union Creek Resort, at the intersection of State Highways 62 and 230, follow mileposts on 230 to milepost 6, at the junction with Forest Road 6530.   Turn right onto Road 6530 and go about 4 mi. to the junction with Road 6530/300. Turn right onto Road 300 and proceed to the National Creek Falls parking lot and trailhead.

FEATURES: This short trail drops down through a mixed conifer forest to the base of the falls.   National Creek is fed by springs in Crater Lake National Park.

HISTORY: "NATIONAL CREEK, FALLS, CAMP: The date of this name is unknown; it may have been given to the creek by members of the Forest Service road building crew in 1910." (USFS quote)

BOUNDARY SPRINGS TRAIL #1057. (See map 2)

TRAIL BEGINS:	-Near Crater Rim Viewpoint, Hwy. 230. ELEV. 4900'
TRAIL ENDS:	-Boundary Springs, Crater Lake Park. ELEV. 5060'
DISTANCE:	-About 2 miles, easy grade. USE: hiker only.
SEASON:	-Usually snow-free June to October.
CONNECTING TR:	-Upper Rogue Trail 1034.
BRING MAPS:	-Prospect Ranger Dist. -Rogue River Ntl. Forest.
	-USFS Rec. Opportunity Guide-Boundary Springs Tr.

ACCESS: Just north of Union Creek Resort, at the junc-
               tion with State Highways 62 and 230, follow the
mileposts northeast on 230, 18.6 miles to Crater Rim Viewpoint on
the right.

Starting from the parking area, take the Upper Rogue River Trail
0.6 mi. to the junction with the Boundary Springs Trail. Turn to
the left (south) onto the Boundary Springs Trail and hike about 2
miles to Boundary Springs. Along the way, the trail comes out to
Lake West Road and crosses the Rogue River at a bridge. The trail
resumes south immediately after crossing the bridge.

FEATURES: This trail begins a 7.2 mile link with the PCNST
                 (Pacific Crest Trail). Hikers are advised to use
special care to protect this sensitive environment....do not camp
here and do not walk on the moss.   Boundary Springs has been ad-
ded to Crater Lake National Park, where DOGS NOT ALLOWED.

"The springs form the origin of the Upper Rogue River; named sub-
sequent to 1905 because of their location at the boundary between
Crater Lake National Park and Rogue River National Forest."
(USFS quote)

VARMINT CAMP TRAIL #1070. (See map 5 and 6)

TRAIL BEGINS:	-Milepost 10 Forest Road 6205.	ELEV. 3600'
TRAIL ENDS:	-Forest Road 830.	ELEV. 5400'
DISTANCE:	-3.1 miles, moderate grades. USE: hiker/horse/mtn. bike/motorbike. Seasonal motorized closure March 1 to June 30.	
SEASON:	-June through October.	
BRING MAPS:	-USFS Prospect Ranger District, Rogue River N.F. -USFS Recreation Opportunity Guide (this trail).	

ACCESS: From the town of Prospect, Oregon, drive east on
County Route 992 leading toward Butte Falls, 1.1
mile to the junction with Red Blanket Road.   Follow Red Blanket
Road 0.3 mile to Forest Road 6205.   Turn left onto Road 6205   and
continue 10.5 mi. to Varmint Camp Trailhead on the left. There is
parking for 1 or 2 vehicles across the road from the trailhead. A
Sign at milepost 4 of Road 6205   indicates the road is closed beyond that point December 1 to April 15.

FEATURES.   From Road 6205 Trailhead, the trail climbs gradually for about 1 mi.,crosses Varmint Creek then
climbs steeply for 1.5 miles through a dense conifer forest.   The
trail crosses a mountain meadow lined with wild onion.   Look for
wildflowers in mid-summer.

Caution should be exercised if using a motorcycle on this trail.
The tread is narrow and rocky in places. The trail ends on Forest
Road #830.

HISTORY: "Varmint Creek,Camp: A turn-of-the-century hunters' and sheepherders' camp,probably named af-
ter the presence of coyotes or other varmints." (USFS quote)

COLD SPRINGS TRAIL #1073. (See map 6)

TRAIL BEGINS:	-Forest Road 6205/100.	ELEV. 6200'
TRAIL ENDS:	-Cold Springs.	ELEV. 5940'
DISTANCE:	-2.6 miles, moderate.	
SEASON:	-May through October.	
USE:	-Hiker, horse, mountain bike, motor bike.	
	Seasonal motorized closure March 1 to June 30.	
BRING MAPS:	-Prospect Ranger Dist.-Rogue River Ntl. Forest.	
	-USFS Rec. Opportunity Guide-Cold Spr. Tr. 1073.	

ACCESS: From Prospect, travel east on County Route 992
              leading toward Butte Falls, and go 1.1 mile   to
the junction with Red Blanket Road.   Follow Red Blanket Road 0.3
mile to Road 6205.   Turn left onto Road 6205 and go 4.0 miles   to
the junction with Road 6205/100. Turn left onto Road 6205/100 and
go about 7 miles to the trailhead on the right.   Parking space is
provided directly across the road.

FEATURES: The trail begins its journey,and after about 1.0
                mile reaches "Paul Bunyan's Grave" on the north
side of the trail.   Look for a hill with loose rocks, and a nearby metallic Forest Service sign tacked to a tree. The trail later
crosses a road, and resumes directly beyond, before ending at the
springs. CARRY WATER, as the springs are muddied and may be dried
up.

The route is sometimes hard to follow when passing through meadows. Rock Cairns, tree blazes, and diamond-shaped markers can be
followed fairly easily.   Elk may be seen, or their sounds may be
heard in the thickets below the trail.   There is an abundance of
wildflowers in season.

GEYSER SPRINGS TRAIL #1087. (See map 11)

TRAIL BEGINS: -Forest Road 3795/300.   ELEV. 4080'

TRAIL ENDS: -Middle Fork of the Rogue River.   ELEV. 3240'

DISTANCE: -1.1 mile, difficult. USE: hikers only.

SEASON: -Summer months.

BRING MAPS: -Prospect Ranger Dist.-Rogue River Ntl. Forest.
             -USFS Rec. Opportunity Guide-Geyser Spr. Trail.

ACCESS: From the town of Prospect, Oregon, drive east on
               County Road 992 leading toward Butte Falls, for
2.5 miles to the junction with Forest Route 37. Turn left onto 37
and go 2.8 miles to the junction with Forest Road 3795. Continue
on 3795, 2.7 miles to Forest Road 3795/300. Follow Road 300, 1.2
miles to the trailhead on the right. Road 300 is gated from Nov.
1 to June 15.

FEATURES: After the first 1/3 mile, Geyser Springs can be
               seen about 25 feet below the trail. There is no
established trail leading to the springs from this point, so care
must be taken to get there and back. The main trail continues to
the Middle Fork of the Rogue River. This is a steep trail dropping about 800 feet from the road to the river. Native rainbow
and brook trout are popular with fishermen.

Geyser Springs is one of the headwater springs that feed the Middle Fork of the Rogue River.

HISTORY: The Geyser Springs Trail was once part of an old Forest
Service trail system and telephone line that ran from the Imnaha
Guard Station,down the Middle Fork Canyon,up to Bessie Rock Guard
Station, and ended at Bessie Rock Lookout. Used for fire watch
communications in the 1920's, the telephone line and much of the
trail were abandoned in the 1960's. (USFS information)

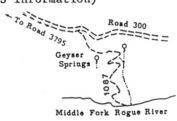

GOLDEN STAIRS TRAIL #1092 (See map 5)

TRAIL BEGINS:	-Near Forest Road 68/550.	ELEV. 3750'
TRAIL ENDS:	-Rogue-Umpqua Divide Trail 1470.	ELEV. 5350'
DISTANCE:	-4.3 mi., moderately steep, limited maintenance.	
SEASON:	-June through October USE: hiker/horse.	
CONNECTING TR.	-Rogue-Umpqua Divide Trail 1470.	
BRING MAPS:	-Prospect Ranger Dist.-Rogue River Ntl. Forest.	
	-USFS Rec. Opportunity Guide-Golden Stairs Trail.	

ACCESS: LOWER TRAILHEAD: From the Prospect Ranger Sta-
               tion (north end of Prospect Oregon), go north on
State Hwy. 62, 6 miles (just beyond milepost 51), to the junction
with Forest Route 68. Turn left onto 68 and follow mileposts to
mile 5 at the junction with Forest Road 550. Turn right onto 550
and continue one mile to an unsigned junction. Keep left and go
2 miles, passing the junction with Road 557, and continue 0.1 mi.
further to the signed trailhead on the right.

UPPER TRAILHEAD: From the junction of State Hwy. 62 and Forest
Route 68, turn left and continue on 68, 2.5 miles to the junction
with Forest Road 6510. Keep right onto 6510 and travel 2.0 miles
to the junction with Forest Road 6510/500.   Turn left onto Road
500 and travel about 4.0 miles to the junction with Roads 700 and
770. Continue straight ahead onto Rd.700, 1.1 mi. to Yellowjacket
Camp. The Rogue Umpqua Divide Trail passes by this point. Follow
this trail 1.0 mile west to the upper end of Golden Stairs Trail.

FEATURES: The lower end of the trail begins through stands
                of fir before continuing along the southern, ex-
posed ridge of Falcon Butte. Along the way, there are good views
of the Rogue River, Elk Creek and Woodruff Creek drainages. Further on toward the Rogue-Umpqua Divide, the face of Elephant Head
and the slopes of Abbott Butte will be seen. The upper end of the
trail junctions with the Rogue-Umpqua Divide Trail about 1.0 mile
west of Forest Road 6510/700. NO WATER

HISTORY: Golden Stairs Trail was "named in part from the Abbott
           brothers alleged gold mine in the area." (USFS quote)

ROGUE-UMPQUA DIVIDE TRAIL #1470. (See maps 5,1B and 2)

TRAIL BEGINS:-Junction of Forest Routes 68 and 30 at Rogue-Umpqua
          Divide, at milepost 30 on Route 68.
TRAIL ENDS: -Three Lakes Camp, Forest Road 3703.
DISTANCE: -31.4 miles USE: hiker/horse. SEASON: summer/fall.
BRING MAPS: -USFS Rogue-Umpqua Divide, Boulder Creek and Mt.
          Thielsen Wildernesses.
          -USFS Tiller, Diamond Lake and Prospect Ranger Dis-
          tricts-Umpqua and Rogue River National Forests.

FEATURES: This National Recreation Trail is the primary route
through the Rogue-Umpqua Divide Wilderness. The trail offers ex-
ceptional views both east and west as it weaves across the crest
of the divide. To the west, lies the irregular and deeply dis-
sected terrain of the Umpqua Drainage;while to the east the trav-
eler sees the broad, open Rogue Basin, with the peaks of the high
Cascades rising above. In addition to the fine vistas,the divide
features a spectacular display of wildflowers in its many meadows
from mid-June until mid-August.

The Divide Trail begins from the southern end of the wilderness.
In places, the trail parallels the old CCC road to Abbott Butte.
Due to a steep and narrow section of trail, horse users are advised to take the old road at one point and loop back into the
trail, avoiding a potential hazard.

The trail passes below Abbott Butte Lookout and descends to a
small pond below a rock cliff called Elephant Head. The old lookout is still standing, but it is unsafe to climb up to the building.

Traveling east, the trail is joined by Golden Stairs Trail #1092,
three miles beyond Abbott Butte. This steep trail leads to the
Rogue River National Forest Road #6800-550. One mile past this
junction, the trail enters Yellowjacket Camp. From here,the trail
follows an old skid road for 1/2 mile. A live creek crosses the
trail just below the road. The trail then climbs the south slope
of Anderson Mountain and opens to a gigantic sub-alpine meadow.
Here,Sandstone trail #1436 joins the divide trail from the Umpqua
side. From the Rogue side of the divide,Anderson Camp Trail #1075
reaches the ridgetop and joins the divide trail.
                          154

From Anderson Mountain, the Divide Trail travels northerly on the crest of a rocky ridge, offering fine views of Crater Lake Rim and Mt. McLoughlin to the east; Highrock Mountain to the west and Abbott Butte to the southwest. Pup Prairie Trail #1434 intersects the Divide Trail just before the trail meets Road 6515-530 at its junction with Road 6515. Here, a spring can be found in the meadow south of this junction. Road 6515-530 becomes the route for the Divide Trail for about 1.5 miles to the junction of Acker Divide Trail #1437. At this intersection the road leads another 1/2 mile to Hershberger Lookout. The Divide Trail however, continues north at this junction, along the route known as the Log Pile Trail. Fish Lake Trail #1570 intersects the Rogue-Umpqua Divide Trail 3/4 mile down this section of trail.

About 1/4 mile further, the Rocky Rim Trail #1572 intersects to the west. The Divide Trail then passes through a saddle onto the eastern face of Weaver Mountain where vistas open to the north and east. The trail then descends to the edge of an ancient shallow glacial lake, now a marshy meadow called Hole-in-the-ground. After passing along the southeast edge of the meadow, the trail forks. The Divide Trail continues on the northerly fork, crossing the meadow to Hole-in the Ground Camp. Here, Buck Canyon Trail #1046 intersects and the Divide Trail heads north for a strenuous one mile climb to Road #3700-870.

This road, at the end of Fish Creek Valley serves as a connecting route between segments of the Divide Trail. To return to the Rogue-Umpqua Divide Trail, follow this road for about 1 mile to Happy Camp. 1/10 of a mile further down the road, the trail continues off to the left of the road. Take this trail to the intersection with the Whitehorse Meadow Trail #1477, and proceed northeast on this trail down the valley. About 3/4 of a mile down the valley, the Whitehorse Meadow Trail turns right and climbs out of the valley. The Divide Trail continues down the valley. This segment of trail passes the Fish Creek Shelter before it climbs out of the valley and crosses Road #3700-870.

The Divide Trail continues up the ridge with some steep stretches and then down the east slope, across Forest Route #37, and on to Buck Camp. Clear Camp lies about 1 mile further down the trail, and the Rogue-Umpqua Divide Trail terminates at THREE LAKES CAMP, on Forest Road #3703. (From Tiller Ranger Dist. Recreation Guide)

155

ACCESS TO ROGUE-UMPQUA DIVIDE TRAIL.

SOUTHERN END OF ROGUE-UMPQUA DIVIDE TRAIL.-Abbott Butte Trailhead.
From the town of Prospect, go north on Hwy. 62 just beyond milepost 51 at the junction with Forest Route 68. Turn left onto 68
and go 13 miles to the Rogue-Umpqua Divide at the junction with
Forest Route 30. The trailhead is on the right.

VIA GOLDEN STAIRS TRAIL #1092.
North of Prospect on Hwy. 62, just beyond milepost 51, turn left
onto Forest Route 68 and follow mileposts to mile 5 at the junction with Forest Road 550.Turn right and go 1 mi. to an(unsigned)
junction. Keep left and go 2 miles, passing the junction with Rd.
557, and continue 0.1 mile further to the signed trailhead on the
right. This steep trail continues 4.3 miles to the Rogue-Umpqua
Divide Trail, about 1 mile west of Forest Road 6510-700.

YELLOWJACKET CAMP.
North of Prospect on Hwy. 62, just beyond milepost 51, turn left
on Forest Route 68 and go about 2.5 miles to Forest Road 6510.
Turn right and follow 6510, 2 miles to Road 6510/500. Follow Road
500 about 4 miles to the junction of Roads 700 and 770. Continue
straight ahead onto Road 700, 1.1 mi. to Yellowjacket Camp.

VIA ANDERSON CAMP TRAIL #1075.
North of Prospect on Hwy. 62, just beyond milepost 51, turn left
onto Forest Route 68 and go about 2.5 miles to Forest Road 6510.
Turn right and follow 6510, 5.8 miles to Forest Road 6515.   Turn
left onto 6515 and go 6.3 miles, looking carefully for the trailhead on the left.   Anderson Camp Trail reaches the Rogue-Umpqua
Divide Trail after 3/4 mile.   To reach Anderson Mountain Summit,
turn left (south) to a sign posted at a short, faint trail to the
summit.

VIA HERSHBERGER ROAD.
North of Prospect on Hwy. 62, just beyond milepost 51, turn left
onto Forest Route 68 and go about 2.5 miles to Forest Road 6510.
Turn right and follow 6510, 5.8 miles to Forest Road 6515.   Turn
left onto 6515 and go 9.6 miles to the junction of Roads 525 and
530.   A spring is located in the meadow south of this junction,
along the east bank of Flat Creek.   The trail follows along Road
530 for about 1.5 miles before continuing as a trail to points
north. -continued

ACCESS TO ROGUE-UMPQUA DIVIDE TRAIL-continued.

VIA HOLE-IN-THE-GROUND TRAIL #1047.
North of Union Creek Resort, at the junction of Hwys. 62 and 230,
follow mileposts on 230 to mile 9.1 (the northern end of loop Rd.
6540). Turn left and go about 4.8 miles (at milepost 6) to the
junction with Forest Road 6540/500. Turn right onto Road 500 and
go 1.5 miles to the trailhead at the end of the road. ELEV. 5200'
Trail 1047 travels along Log Creek and joins Rogue-Umpqua Divide
Trail at the edge of a small glacial meadow. Hole-in-the-Ground
Camp is east of the meadow, just inside the trees.   The junction
with Buck Canyon Trail #1046 appears at this camp ELEV. 5600'.

TO WHERE THE DIVIDE TRAIL CROSSES FOREST ROUTE 37.
Follow mileposts on State Highway 230 to mi. 12.1 at the junction
with Forest Road 6560. Turn left onto Road 6560 and go 4 miles to
the Rogue-Umpqua Divide, where the route number becomes Route 37.
Follow Route 37, 0.4 miles further and look carefully for a sign
far to the left, indicating the Divide Trail leading southwest.On
the right side of Route 37,look just beyond for a road track from
where the Divide Trail leads northeast to Three Lakes Camp.

ALONG FISH CREEK VALLEY ROAD 870.
Continue 0.1 mi. further on Route 37 to the junction with Forest
Road 800. Turn left onto Road 800 and go 3 miles to Fish Creek
Valley Road 870. Turn left onto Road 870 and go 0.9 mile to where
the Divide Trail crosses left from Road 37 and right toward the
Fish Creek Shelter.

Fish Creek Valley Road continues about 3 miles to where the Divide Trail merges from the right (from Fish Creek Valley) to follow Road 870, about 1.1 mi. to its end. A sign reads: "Hole-in-
the-ground 1 mile, Hershberger Lookout 5 miles, Abbott Butte 19
miles".

FROM THREE LAKES ROAD 3703.
North of Union Creek Resort, follow mileposts on Hwy. 230 to mile
20.6   Turn left onto Three Lakes Road 3703 and go 5.7 mi. to the
junction of Road 3703/400. Turn left on Road 400 and go 0.2 mile
to a parking area at the west end of the lake.   Follow blazes on
an old road, 0.8 mi. to the beginning of the trail.

The Rogue-Umpqua-Divide Trail 1470 lies within the Rogue-Umpqua Divide Wilderness, created by the Oregon Wilderness Act of 1984.

WILDERNESS REGULATIONS INCLUDE:

-PACK OUT ALL LITTER, especially foil packaging that doesn't burn.

-BURY HUMAN WASTE 6 to 8 inches deep, 200 feet or more from open water.

-CAMPFIRES only in safe spots, keep small. It is best to carry stoves.

-CAMPING: Pitch your tent so no drainage ditch is required. Replace rocks and other materials removed from sleeping areas.

-MOTORIZED and MECHANICAL equipment, including bicycles, are prohibited in the wilderness.

(EXCERPTS: "New Wilderness on the Umpqua National Forest" brochure)

As You Hike Under The Forest
Canopy These Guys Will dispute Your
Passage.

ROCKY RIM TRAIL #1572. (See map 1B)

TRAIL BEGINS:	-UPPER TRAILHEAD: Rogue Umpqua Divide Trail 1470, 1 mile north of Hershberger Mtn. ELEV. 5680'
TRAIL ENDS:	-LOWER TRAILHEAD: Beaver Swamp Trailhead, Umpqua Forest Road 2840/400 near Fish Lake. ELEV. 4000'
DISTANCE:	-6.8 miles, moderate. USE: hiker/horse.
SEASON:	-Upper end snow-free July to October.
CONNECTING TR.:	-Rogue-Umpqua Divide Trail 1470.
	-Rocky Ridge Trail 1571, (partially abandoned).
BRING MAPS:	-Tiller Ranger District-Umpqua National Forest.
	-USFS -Rogue Umpqua Divide, Boulder Creek and Mt. Thielsen Wildernesses.
	-USFS Recreation Opportunity Guide Rocky Rim Tr.

ACCESS: -UPPER END: North of Prospect on Hwy. 62 just be-
              yond milepost 51, turn left onto Forest Route 68
and go about 2.5 miles to Forest Road 6510. Turn right and follow
6510, 5.8 miles to Forest Road 6515.   Turn left onto 6515 and go
9.6 miles to the junction of Roads 525, 530 and the Rogue-Umpqua
Divide Trail 1470.A spring is located in the meadow south of this
junction along the east bank of Flat Creek. Follow Road 530 about
1.5 miles to where the Divide Trail continues.   Take the Divide
Trail 1 mile north to the beginning of Rocky Rim Trail.

FEATURES: This description uses only the 4 mile portion of
                Rocky Rim Trail from its upper end near Hershber-
ger Mountain to the junction with the Rocky Ridge Trail and return, a very attractive day hike.   From the Rogue-Umpqua Divide
Trail, Rocky Rim Trail travels northwest through timber and sub-
alpine meadows before meeting the narrow backbone of Rocky Ridge.
The trail features a birdseye view of Fish Lake, the Castle Creek
drainage, and of the high Cascade Mountains. Wildflowers usually
are in great numbers, well into the summer months.

159

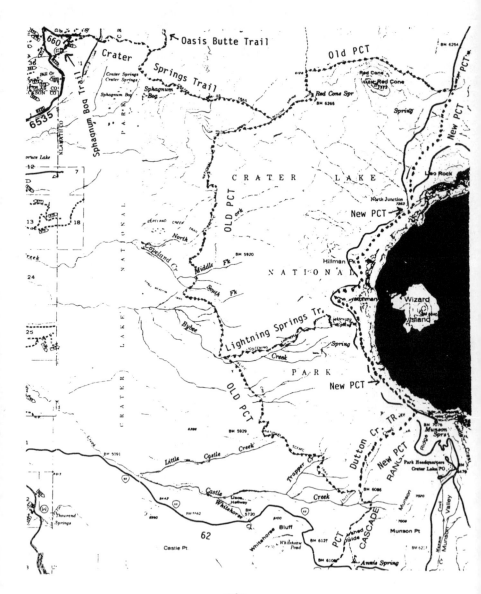

CRATER LAKE NATIONAL PARK BACKCOUNTRY USE REGULATIONS.

BACKCOUNTRY USE PERMITS ARE REQUIRED FOR ALL OVERNIGHT STAYS. The only exception is for overnight hikers who enter on the Pacific Crest Trail and exit the PCT at the opposite boundary. Free permits are available at entrance stations, information and visitor centers, from park rangers (after hours) or by mail. OTHER REGS:

1. CAMPING AND CAMPFIRES Open campfires allowed where not specifically prohibited.. Use only dead and down wood. No cutting or damaging living or standing vegetation, or collecting wood above 6900 ft. Use established fire rings at existing sites.In un-designated sites, remove all signs of fire by scattering rocks and churning the soil. Prior to leaving the campsite, make sure the fire is out and cold.
   CAMPING AND OPEN FIRES are prohibited between Rim Drive and Crater Lake; on Phantom Ship; Wizard Island; on Mt. Scott or its summit trails; within any meadow; within one mile of any paved road, nature trail or developed area; within 1/4 mile of Boundary Springs or Sphagnum Bog; within 100 ft. of any water source, trail or other camping party except when using a designated campsite.
2. PARTY SIZE(overnight trips) Limit 8 persons, 12 head of stock.
3. STAY ON TRAILS: NO HIKING OR CLIMBING INSIDE THE RIM except on the Cleetwood Trail.
4. PETS ARE NOT ALLOWED ON ANY PARK TRAIL, NOR ANYWHERE ELSE IN THE BACKCOUNTRY.
5. FIREARMS, bicycles, and motorized vehicles ARE NOT PERMITTED IN THE BACKCOUNTRY.
6. HORSES/PACK ANIMALS permitted only on designated trails. Horse Regulation handouts are available at park visitor centers.
7. SANITATION: Pack out all litter and leave clean campsite. Use privies where available, otherwise make your toilet in a shallow slit trench and cover when finished, away from camp and over 100 feet from any water source. BOIL OR TREAT ALL WATER.
8. PROTECTION FROM BEARS: Suspend food items from a tree branch, at least 10 ft. above ground and 4 ft. horizontally from the trunk. Store and prepare food away from sleeping areas. Food is defined as any packaged, bottled or canned consumables, drinks, toiletries, perfumes, soaps, etc. (Excerpts "Crater Lake Backcountry Use" leaflet).

UNION PEAK TRAIL, CRATER LAKE NATIONAL PARK. (See map 7)

TRAIL BEGINS: -Pacific Crest Trail, about 3 miles southwest of
                State Highway 62.   ELEV. 6550'
TRAIL ENDS: -Union Peak summit.   ELEV. 7709'
DISTANCE: -About 2.5 miles, moderate to steep grades.
USE: -Hikers only.
SEASON: -Usually snow-free July through September.
CONNECTING TR. -Pacific Crest National Scenic Trail.
BRING MAPS: -USFS Pacific Crest Trail-Oregon Central Portion.
               -CRATER LAKE map/brochure-National Park Service.

ACCESS: Just north of Union Creek Resort, at the inter-
                section of State Hwys. 230 and 62, travel north-
east on 62, 15.7 miles to a point where the Pacific Crest Trail
(PCNST) crosses the highway. ELEV. about 6200'. After parking,
go southwest on the PCNST about 3 miles to the junction with the
Union Peak Trail. Follow the Union Peak Trail about 2.5 miles to
the summit of Union Peak. CARRY WATER.

To the south you can see Mt. McLoughlin. Diamond Peak, Mt. Bailey
and Mt. Thielsen are to the north. The Crater Lake Rim, with its
lofty peaks, appears in the northeast.

NOTE: PLEASE OBSERVE CRATER LAKE NATIONAL PARK BACKCOUNTRY USE
REGULATIONS LISTED AT THE BEGINNING OF THIS CHAPTER.

HISTORY: "UNION PEAK (7709 feet), located in the southwest
                corner of the park, was so-named during the Civil
War by Northern sympathizers in the Rogue River Valley."
(USFS quote)

DUTTON CREEK TRAIL- CRATER LAKE NATIONAL PARK. (See map 7)
(Southern leg of a Pacific Crest Trail alternate route)

TRAIL BEGINS: -Pacific Crest Trail (PCNST).   ELEV. 6100'
TRAIL ENDS: -Park Headquarters Road, 200 feet   south of its
                     junction with the Rim Drive.   ELEV. 7100'
DISTANCE: -2.5 miles one way. Steep grades.
SEASON: -Usually snow-free July through September.
CONNECTING TRAIL: -Pacific Crest National Scenic Trail.
BRING MAPS: -USGS Crater Lake West, 7.5' series, 1985.
                    -Pacific Crest Trail, Oregon Central Portion.
                    -CRATER LAKE map/brochure-National Park Service.

ACCESS: LOWER TRAILHEAD: North of Union Creek Resort
                        at the junction of State Highways 62 and 230,
go 15.7 miles on Hwy. 62 to where the Pacific Crest Trail crosses
the highway. Park at this location and hike north, 1.7 miles to
the junction with the lower end of the Dutton Cr. Tr.(the southern leg of the new PCT alternate route). After leaving this older
section of the PCT, the Dutton Creek Trail leads 2.5 miles to its
upper trailhead on Park Headquarters Road near West Rim Drive.

UPPER TRAILHEAD: From the south entrance station of Crater Lake
National Park, travel beyond the Park Headquarters, and continue
north to within 200 feet of the junction with the West Crater Lk.
Rim Drive. Dutton Creek Trail leads downhill left (southwest).

From the upper trailhead,the PCT alternate route crosses West Rim
Drive and follows 6 miles along the west rim of Crater Lake.After
crossing the East Rim Drive at North Junction, the route descends
from Llao Rock and, after 2 miles, reaches the intersection where
this alternate route meets the older section of the PCT.

HISTORY: Captain Clarence E. Dutton   commanded   a U.S.
                    Geological Survey party to sound the depth of
Crater Lake from their boat, the Cleetwood.   Their deepest wire
soundings indicated the lake depth at 1996 feet, amazingly close
to sonar measurements of 1932 feet officially recorded in 1959.
(From "Crater Lake National Park" brochure) PLEASE SEE BEGINNING
OF THIS CHAPTER FOR BACKCOUNTRY USE REGULATIONS   IN CRATER LAKE
PARK.

LIGHTNING SPRINGS TRAIL. (See map 7)

TRAIL BEGINS:	-Crater Lake Rim Drive.	ELEV. 7170'
TRAIL ENDS:	-Pacific Crest Trail.	ELEV. 5850'
DISTANCE:	-4 miles, steep grades.	
SEASON:	-Usually snow-free July through September.	
CONNECTING TR.	-Pacific Crest National Scenic Trail.	
BRING MAPS:	-USGS Crater Lake West, 7.5' series, 1985.	
	-USFS Pacific Crest Trail-Oregon Central Portion.	
	-CRATER LAKE map/brochure-National Park Service.	

ACCESS: The Lightning Springs Trail begins from the west
               portion of Crater Lake Rim Drive, about 2.3 miles
northwest of Rim Village.   (This point can also be reached from
Highway 238 at the junction with the North Rim Access Road.   Take
the North Rim Access Road to the Crater Lake Rim Drive and turn
right for about 3.5 miles to Lightning Springs Trailhead.)

FEATURES: The trail switchbacks sharply downhill,   reaching
                 Lightning Springs in less than 1 mile.   Water is
available here, but should be boiled before drinking.   From the
springs, a stream follows the trail as it continues to the Pacific Crest Trail (PCNST) near Bybee Creek. Travelling south on the
PCNST leads 6.3 miles to State Highway 62. BACKCOUNTRY USE REGU-
LATIONS IN CRATER LAKE PARK ARE LISTED   AT THE BEGINNING OF THIS
CHAPTER.

Build Campfires only in safe
places, and make small fires.

164

CHAPTER 12 - DIAMOND LAKE AREA

MT. THIELSEN TRAIL #1456. (See map 1A)

TRAIL BEGINS:	-State Highway 138 near milepost 81. ELEV. 5400'
TRAIL ENDS:	-Mt. Thielsen Summit. ELEV. 9182'
DISTANCE:	-4.9 miles. more difficult.
SEASON:	-Summer and fall; hiker,horse. Winter skiing.
CONNECTING TR:	-Spruce Ridge Trail 1458, Pacific Crest Trail.
BRING MAPS:	-USFS Recreation Guide, Diamond Lake Ranger Dist.
	-Mt. Thielsen Wilderness information-USFS Diamond Lake, Chemult, Crescent Ranger Districts.
	-USFS Pacific Crest Trail-Central Oregon Portion.
	-USGS "Diamond Lake" and "Mount Thielsen", 7.5' series 1985.

ACCESS: Near the southeast corner of Diamond Lake, State Highways 230 and 138 intersect. From this point, go 1.5 miles north on 138 to Mt. Thielsen Trailhead on the right (east) side of the road between mileposts 81 and 82.

FEATURES: The trail leads upwards 1.6 miles to the junction with Spruce Ridge Trail 1458, and 1.3 miles further to the Pacific Crest Trail.

After crossing the Pacific Crest Trail, a 2 mile scramble begins a steep climb along a ridge to the east side of the summit pinnacle. The route up to the pinnacle must be well chosen to allow for proper hand and foot placements. This portion is steep. The use of a climber's rope is not absolutely necessary, but could be set in place as guidance and support to others in your party who may need it. Views from the summit extend north to Mt. Hood and south to Mt. Shasta.

HISTORY: Mt. Thielsen has been referred to as the "Lightning Rod of the Cascades," and was named for Hans Thielsen, a prominent railroad engineer and builder. The peak is one of several old volcanoes formed by lava flow about 2 million years ago when geologic forces folded and fractured the High Cascades. (USFS Information)

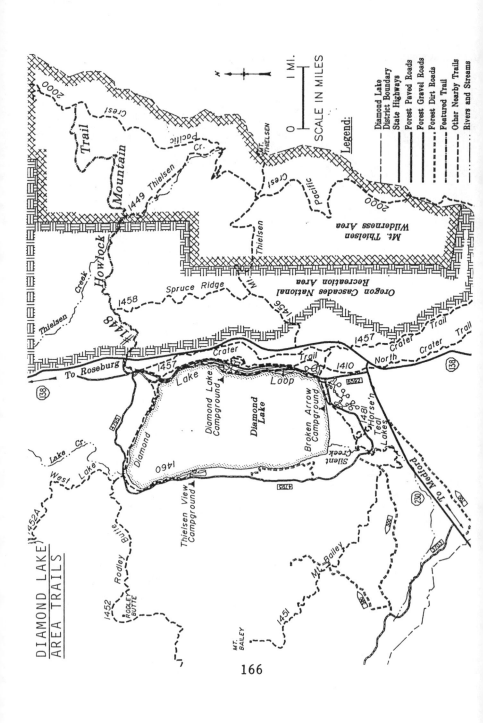

DIAMOND LAKE
AREA TRAILS

SCALE IN MILES

0   1 MI.

Legend:

Diamond Lake
District Boundary
State Highways
Forest Paved Roads
Forest Gravel Roads
Forest Dirt Roads
Featured Trail
Other Nearby Trails
Rivers and Streams

Mt. Thielsen
Wilderness Area

Oregon Cascades National
Recreation Area

MT. THIELSEN

Pacific Crest

Crest 2000

Crest 2000

Howlock Mountain Trail

Thielsen Cr.

1449 Thielsen

Thielsen Creek

Spruce Ridge

1448

1458

Mt. Thielsen

1456

1457   Crater Trail

North Crater Trail

Crater Trail

To Roseburg

1457   Crater

38

38

Lake   Trail

Loop

1410

65394

Diamond Lake Campground

Diamond Lake

Broken Arrow Campground

Teal Horse'n Lakes

1481

Diamond

1460

Silent Creek

4795

To Medford

230

700

Lake Cr.

West Lake

1452A

1452

Rodley Butte

RODLEY BUTTE

Thielsen View Campground

Mt. Bailey

1451

MT. BAILEY

4793

4701

166

HOWLOCK MTN. TRAIL #1448. (See map 1A)

TRAIL BEGINS:	-Forest Road 4795 near Diamond Lake.	ELEV. 5390'
TRAIL ENDS:	-Pacific Crest Trail (PCNST).	ELEV. 7220'
DISTANCE:	-7 miles, difficult. USE: hiker/horse/skiers.	
SEASON:	-Hikers, July through September. Winter skiing.	
CONNECTING TR.	-Spruce Ridge Trail 1458, Thielsen Creek Trail 1449 and Pacific Crest National Scenic Trail.	
BRING MAPS:	-USFS Recreation Guide, Diamond Lake Ranger Dist. -Mt. Thielsen Wilderness information-USFS Diamond Lake, Chemult, Crescent Ranger Districts. -USFS Pacific Crest Trail-Oregon Central Portion.	

ACCESS: Just north of the Union Creek Resort at the junc-
                  tion with Highways 62 and 230, follow mileposts
on 230, 23.9 mi. to the junction with State Hwy. 138.   Turn left
and go north on 138, 4.3 miles to the junction of Road 4795, the
north entrance to Diamond Lake Recreation Area.   Turn south onto
Road 4795 and go 0.3 mile to the Howlock Mtn. Trailhead parking
area on the left.

FEATURES: From the Howlock Mtn. Trailhead, the Spruce Ridge
                  Trail is 1.2 miles, Timothy Meadows about 3 mi.,
Thielsen Creek Trail 3.5 miles(the last source of water along the
Howlock Mtn. Trail), and Pacific Crest Trail 7 miles. This point
on the Pacific Crest Trail is nearly 1 mile northwest of and 1000
feet lower elevation than Howlock Mountain.

From the upper Howlock Mtn. Trailhead, Windego Pass is 19 miles
north along the PCNST and the PCNST Trailhead on Hwy. 138 is 11.0
miles south.

The views of Howlock Mountain, Mt. Thielsen, Mt. Bailey and of
open meadows are outstanding. A loop hike using the Howlock Mtn.
Trail 1448 can be made by hiking right (south) along the Pacific
Crest Trail 3 miles to the Thielsen Creek Trail junction.   Turn
right onto Thielsen Creek Trail 1449 and go about 2 1/4 miles to
the Howlock Mountain Trail. Keep left and follow the Howlock Mtn.
Trail 3 1/2 miles back to its trailhead. The total loop distance
is nearly 16 miles.

THIELSEN CREEK TRAIL #1449.   (See map 1A)

TRAIL BEGINS:	-(LOWER END): Howlock Mtn. Trail.	ELEV. 5600'
TRAIL ENDS:	-(UPPER END): Pacific Crest Trail.	ELEV. 6500'
DISTANCE:	-2.1 miles, more difficult. USE: hiker and horse in summer and fall. Winter skiing.	
CONNECTING TR.	-Howlock Mtn. Trail 1448 and Pacific Crest Trail.	
BRING MAPS:	-USFS Recreation Guide, Diamond Lake Ranger Dist.	
	-Mt. Thielsen Wilderness information USFS Diamond Lake, Chemult, Crescent Ranger Districts.	
	USFS Pacific Crest Trail-Oregon Central Portion.	

ACCESS: Follow the directions to Howlock Mtn. Trailhead
                 on the previous page. Take the Howlock Mtn. Trail
3.5 mi. to the LOWER END of the Thielsen Creek Trail.   Turn right
and go 2.1 miles southeast to the Pacific Crest Trail.

From the upper Thielsen Creek Trailhead, Windego Pass is 22 miles
north along the PCNST and the North Crater Trailhead on Hwy. 138
is 8 miles south.

FEATURES: Thielsen Creek Camp is along the upper end of the
                 Thielsen Creek Trail about 1/8 mile below the Pa-
cific Crest Trail. Water is available. A 16 mile loop trip back
to the Howlock Mtn. Trailhead could be made by using the Thielsen
Creek Trail, taking the Pacific Crest Trail 3 miles north to the
Howlock Mtn. Trail, then turning left and following Howlock Mtn.
Trail 7 miles back to its trailhead.

Always take extra clothing
along. You may need some
dry things to put on.

<u>MT. BAILEY TRAIL #1451.</u> (See maps 1A or 3)

<u>TRAIL BEGINS:</u>	-Forest Road 4795/300.	<u>ELEV.</u> 5200'
<u>TRAIL ENDS:</u>	-Mt. Bailey summit.	<u>ELEV.</u> 8363'
<u>DISTANCE:</u>	-5 miles, moderate grades.	<u>USE:</u> hiker only.
<u>SEASON:</u>	-Hikers July to October.	
<u>BRING MAPS:</u>	-Diamond Lake Ranger Dist.-Umpqua Ntl. Forest.	
	-USFS Rec. Opportunity Guide-Mt. Bailey Trail.	
	-USGS Diamond Lake, 7.5' series, 1985.	

<u>ACCESS #1.</u>   From the southeast corner of Diamond Lake, go about 2 miles west on Road 4795 to the junction of Road 4795/300. Turn left onto Road 300 and go 0.4 mile to the trailhead parking lot. Mt. Bailey Trail begins on the right of the parking area.   ELEV. about 5200'.

<u>ACCESS#2.</u>   INTERCEPTS THE MT. BAILEY TRAIL, 2-1/4 MILES HIGHER ON THE MOUNTAIN SLOPES, ELEV. ABOUT 6075'.   Near milepost 21 on State Highway 230, find the junction with Forest Road 3703. Turn onto Road 3703 and travel northwest, about 2 miles to the junction with Forest Road 4795/300. Turn right onto 300 and go about 0.1 mi. to Forest Road 4795/380 on the left. Road 380 is narrow, rocky and undriveable. It is a 1.5 mile hike up Road 380 to the point where Mt. Bailey Trail crosses and climbs to the summit.

<u>FEATURES:</u>   No technical ability is required to reach the summit.   The last 0.5 mi. is quite steep and rocky and may be too difficult for small children.   Mt. Thielsen and Diamond Lake are in the foreground.   To the north you can see Mt. Jefferson, Three Fingered Jack, Mt.Washington, the Three Sisters,   Broken Top, Diamond Peak, Bachelor Butte and nearby Cowhorn Mountain.

To the south you can see the Crater Lake Rim, Union Peak, Mt. Mc-Loughlin and Mt. Shasta.

Rogue River National Recreation Trail

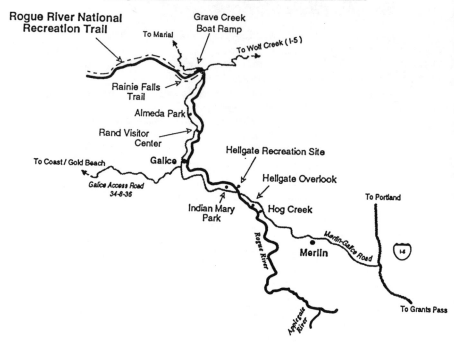

Rogue River National Recreation Trail

Grave Creek Boat Ramp

To Marial

To Wolf Creek (I-5)

Rainie Falls Trail

Almeda Park

Rand Visitor Center

Galice

Hellgate Recreation Site

To Coast / Gold Beach

Galice Access Road 34-8-36

Indian Mary Park

Hellgate Overlook

Hog Creek

To Portland

Rogue River

Merlin

Merlin-Galice Road

To Grants Pass

Applegate River

CHAPTER 13 - LOWER ROGUE AREA

LOWER ROGUE RIVER TRAIL #1160-Grave Creek to Foster Bar.

TRAIL BEGINS:	-Grave Creek Trailhead, Merlin-Galice Road, 27 miles northwest of Grants Pass. ELEV. 650'
TRAIL ENDS:	-Foster Bar near Illahe. ELEV. 207'
DISTANCE:	-40 miles, moderate grades. USE: hiker only.
SEASON:	-Open all year, canyon very hot in summer months.
BRING MAPS:	BLM/USFS "The Wild and Scenic Rogue River".

ACCESS: From Interstate Highway 5, Merlin exit, take the Merlin-Galice Road, 27 miles northwest to the Grave Creek boat landing just after crossing the Rogue River. The last commercial facilities are located at Galice   (store/restaurant, gas and car shuttle services that will arrange to have your car at the Foster Creek landing at your designated time).

DAY HIKING: From the boat landing;hike to Rainie Falls (mile 2.0), Whiskey Creek cabin (mile 3.3), Big Slide (mile 3.7) or Russian Creek (mile 5.8) and return.   The cabin at Whiskey Creek is a Registered National Landmark maintained by the BLM. To find it, cross the bridge over Whiskey Creek and take the side trail immediately to the right. OVERNIGHT CAMPING is available at Whiskey Creek, Big Slide and Russian Creek campsites.

40 MILE TRIP: The 40 mile trip is comfortably hiked in 5 days.   The BLM/USFS map/brochure gives a detailed log for hikers and boaters, as well as trail tips and precautions concerning heat, ticks, poison oak, rattlesnakes, etc. Information about Federal agencies, river guides, motels, lodge accommodations, fishing and hunting regulations, USGS topo maps, vegetation, animals, fish, and birds; is also given.

The upper 24 miles are administered by the Medford District Bureau of Land Management, and the lower 16 miles by USFS, Siskiyou National Forest.   FOR MORE INFORMATION CONTACT:
-Medford Dist. B.L.M., 3040 Biddle Road, Medford, OR. 97504
-Siskiyou Ntl. Forest, 200 N.E. Greenfield Rd., Grants Pass 97526
-Galice Ranger Dist., 1465 N.E. 7th, Grants Pass, OR.97526
-Gold Beach Ranger Dist.,1225 S. Ellensburg, Gold Beach OR, 97444

CHAPTER 14 - PACIFIC CREST TRAIL ROAD ACCESS

COOK AND GREEN PASS-FOREST ROAD 1055. (See map 26)

SEASON: -Usually snow-free July through October.
CONNECTING TR. -Cook and Green Trail 959, Horse Camp Trail 958.
BRING MAPS: -USFS Rogue River and Klamath National Forests.
                -USFS Pacific Crest Trail-Oregon Southern Portion.
                -USFS brochure-Red Buttes Wilderness.

ACCESS: From the town of Ruch, Oregon, follow mileposts
                 south on Upper Applegate Road, 18.8 miles to the
junction with Carberry Creek Road (County Route 777). Keep left
and go beyond milepost 20 to the California-Oregon border, at the
signed junction with Forest Roads 1040 and 1050. Turn left onto
Road 1050 and go 0.9 mi. to the junction with Forest Road 1055 on
the right. Travel south on Road 1055 to Cook and Green Pass near
milepost 10. The Pacific Crest Trail comes in on the left (east),
and then follows south along the undriveable Kangaroo Road about
3.5 miles. Near Lily Pad Lake, look left for the junction where
the Pacific Crest Trail continues as a trail to points south.

FEATURES: WATER is located from a spring near the Cook and
                 Green Pass. Hike down Cook and Green Trail less
                 than 1/4 mile.

HISTORY: "COOK AND GREEN PASS, CAMPGROUND: Robert Cook and
                 the two Green brothers were partners in several
mining ventures in this vicinity during the 1870's and 1880's and
the name undoubtedly resulted from their activities."
(USFS quote)

PACIFIC CREST TRAIL ACCESS, FOREST ROAD 2025. (See map 27)

SEASON: -Usually snow-free July through October.
BRING MAPS: -USFS Rogue River and Klamath National Forests.
               -USFS Pacific Crest Trail-Oregon Southern Portion.

ACCESS: From the the town of Ruch, Oregon, follow mileposts
               south on Upper Applegate Road to mile 9.3, at the
junction with Beaver Creek Road (Forest Route 20). Turn left onto
20 and follow mileposts to mile 14.1 at the junction with Forest
Road 2025.

Turn right onto 2025 and follow mileposts to:
-Mile 4.3 Pacific Crest Trail crosses the road, look for signs.
-Mile 5.1 Pacific Crest Trail crosses the road at the junction
           with Forest Road 40-S-01. Look for signs.

Forest Road 2025 can also be reached via Forest Route 20 from the
east, but portions of the road could be bumpy and not recommended
for passenger cars.

FEATURES: Watch carefully for trail signs, as road spurs and
               other evidence of timber harvesting can add confu-
sion. For water sources along the trail, check with Star Ranger
Station near milepost 7 on Upper Applegate Road.

ALWAYS READ THE POSTED SIGNS
AT THE TRAILHEAD.

173

PACIFIC CREST TRAIL ACCESS, FOREST ROUTE 22. (See maps 20 and 28)

SEASON: -Usually snow-free July to October. Wildflowers in
                abundance throughout the summer months.
BRING MAPS: -USFS Rogue River and Klamath National Forests.
                -USFS Pacific Crest Trail-Oregon Southern Portion.

ACCESS: From Talent, Oregon, at the intersection of Talent
                Avenue and Main Street, go south on Main St., which
becomes Wagner Creek Road in about 1 mile. Follow mileposts on
Wagner Creek Road to the following mileage points:

-Mile 4.5   Pavement ends.
-Mile 7.1   Bald Mt. Road junction, keep left.
-Mile 9.1   Wagner Gap (three-way junction) keep left on Forest
            Route 22.

Continue on Forest Route 22, approx. 8 miles to the junction with
Forest Route 20 on the Siskiyou Crest. Turn right on Forest Route
20 and go 0.1 mi. to the junction of Forest Roads 2040 and 40S16.
Look to the left where the Pacific Crest Trail crosses 40S16.

FEATURES: Forest Route 22 is unpaved, and there are some curves
            at its lower elevations. It is best to be cautious.
Otherwise, this road provides a good access to the Pacific Crest
Trail as it continues along the Siskiyou crest. For other access
points along Forest Route 20, see details on the following page.

PACIFIC CREST TRAIL ACCESS-ALONG FOREST ROUTE 20 and Hwy. 99
(Maps 24,27,28)

SEASON: -Usually snow-free by late July at higher elevations, (Mt. Ashland and Dutchman Peak areas).

BRING MAPS: -USFS Pacific Crest Trail-Oregon Southern Portion.
-USFS Rogue River and Klamath National Forests.
-BLM Medford District, Pacific Crest Trail Log.

ACCESS: From Interstate Highway 5,Ashland Exit 14, continue 9 miles to Mt. Ashland Exit 6 leading to a junction with Old Highway 99 South. Keep right and go 0.6 mile to a -hiker trail- sign on the right indicating the Pacific Crest Trail leading west toward Mt. Ashland and California. Continue 0.1 mile to Mt. Ashland Access Road, and follow this road to mile readings:

Mile 7.0   PCNST crosses the road at the National Forest Boundary, FROM THIS POINT THE ROAD BECOMES FOREST ROUTE 20.

Mile 11.1   Grouse Gap, PCNST parallel to road on the left(south).

Mile 16.1   Junction with Forest Roads 40S16 and 40S20, look left to where the PCNST crosses.

Mile 16.9   PCNST crosses Route 20 at Siskiyou Gap.

Mile 19.9   Wrangle Gap, Jnc. Road 2030, PCNST on right (north).

Mile 20.1   PCNST crosses Route 20.

Mile 21.9   Track on left (south) leads about 0.1 mile to Sheep Camp Springs.

Mile 22.3   Jackson Gap. To reach the PCNST turn left onto Road 40S01 and go 0.6 mile to where the PCNST crosses.

Mile 23.7   (Appx.) Junction with Forest Road 2025. To reach the PCNST, turn left and go 4.3 miles to where the PCNST crosses.

FEATURES: Food and a pay telephone are located at Callahan's Restaurant on Old Highway 99S just east of Interstate 5 Mt. Ashland exit. Route 20 between Grouse Gap and Road 2025 may be too rough for passenger cars. Water is scarce along this portion of the trail.ORVs including bicycles-NOT ALLOWED on the PCT.

PACIFIC CREST TRAIL ACCESS-PILOT ROCK ROAD. (See map 29)

SEASON: -Usually snow-free by early May.
BRING MAPS: -USFS Pacific Crest Trail-Oregon Southern Portion.
                  -BLM Medford District-Pacific Crest Trail Log.

ACCESS: From Ashland Exit 14, continue southeast on Inter-
                state Hwy. 5, 9 miles to Mt. Ashland Exit 6.   The
off-ramp leads to a junction with Old Highway 99 South. Keep to
the right at this junction and go 1.9 miles to the junction with
Pilot Rock Road 40-2E-33. ALONG THE WAY, THE PACIFIC CREST TRAIL
FOLLOWS OLD HIGHWAY 99S FOR A DISTANCE OF 1/2 MILE SOUTH OF THE
FREEWAY OVERPASS.   LOOK ON THE LEFT FOR A TRAIL SIGN NAILED TO A
TREE WHERE THE PCNST LEAVES THE ROAD AND HEADS TOWARD PILOT ROCK.

Turn left (east) onto Pilot Rock Road using your odometer to note
the following Pacific Crest Trail (PCNST) crossings:

Mile 1   PCNST crosses road in a saddle, look for trail signs.
Mile 2.1 Keep left downhill at a junction. (A right turn would
          lead 0.8 mile to the base of Pilot Rock and an access
          to the PCNST.)
Mile 2.9 Road junction, stay uphill to the right.
Mile 3.8 Road junction, stay right.
Mile 3.9 PCNST crosses at the crest of a ridge near a road gate
          in a recent logging area. Look for trail signs. From
this point, the PCNST LEADS RIGHT passing the base of Pilot Rock
and reaches Old Highway 99S in about 5.8 miles.   The PCNST LEADS
LEFT (northeast) to State Hwy. 66 (Greensprings Hwy.) in 11 mi.,
passing the slopes of Soda Mtn. and Hobart Bluff. CARRY WATER.

HISTORY: "PILOT ROCK, a volcanic plug so named because of its
              prominence as a landmark to early travelers on the
Oregon-California Trail. Although the chute on the north face of
the rock can be scaled without special equipment, climbers should
be cautious of loose rock." (USFS quote)

PACIFIC CREST TRAIL ACCESS, BALDY CREEK ROAD 40-3E-5.(Maps 22,29)

SEASON: -Usually snow-free late May to October.
BRING MAPS: -USFS Pacific Crest Trail-Oregon Southern Portion.
               -BLM Transportation Map-Medford District-Klamath
               Resource Area.
               -BLM Medford District-Pacific Crest Trail Log.

ACCESS: From Ashland Interstate Highway 5 Exit 14, travel
               14.8 miles (southeast) on State Highway 66. Turn
right onto Tyler Creek Road and go 1.4 miles to the junction with
Baldy Creek Road 40-3E-5. Take 40-3E-5, 5.7 miles to the crest of
a ridge at the junction with Road 40-3E-30. The PCNST crosses the
road (40-3E-5) just before reaching a cattle guard.

TURNING RIGHT (SOUTH) onto the PCNST leads 9.4 mi. to Interstate
Hwy. 5 (passing Porcupine Mtn. at mile 2.6 and Pilot Rock at mile
5.3)

TURNING LEFT (NORTH) onto the PCNST leads 7.4 mi. to Hwy 66 (passing the western slopes of Soda Mountain at mile 1.5 and crossing
Soda Mountain Road near mile 3.0).

FEATURES: The Baldy Creek Road provides access to the Pacif-
               ic Crest National Scenic Trail, southwest of Soda
Mountain Lookout, at the near mid-point of the Highway 66-Inter-
state Highway 5 section of the trail. CARRY WATER when hiking in
this area.   The Pacific Crest Trail passes through BLM and private lands. Watch carefully for the trail as it travels through
areas of timber harvesting. Numerous roads and cattle trails can
add to the confusion. Wildflowers are abundant from May to July.

PACIFIC CREST TRAIL ACCESS, STATE HIGHWAY 66.

SEASON: —Usually snow-free late May through October. Wild-
            flowers abundant May to July.
BRING MAPS: —USFS Pacific Crest Trail-Oregon Southern Portion.
            —BLM Transportation Map -Medford District -Klamath
            Resource Area.
            —BLM Medford District-Pacific Crest Trail Log.
USE: CLOSED TO MOTORIZED/MECHANICAL VEHICLES, INCLUDING
            BICYCLES.

ACCESS: From Interstate Hwy. 5, Ashland Exit 14, follow the
            mileposts east on State Hwy. 66, 15.7 miles to the
highway summit at Soda Mtn. Road. The Pacific Crest Trail crosses Hwy. 66 just beyond.

From this point the trail leads RIGHT, south and west, 16.8 miles
to Interstate Highway 5. Hobart Bluff, Soda Mountain Road, Soda
Mountain, and Pilot Rock are landmarks along the way.

Leading from the LEFT of Highway 66, the PCNST travels 4.6 miles
to Little Hyatt Reservoir then approx. 1.5 miles further to Hyatt
Prairie Road.

FEATURES: In this area of the Pacific Crest Trail, there are
            views of the Rogue River Valley, Mt. Shasta in nor-
thern California and the Klamath Basin. The trail passes through
mixed private and BLM administered lands. Watch for trail insignias. The trail may be hard to follow due to timber harvesting,
cattle trails, and numerous roads. CARRY DRINKING WATER, as on-
route supplies are very limited. Check with Ashland Ranger Station or Medford BLM office for exact locations.

HISTORY: "State Highway 66.......Known locally as the Green-
            springs Highway, this road parallels the 'Old Ap-
plegate Trail' which was used during the 1840's by pioneers who
branched off the main Oregon Trail at Fort Hall Idaho and crossed
the sagebrush desert of northern Nevada." (USFS quote)

178

PACIFIC CREST TRAIL ACCESS- HYATT LAKE RESERVOIR. (See map 22)

SEASON: -Usually snow free mid-May through October. Wild-
               flowers at their best late spring and early summer.
BRING MAPS: -USFS Pacific Crest Trail-Oregon Southern Portion.
               -BLM Transportation Map-Medford District -Klamath Re-
               source Area.
               -BLM Medford District-Pacific Crest Trail Log.

ACCESS: HYATT LAKE RESERVOIR.   From Interstate Hwy. 5, Ash-
               land-Klamath Falls Exit 14, follow mileposts east on
State Hwy. 66, 17.5 mi. to the junction of East Hyatt Lake Road.
Turn left onto this road and travel 3.1 miles north to the south
end of Hyatt Lake at the junction with West Hyatt Lake Road. The
Pacific Crest Trail crosses at this road junction.

Hyatt Lake (BLM) Campground is located near this access point. A
hikers' camp is located just off the Pacific Crest Trail.   There
are hot showers at the campground.   Food, phone and maildrop are
available at Hyatt Lake Resort.   A horse camp with ample feed is
located at Little Hyatt Lake.

From Hyatt Lake Campground, the Pacific Crest Trail leads SOUTH-
WEST 1.5 miles to Little Hyatt Lake, and 4.6 miles further to the
Greensprings Highway 66.   Leading NORTHEAST from the campground,
the trail goes along the east shore of Howard Prairie Lake and on
to points north.

LITTLE HYATT LAKE RESERVOIR.   From the above Pacific Crest Trail
crossing near Hyatt Lake Campground,   travel about 1 mile west on
West Hyatt Lake Road to the junction with Old Hyatt Prairie Road.
Turn left onto this road and travel 1.5 miles southwest to Little
Hyatt Reservoir.

MOTORIZED VEHICLES NOT ALLOWED ON THE PCT,   CARRY WATER!

PACIFIC CREST TRAIL ACCESS, KENO ACCESS ROAD 39-7E-31. (Map 23)

SEASON: -Usually snow free mid-May through October.
BRING MAPS: -USFS Pacific Crest Trail-Oregon Southern Portion.
                 -BLM Transportation Map-Medford District-Klamath
                 Resource Area.
                 -BLM Medford District-Pacific Crest Trail Log.

ACCESS: From Interstate Hwy. 5, Ashland-Klamath Falls Exit
                 14, travel east on State Highway 66, 0.6 mi. to the
junction with Dead Indian Memorial Road. (County Route 722). Turn
left (northeast) onto this road and follow mileposts to mile 18.5
at the junction with Keno Access Road 39-7E-31.   Turn right onto
39-7E-31 and go 5.0 mi. to where the Pacific Crest Trail crosses
the road.

FEATURES: Hiking NORTHEAST from this point leads three miles
                 to Big Springs at Griffin Pass on Forest Road 2520.
Big Springs is the only year-round on route water supply in the
area. It is best to CARRY WATER.

Hiking SOUTHWEST from the Keno Access Road leads 3 miles to the
southern shore of Howard Prairie Lake and Road 38-4E-32.   Willow
Point Campground is located 1.8 mi. northwest along this road, on
the southwest shore of Howard Prairie Lake.

The trail in both directions continues through mixed private and
BLM administered lands. Watch carefully for trail blazes. MOTOR-
IZED VEHICLES ARE NOT ALLOWED ON THE PACIFIC CREST TRAIL.

PACIFIC CREST TRAIL ACCESS, GRIFFIN PASS, ROAD 2520. (See map 23)

SEASON: -Usually snow free mid-June through October.
BRING MAPS: -USFS Pacific Crest Trail-Oregon Southern Portion.
                -USFS Ashland Ranger Dist.-Rogue River Ntl. Forest.
                -BLM Transportation Map-Medford District-Klamath
                 Resource Area.
                -BLM Medford District-Pacific Crest Trail Log.

ACCESS: From Interstate Hwy. 5, Ashland-Klamath Falls Exit
                14,travel east on Hwy. 66, 0.6 mile to the junction
with Dead Indian Memorial Road (County Route 722). Turn left onto
this road and follow mileposts to mile 23.7 at the junction with
Forest Road 2520. Turn right onto 2520 and continue 4.0 miles to
Griffin Pass at the point where the Pacific Crest Trail crosses
the road.

FEATURES: Big Springs, at Griffin Pass is the only year-round
                on-route water supply in the area.   After reaching
the Pacific Crest Trail crossing,go 600 ft. further south on Road
2520 to a faint trail on the left that leads a short distance to
the spring. A metal storage container is located at the spring.
PLEASE COVER THE CONTAINER SO AS TO KEEP OUT VARMINTS. WILDERNESS
WATER SHOULD BE TREATED BEFORE DRINKING.

From Griffin Pass the Pacific Crest Trail climbs NORTHEAST to the
eastern slopes of Old Baldy Mountain, and on to Dead Indian Memorial Road. (CARRY WATER)

SOUTHWEST, the trail descends to Keno Access Road, Howard Prairie
Lake, and to points south through mixed private and BLM adminis-
tered lands. Watch carefully for route marker insignias. MOTOR-
IZED VEHICLES OR BICYCLES NOT ALLOWED ON THE PACIFIC CREST TRAIL.
CARRY WATER.

HISTORY: "GRIFFIN PASS: The origin and date of this name are
                unknown, although the Griffin family settled in the
Phoenix area of the Bear Creek Valley in the 1850s."
(USFS quote)

181

PACIFIC CREST TRAIL ACCESS-OLD BALDY MTN. ROAD 2520/600. (Map 23)

SEASON: -Usually snow-free July through October.
BRING MAPS: -USFS Pacific Crest Trail-Oregon Southern Portion.
                 -USFS Ashland Ranger Dist.-Rogue River Ntl. Forest.
                 -BLM Medford District-Pacific Crest Trail Log.

ACCESS: From Interstate Hwy. 5, Ashland-Klamath Falls Exit
                 14,travel east on Hwy. 66, 0.6 mile to the junction
with Dead Indian Memorial Road (Jackson County Route 722).   Turn
left onto this road and follow mileposts northeast to mile 23.7
at the junction with Forest Road 2520. Turn right onto 2520, and
go 2.4 miles to the junction with Forest Road 2520/640. Turn left
onto Road 640 and go 0.6 miles to the merger with Road 600. Continue uphill right on 600, passing junctions with Roads 680 and
650, 1.0 mi. to a parking place at the end of the road just below
Old Baldy Mountain.

FEATURES: There are no signs giving directions to the Pacific
                 Crest Trail (PCNST). Go to the very end of the road
to where a log blocks the uphill Jeep track. From the log, turn
left and go cross-country, keeping east, about 200 ft. to the Pacific Crest Trail. It would be well to mark the trail for the return trip to the parking area.

Turning RIGHT onto the Pacific Crest Trail leads 600 ft. to a
gate at the Rogue River National Forest boundary. The trail then
descends to Griffin Pass and points south. Turning LEFT onto the
PCNST leads downhill 1.7 miles to where Burton Flat Road crosses
and 1.9 miles further north to Dead Indian Memorial Road.

A SIDETRIP TO THE TOP OF OLD BALDY MOUNTAIN (ELEV. 6340') can be
made from the above parking area and hiking about 1/4 mile along
the old uphill Jeep road. From the summit, Mountain Lakes Wilderness can be seen to the northeast, Mt. McLoughlin to the north,
and Mt. Shasta to the south.   Motorized vehicles are not allowed
on the Pacific Crest Trail. CARRY WATER.

PACIFIC CREST TRAIL ACCESS, DEAD INDIAN MEMORIAL ROAD. (Map 23)

SEASON: -Usually snow-free July through October.
BRING MAPS: -USFS Pacific Crest Trail-Oregon Southern Portion.
                       -USFS Ashland Ranger Dist.-Rogue River Ntl. Forest.

ACCESS: From Interstate Hwy. 5, Ashland-Klamath Falls Exit
                       14,travel east on Hwy. 66, 0.6 mile to the junction
with Dead Indian Memorial Road (Jackson County Route 722, Klamath
County 533). Turn left (northeast) onto this road and go 27.2 mi.
to the Pacific Crest Trailhead (Pederson Snow Park). Parking and
turn-around is available.

FEATURES: The Pacific Crest Trail from the SOUTH shoulder of
                       the   road   leads 1.9 miles SOUTH to the crossing of
Burton Road and 1.7 miles further to the east slopes of Old Baldy
Mountain (ELEV. 6340'). It then continues about 2 mi. to Griffin
Pass (Big Springs year-round water supply). ALL WATER IN WILDER-
NESS SHOULD BE TREATED!

From the NORTH shoulder of Dead Indian Memorial Road, the Pacific
Crest Trail leads 2 miles NORTH to a side trail leading to Brown
Mountain Shelter where water may be available. The PCNST contin-
ues, passing the junction with Brown Mtn. Trail, and the forks of
Little Butte Creek. The junction with Fish Lake and High Lakes
Trails are met, just before reaching Highway 140.   CARRY WATER!
Cascade Canal just north of Hwy. 140, is a water source but not
always available. (Total of 12.5 PCT miles in this section).

Water, food, lodging and telephone are available at Fish Lake Re-
sort. Fish Lake and High Lakes Trails are co-located for one mile
west before Fish Lake Trail continues left, less than one mile to
Fish Lake Resort and Campgrounds, WHERE STOCK ANIMALS ARE NOT AL-
LOWED. SEE LATEST USFS RECREATION INFORMATION FOR A NEARBY TETH-
ERING LOCATION.

HISTORY: DEAD INDIAN MEMORIAL ROAD is an early link between
                       Ashland and the Klamath Basin. This road supposedly
got its name in the 1850s when settlers found a party of dead Indians on the plateau.

PACIFIC CREST TRAIL ACCESS, HIGHWAY 140. (See map 16)

SEASON: –Usually snow-free July through October.
BRING MAPS: –USFS Pacific Crest Trail-Oregon Southern Portion.
               –USFS Sky Lakes Area-Rogue River and Winema National
                Forests.
               –USFS Rogue River and Winema National Forests.

ACCESS: From White City, Oregon, follow mileposts east on
               State Highway 140 to mile 32.5 at the Pacific Crest
Trail parking area, located on the left (NORTH) side of the highway.

If travelling from Ashland, travel 36.3 miles on Dead Indian Memorial Road (Jackson County Route 722, Klamath County 533) to the
junction with State Highway 140. Turn left onto Hwy. 140 and go
5.1 miles to the Pacific Crest parking area between mileposts 32
and 33.

FEATURES: Water is sometimes available from the Cascade Canal
               immediately north of Highway 140. CARRY WATER on
the PCNST as supplies could be dried up in summer.

The Pacific Crest Trail SOUTH from Highway 140 reaches the junction with High Lakes and Fish Lake Trails in 0.5 mile before continuing along the western slopes of Brown Mountain through lava
beds formed 15 to 20 thousand years ago by volcanic eruptions.Red
cinder rock imported for trail surface makes walking difficult
especially for horses. The trail passes the forks of Little Butte
Creek, the junction with Brown Mountain Trail,before reaching Rd.
700 at the 9.2 mile point. After passing Road 700, the PCNST soon
reaches a short spur to Brown Mountain Shelter where water may be
available. It is 2.0 trail miles further to Dead Indian Memorial
Road (Klamath County Route 533, Jackson County 722).

The Pacific Crest Trail NORTH from Hwy. 140 enters the Sky Lakes
Wilderness in about 2 miles and crosses the Mt. McLoughlin Trail
near Freye Lake in another 1.5 miles. The trail then continues
through the Sky Lakes Wilderness, Crater Lake National Park, and
on to other points north.Water may be available from nearby Freye
Lake, or lakes in Sky Lakes Wilderness.

PACIFIC CREST TRAIL ACCESS, HIGHWAY 62 (Crater Lake Park).
(See map 7)

SEASON: -Usually snow-free late June through September.
BRING MAPS: -USFS Pacific Crest Trail-Oregon Central Portion.
               -CRATER LAKE map/brochure, National Park Service.

ACCESS: STATE HIGHWAY 62 NEAR ANNIE SPRING: Just north of
               Union Creek Resort at the junction with State High-
ways 230 and 62, go 15.7 miles northeast on Highway 62 to where
the Pacific Crest Trail crosses the highway (ELEV. about 6200ft.)
This point is 0.8 mi. west of Annie Spring, the south entrance to
Crater Lake National Park.

FEATURES: An older section of the Pacific Crest Trail leads
NORTH, 31 miles below and west of the lake. A SHORTER, SCENIC AL-
TERNATE ROUTE HAS BEEN ESTABLISHED THROUGH THE PARK, THAT FOLLOWS
THE WESTERN RIM OF THE LAKE, BEFORE REJOINING THE OLDER SECTION.
After travelling 1.7 miles along the PCT, the junction is reached
with the lower end of the DUTTON CREEK TRAIL (the southern leg of
the new PCT alternate route). The route uses the 2.5 mile Dutton
Creek Trail, crosses the West Rim Drive and follows about 6 miles
along the west rim of the lake. After crossing the East Rim Drive
at North Junction, the new PCT descends from Llao Rock and, after
2 miles, reaches the intersection to where the new and old trails
meet.

SOUTH of Hwy. 62, the PCT leads about 3 mi. to the Union Peak Tr.
junction and beyond through Sky Lakes Wilderness.

For CRATER LAKE BACKCOUNTRY USE REGULATIONS, see the beginning of
Chapter 11.

HISTORY: Crater Lake National Park, the Nation's sixth Na-
               tional Park , was established by President Theodore
Roosevelt in 1902.   The lake is the deepest in the U.S. at 1932
feet and was formed approx. 6800 years ago when then 14,000 foot
Mt. Mazama erupted and collapsed.

PACIFIC CREST TRAIL ACCESS, STATE HIGHWAY 138. (See maps 1A or 3)

SEASON: -Usually snow-free late June through September.
BRING MAPS: -USFS Pacific Crest Trail-Oregon Central Portion.
               -USFS Diamond Lake Ranger Dist.-Umpqua Ntl. Forest.
               -USFS Winema National Forest.

ACCESS: From the southeast corner of Diamond Lake, Oregon,
               at the intersection of State Highways 230 and 138,
travel 4 miles southeast on 138, to where the Pacific Crest Trail
crosses the highway. This crossing is 3/4 mile east of the north
entrance to Crater Lake National Park.

FEATURES: The Pacific Crest Trail north from Highway 138 pas-
               ses the junctions of North Crater Trail 1410, Mt.
Thielsen Trail 1456, Thielsen Creek Trail 1449 and Howlock Mountain Trail 1448. These 4 trails offer sidetrips to Diamond Lake
Resort, where food, supplies, lodging, showers and telephone are
available.

If traveling SOUTH through Crater Lake National Park; it is possible to start from Hwy.138,or from the Pacific Crest Trail parking area located 7 miles south of Highway 138 along the NORTH RIM
ACCESS ROAD. From a junction near the parking area,an older section of the PCT leads west from the North Rim Access Road, a long
16.9 miles to Highway 62.   A SHORTER 10.5 MILE ALTERNATE ROUTE
stays east of North Rim Access Road and travels about 2 miles to
the East Rim Drive at North Junction. The route then continues 6
miles along the Caldera Rim to Rim Village at the junction of the
Park Headquarters Road. 200 feet south of this junction, DUTTON
CREEK TRAIL provides a 2.5 mile route to rejoin the older section
of the Pacific Crest Trail.

PLEASE SEE BEGINNING OF THIS CHAPTER FOR BACKCOUNTRY USE REGULA-
TIONS IN CRATER LAKE NATIONAL PARK.

HISTORY: "Mt. THIELSEN: To the east of Diamond Lake is this
               9,182 foot peak often referred to as the 'Light-
ning Rod of the Cascades.   It was named about 1872 in honor of
Hans Thielsen, prominent railroad engineer and builder."
(USFS Quote)

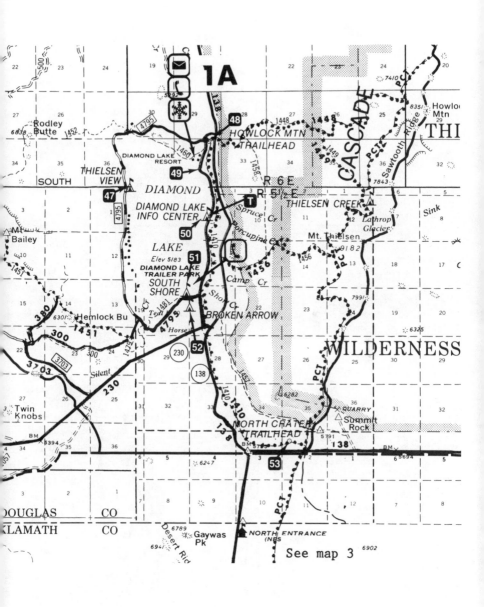

1A

22   23   24   19   22   23   24   20

27   26   Rodley   Butt   30   4795   28   27   835/   Howlo
6639   Butte   1452   1448   1448   Mtn

34   35   36   THIELSEN   33   1456   34   36   32
SOUTH   VIEW   R 6 E   7843
            DIAMOND LAKE   R 5½ E

47   DIAMOND   DIAMOND LAKE   T   THIELSEN CREEK   Sink
    INFO CENTER   Spruce   Cr   10   11   Lathrop
Mt.   LAKE   Porcupine Cr   Mt. Thielsen   Glacier
Bailey   Elev 5183   50   9182
    DIAMOND LAKE   51   1456   PCT
    TRAILER PARK   1456   14   13   18   17
1451   SOUTH   1410   1456
    SHORE   Camp   Cr
15   14   13   BROKEN ARROW   23   24   19   20
    Hemlock Bu   Teal   799/   6325
380   630f   Short   Cr   22
300   Horse   52   WILDERNESS
22   23   300   24   230   27   26   25   30   29
3703   Silent   6282
27   26   230   32   QUARRY   36   Summit   31   32
Twin   25   138   Rock
Knobs   5394   1410   NORTH CRATER   5391   5694
34   35   36   138   TRAILHEAD   138   BM

3   2   1   8   6247   9   10   53   11   12   7   8

DOUGLAS   CO
KLAMATH   CO   6789   Gaywas   NORTH ENTRANCE   6902
    Desert Rid   Pk   (NES)
    694/

See map 3

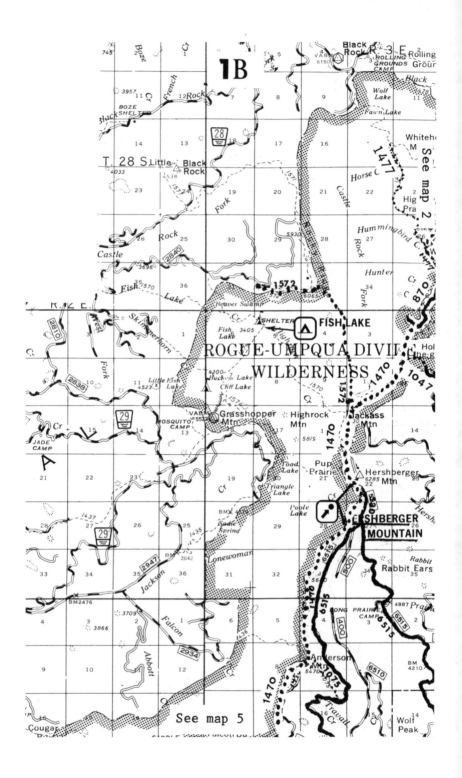

2

See map 1B

See map 3

See map 6

R. 4 E.

R.

O R E S T

R. Q

Crater Lake Park

BEAVER SHELTER

OLD MAN CAMP

Garwood Butte

Skookum Prairie

INCENSE CEDAR GROVE

Skookum

Three Lakes

THREE LAKES CAMP

3703

Happy Valley Cr

Clear Cr

Fish

Lesson

CLEAR CR CAMP

1470

Creek

Sherwood Butte

BUCK CAMP

Rim Rock

Sherwood Mdw

PRINEVILLE CAMP

Beaver

230

230

1034

1470

Lonesome Mtn

CREEK SHELTER

Mosquito L.

1477

Buck Mtn

400

West Fork

Buck Cr

Buck Rk

Sandy Gap

Devils Slide

1046

WILEY WEST CAMP

Fish Mtn

ing ound

Alkali Mdw

ALKALI CAMP

1046

ROGUE

RIVER

Mazama Cr

Soda Springs Cr

Hamaker Bluff

Boundary Springs

SODA SPRING

La West

BM 4407

1039

1034

780

730

850

HAMAKER CAMP

500

550

Park Mdws

Crescent Ridge

Wiley

Foster

Cr

HAMAKER

MEADOW

BEAR CAMP

700

900

Rogue

6540

6540

6520

6540

6530

6530

Cr

National

FURRY CAMP

National

6530

Bobs Bog

Beartree

Creek Middle Fork

South Fork

400

Oasis Spri

Oasis Bu

Roque

1034

100

210

150

NATIONAL CREEK FALLS

660

6535

6535

Log Cr

Cr

1038

Crater Sprs

Sphagnum Bog

TRAILHEAD

WIZARD CAMP

NATIONAL WIZARD CAMP

Bert

DOUGLAS CO.

JACKSON CO.

Bill Jackson

6535

560

800

6535

Crater

Spruce Lake

Copeland

850

900

970

977

230

BM 3756

SUNDAY CAMP

North

BM

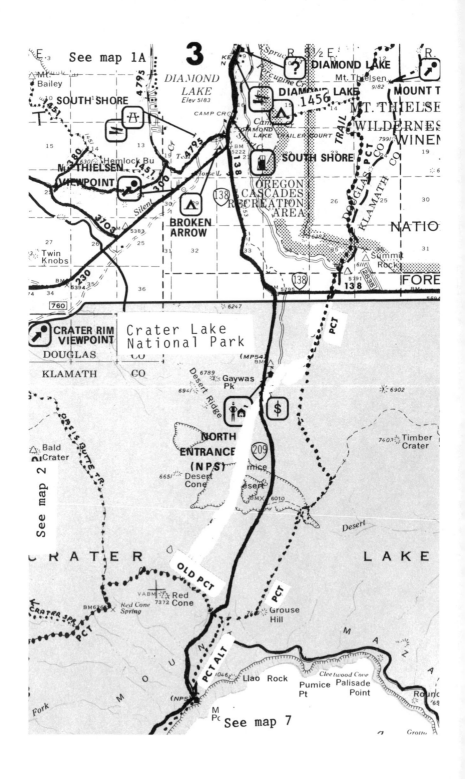

See map 1A

3

E .3

Mt.
Bailey

*DIAMOND
LAKE*
Elev 5183

SOUTH SHORE

Spruc R 5½ E.

KE

Porcupine Cr

DIAMOND LAKE
Mt. Thielsen

9/82

R.

DIAMOND LAKE

1456

14

MOUNT T

MT. THIELSE

15   13

Hemlock Bu

19

CAMP CROS

*DIAMOND
LAKE* TRAILER COURT

BM
5222

SOUTH SHORE

MT. THIELSEN
VIEWPOINT

Horse L

**OREGON
CASCADES
RECREATION
AREA**

6

25   30

WILDERNES
WINEM

799

24

KLAMATH CO

DOUGLAS PCT

TRAIL

NATIO

Silent

30
53

Twin
Knobs

**BROKEN
ARROW**

5383

27   26   25

31   32   33

26

6282

25   30

Summit
Rock

31

6111

5391

R35

230

5394

74 34   35   36

6 5795

138

138

6 5594

BM

FORE

760

6247

CRATER RIM
VIEWPOINT

Crater Lake
National Park

DOUGLAS   CO

KLAMATH   CO

(MP54)
BM

PCT

6789
6941   Gaywas
Pk

Desert Ridge

6902

See map 2

Bald
Crater

OREIS BUTE TR.

**NORTH
ENTRANCE
(NPS)**

$

209

7403 Timber
Crater

6651   Desert
Cone

umice

esert

6010

BMX

Desert

C R A T E R

L A K E

OLD PCT

Red Cone
Spring

VABM
7372 Red
Cone

BM6266

CRATER SPR.

PCT

PCT

PCT ALT

N

U

O

M

Grouse
Hill

6046 Llao Rock

(NPS)

Fork

M

Pc

Pumice
Pt

Palisade
Point

Cleetwood Cove

M   A

Z

N

Roun

Grotto

See map 7

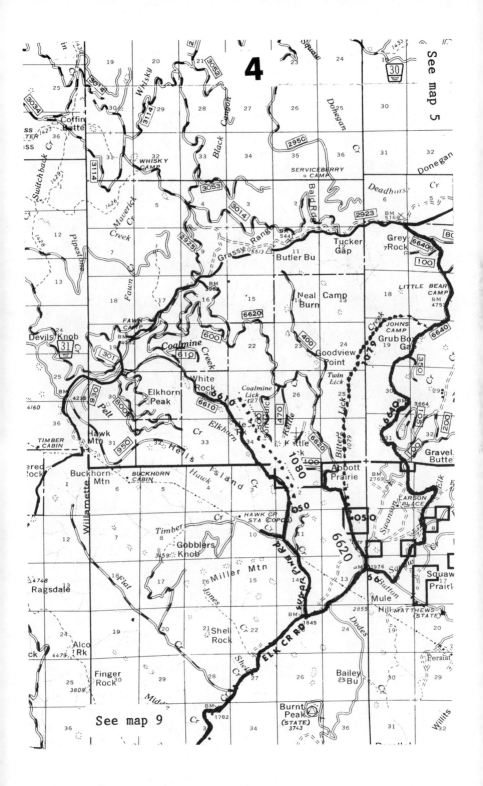

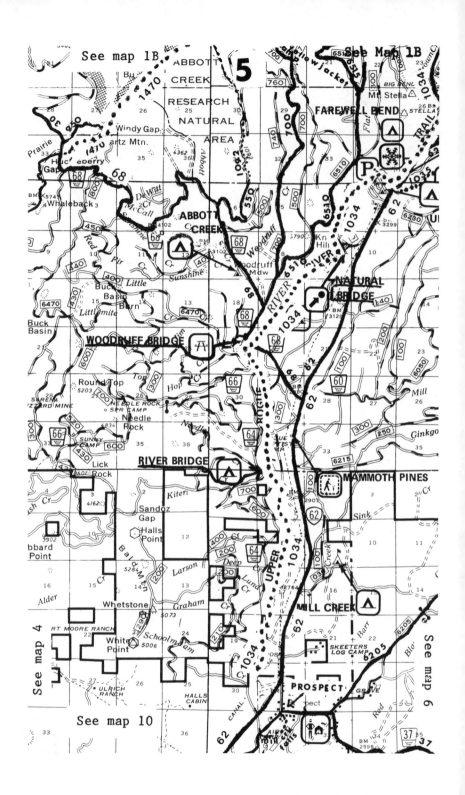

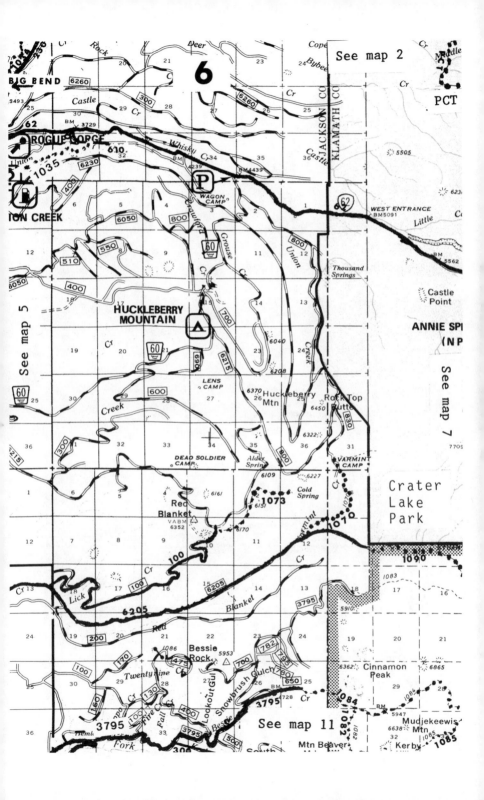

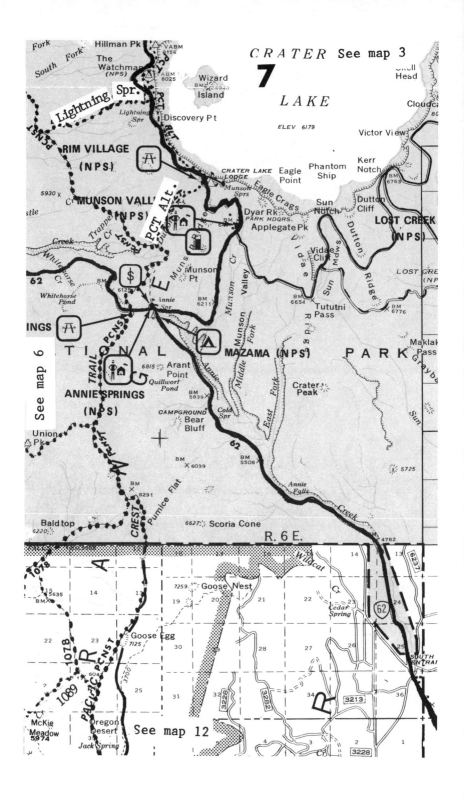

CRATER See map 3

7

LAKE

Fork · Hillman Pk · VABM 8156

The Watchman (NPS) · ABM 8025 · BM 6940 Wizard Island

Skull Head

South Fork

Lightning Spr.

Lightning Spr · Discovery Pt

ELEV 6179

Cloudc...

Victor View

PCT Alt

RIM VILLAGE (NPS)

CRATER LAKE LODGE

Eagle Point

Phantom Ship

Kerr Notch · BM 6763

5930 x

Cr MUNSON VALL (NPS)

Munson Sprs

Eagle Crags

Sun Notch

Dutton Cliff

LOST CREEK (NPS)

Creek · Trapper Cr

PCT Alt.

Dyar Rk

PARK HDQRS.

BM

Applegate Pk

Vidae Cliff

LOST CRE (NP

Whitehorse Cr

BM 6125

Munson Pt

BM 6211

Munson Valley

Munson Cr

BM 6654

Tututni Pass

BM 6776

62

Whitehorse Pond

Annie Spr

Sun Notch

Dutton Ridge

Sun Creek

Maklak Pass

INGS

PCNS

TRAIL

MAZAMA (NPS)

PARK

Graybs

See map 6

TIONAL

6815

Arant Point

Quillwort Pond

Munson Fork

Middle Fork

Crater Peak

5725

ANNIE SPRINGS (NPS)

Union Pk

CAMPGROUND · Bear Bluff

BM 5839

Cold Spr

East Fork

Annie

BM x 6039

BM 5508

62

Annie Falls

Creek

BM x 6291

Pumice Flat

Baldtop 6220

CREST

6627 Scoria Cone

R. 6 E.

BM 4782

6237

1018

A

Wildcat Cr

14

13

15 5635 BM x

14

7259 Goose Nest

19

20

21

22

23

24

Cedar Spring

62

1078

R

22

23

Goose Egg 7125

30

29

28

27

26

25

SOUTH CENTRAL

1089

Cr

PACIFIC PCNS

6044

3700

25

31

32

3228

3262

34

3213

36

McKie Meadow 5974

Oregon Desert

See map 12

Jack Spring

4

3

2

1

3228

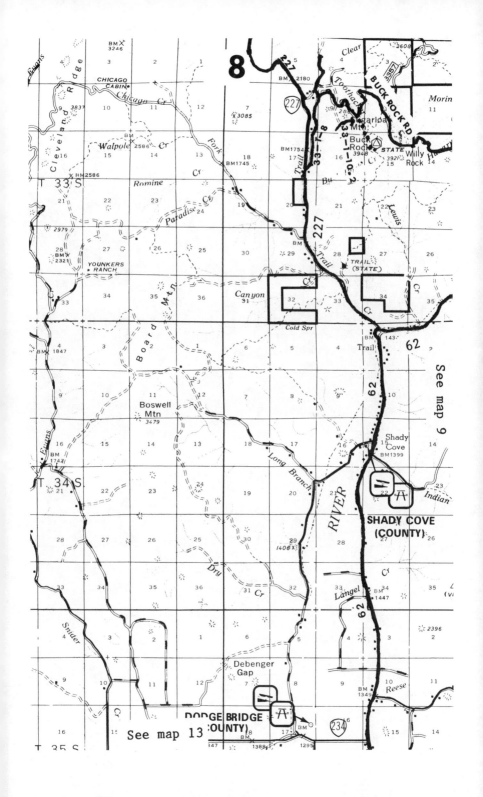

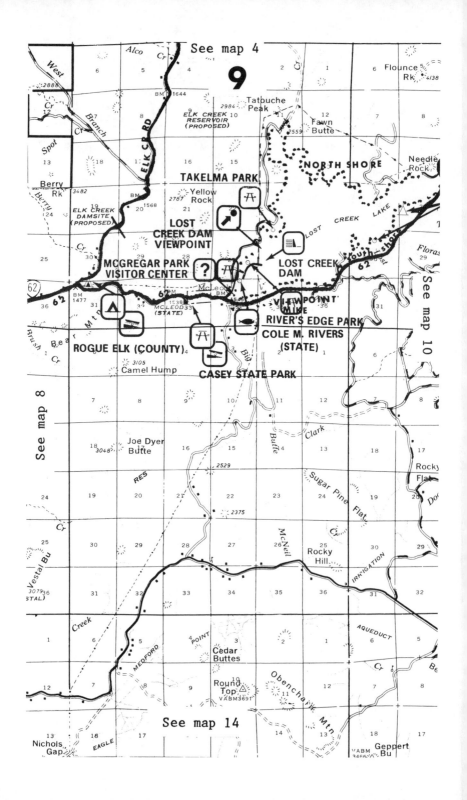

See map 4

9

See map 8

See map 10

See map 14

West

Alco
Cr.

Cr.

Flounce
Rk.

2888

Cr.
12

Branch

BM 1644

Tatouche
Peak

2984

ELK CREEK
RESERVOIR
(PROPOSED)

Fawn
Butte

2559

Spot

ELK CR. RD

NORTH SHORE

Needle
Rock

Berry
Rk

Berry

Yellow
Rock

TAKELMA PARK

3482

BM
1568

2787

CREEK

LAKE

ELK CREEK
DAMSITE
(PROPOSED)

LOST
CREEK DAM
VIEWPOINT

LOST

Cr.

McGREGAR PARK
VISITOR CENTER

LOST CREEK
DAM

Floras

South shore

62

See map 10

62

BM
1477

McLeod
BM

VIEWPOINT
MIKE

31

McLEOD
(STATE)

1538

River's Edge Park

RIVER'S EDGE PARK

Brush

Bear Mt.

ROGUE ELK (COUNTY)

COLE M. RIVERS
(STATE)

Cr.

3105
Camel Hump

CASEY STATE PARK

Big

Joe Dyer
Butte

3048

Butte

Clark

Rocky
Flat

2529

RES

Sugar Pine Flat

Doe

2375

Cr.

McNeil

Rocky
Hill

IRRIGATION

Vestal Bu

3079
(STAL)

Creek

AQUEDUCT

Cr.

Be

MEDFORD

POINT

Cedar
Buttes

Obenchain

Cr.

Round
Top
VABM 3691

Mtn

Nichols
Gap

EAGLE

Geppert
Bu

VABM

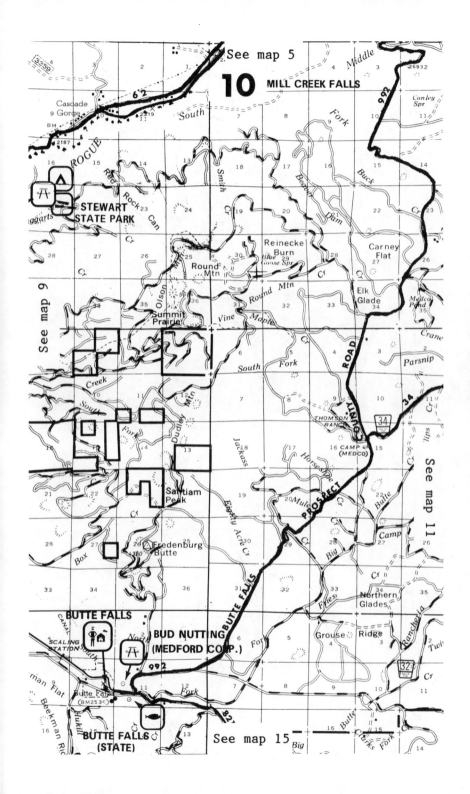

See map 5

10 MILL CREEK FALLS

See map 9

See map 11

See map 15

STEWART STATE PARK

BUTTE FALLS

BUD NUTTING (MEDFORD CORP.)

BUTTE FALLS (STATE)

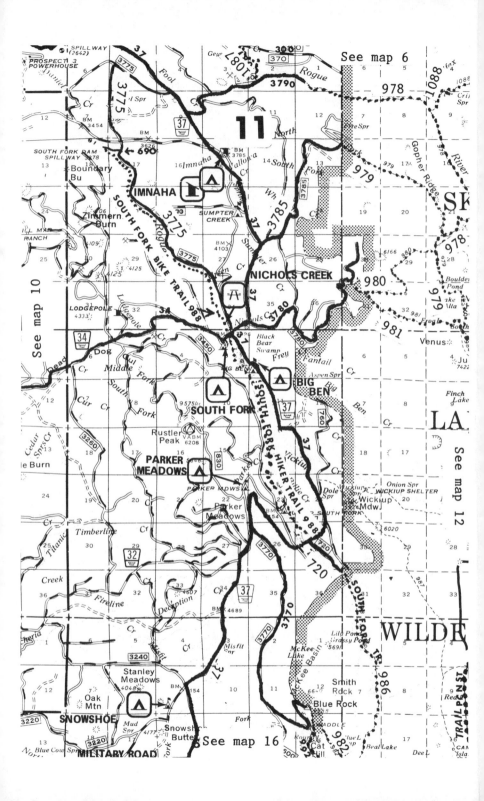

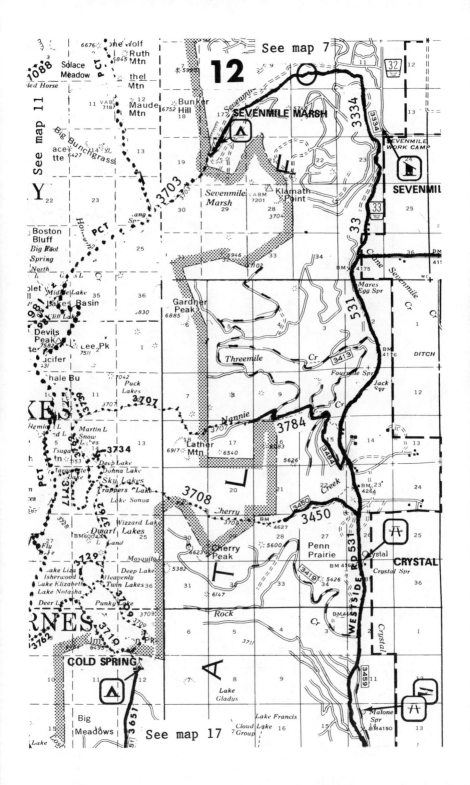

See map 7

12

See map 11

SEVENMILE MARSH

SEVENMILE WORK CAMP

SEVENMIL

Solace
Meadow

one Wolf
Ruth
Mtn
thel
Mtn

6676
845

led Horse

1088

Maude
Mtn

Bunker
Hill

6752
18

VABM
718
11

Y

22

ace
tte

Big Bunchgrass

6427

13

22

23

3703

3334

32

12

11

13

33

3704

Sevenmile
Marsh
29

30

VABM
7201

Klamath
Point
28

25

26

36

Boston
Bluff
Big Foot
Spring
North

Middle Lake
Lakes Basin

Cliff Lake

Devils
Peak
582
cifer
31

Lee Pk
751

hale Bu

Puck
Lakes

PCT

Cone
Sevenmile
Cr

Cr

BM 4175

Mares
Egg Spr

BM
415

Cr

35

36

830

Gardner
Peak
6885

33

34

3102

6946

3

2

1

1

Threemile

Cr

3413

4

Fourmile Spr

BM
4176

DITCH

Jack
Spr

12

3707

3707

Nannie

3784

Cr

7

8

9

Martin L
Snow
Lakes
Tsuga
tn

3734

Deep Lake
Donna Lake
Sky Lakes
Trappers Lake
Lake Sonya

Lather
Mtn
6917

17
6540

18

5683

5626

15

14

13

3481

13

Hemlo L
ed L
153

5

3711

20

21

Creek

3450

22

BM 23
4264

24

3708

3729

Wizzard Lake
Dwarf
Lakes
BM6004

L Land

Lake Liza
Isherwood
Lake Elizabeth
Lake Notasha

Deer L

Cherry

3707

Mosquito L

Deep Lake
Heavenly
Twin Lakes

Punky Lake

5382

6623

Cherry
Peak

6147

BM
4627

5600

28

3450

3450

Penn
Prairie

27

BM 416

26

25

27

31

32

3419

5426
34

Crystal

Crystal Spr

CRYSTAL

36

3709
3709

3762

RNES

3710

Jm

6495

COLD SPRING

Rock

371

Cr

3

BM4

WESTSIDE RD 531

Crystal

2

1

6

5

4

Big
Meadows

3651

See map 17

7

8

Lake
Gladys

9

Lake Francis

Cloud
Group

Lake

Malone
Spr

BM4150

11

13

15

3459

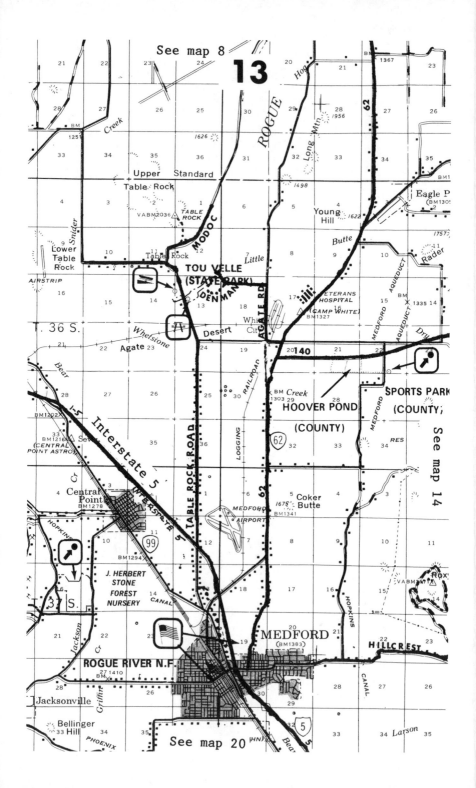

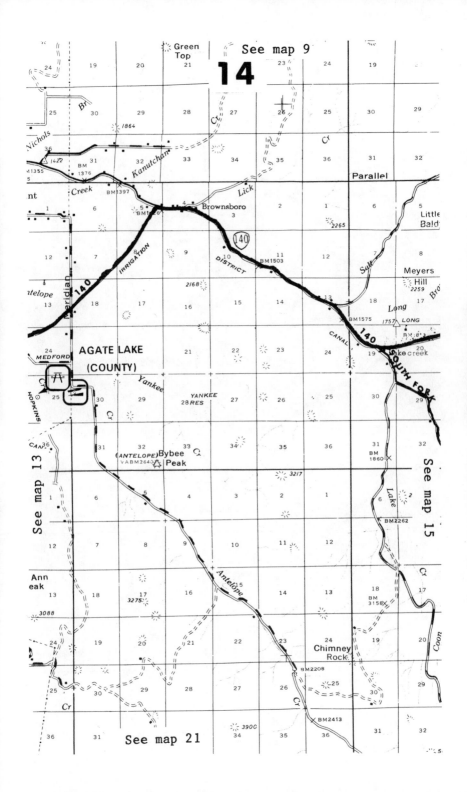

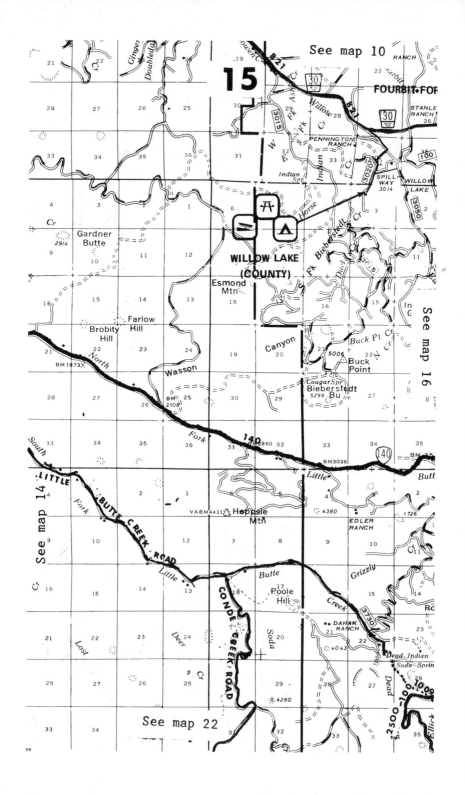

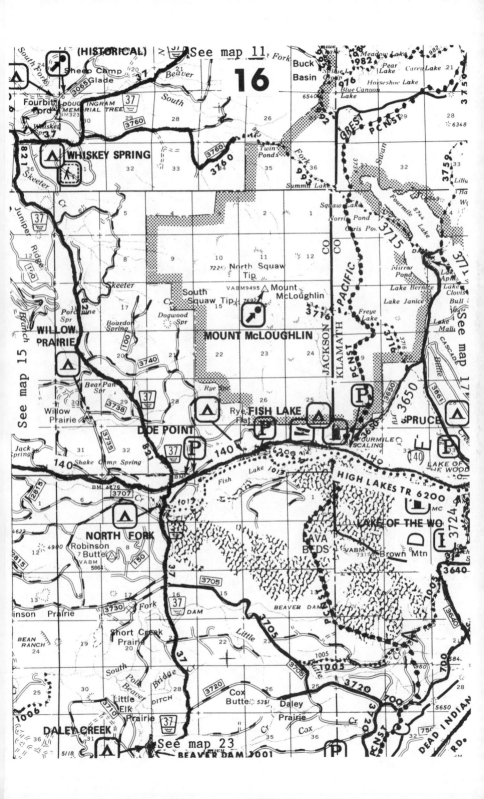

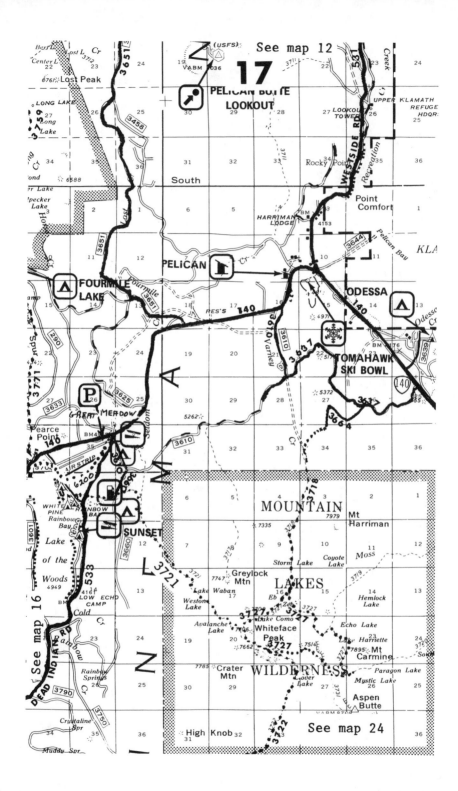

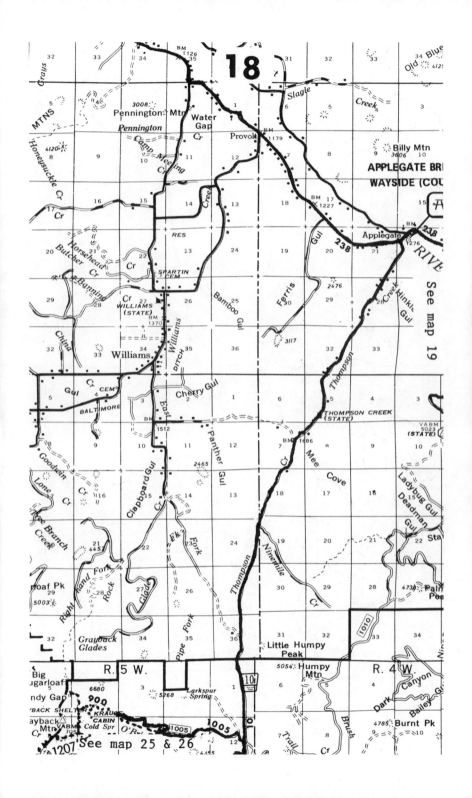

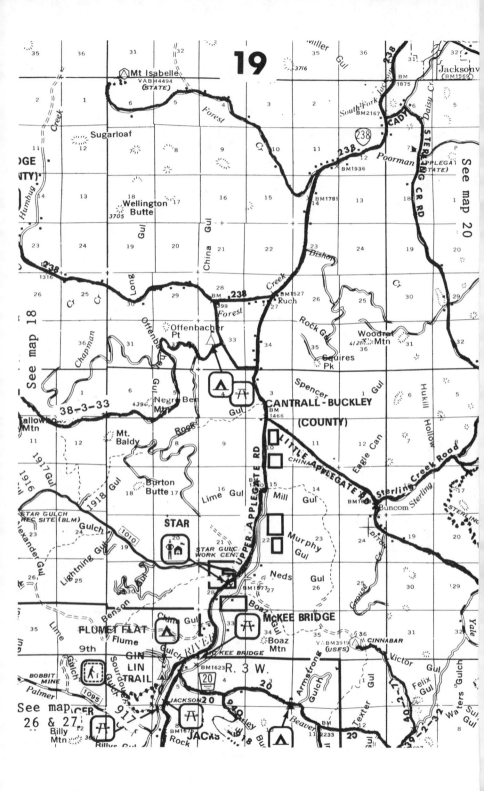

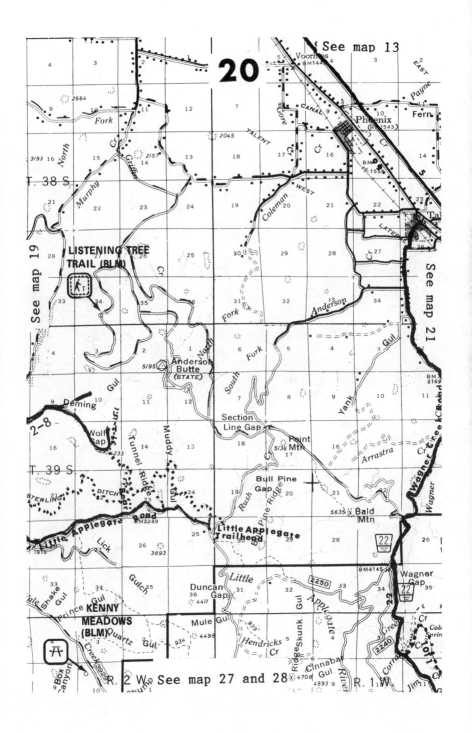

20

See map 13

See map 19

See map 21

Voorhees
BM 1443

Phoenix
BM 1543

Fern

Payne

EAST

Core

CANAL

TALENT

2045

T. 38 S.

North Fork

Murphy Cr

Griffin Cr

2/57

Coleman

WEST

Cr

BM 1555

Tal

LATERAL

LISTENING TREE TRAIL (BLM)

Cr

2664

Anderson

Fork North

Anderson Butte (STATE)
5/95

South Fork

Yank Gul

Wagner Creek

BM 2169

Deming

Gul 1st

Wolf Gap

BM 4233

Tunnel Ridge

Muddy Gul

Section Line Gap

Point Mtn
5/36

Arrastra Cr

T. 39 S.

2-8-

STERLING

DITCH

POND
BM 2249

Bull Pine Gap

Rush Creek

Pine Ridge

Bald Mtn
5635

Wagner

Little Applegate

Lick

Little Applegate Trailhead

22

BM 4145

Wagner Gap

22

Shake Gul

Prince Gul

KENNY MEADOWS (BLM)

Gulch

Quartz Gul

Duncan Gap
4411

Mule Gul

Little

Applegate River

2250

BM4145

2240

Box Canyon

Creek 5929

R. 2 W. See map 27 and 28

4708 Gul

Cinnabar

4593

R. 1 W

Ridgeskunk Gul

Hendricks Cr

3893

4498

934

Cor

Col Spring

Cr

Jim

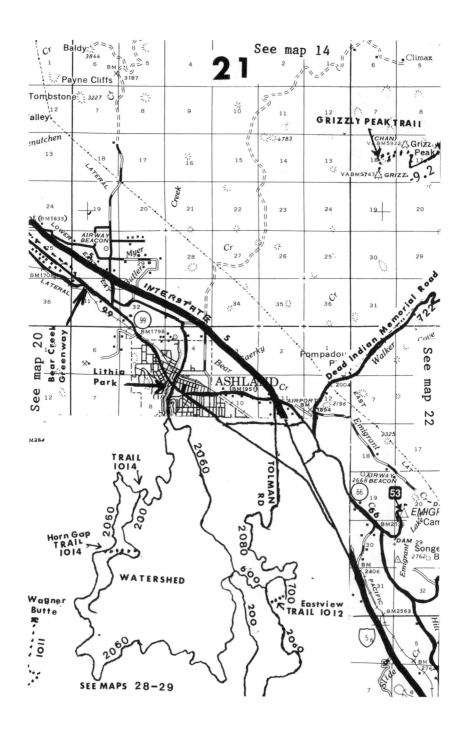

See map 14

21

Baldy
3844

Payne Cliffs
3187

Tombstone *3227*

alley

mutchen

Climax

GRIZZLY PEAK TRAIL

4783

CHAN
V BM5922 △ Grizzly Peak
18
V ABM5747 △ GRIZZ -9.2

LATERAL

Creek

(BM1635)

AIRWAY
BEACON

Myer
29

LOWER

EAST

Butler

BM1708

LATERAL

INTERSTATE 5

Cr

Cr

Cr

99
99

BM1798

See map 20

Bear Creek Greenway

Lithia
Park

aerky

Bear

Pompador
P

Dead Indian Memorial Road 722

cove

Walker

See map 22

ASHLAND
(BM1951)

Cr

AIRPORT
BM 1894
2196
2004

EAST ST

Emigrant

M254

2325

TRAIL
1014

2060

TOLMAN
RD

AIRWAY
2668 BEACON

66

53

C66

EMIGR
20 D.
19
Lake Cam
BM2125

Horn Gap
TRAIL
1014

2060

200

2080

600

30
DAM 29
Songe
2762 B

BM
2406

31

32

WATERSHED

Wagner
Butte

1011

700

200

Eastview
TRAIL 1012

2060

PACIFIC

BM2563

5 6

Cr
BM
276

SEE MAPS 28-29

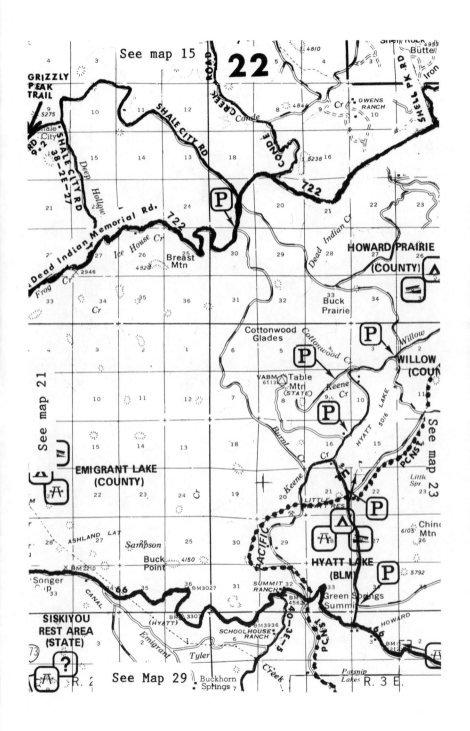

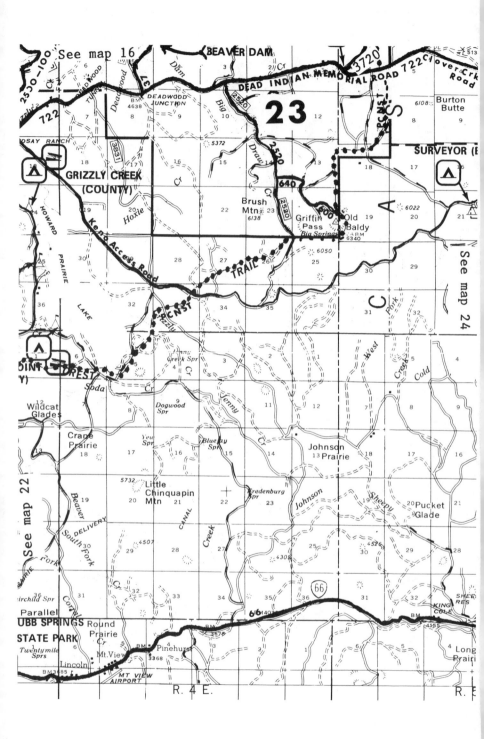

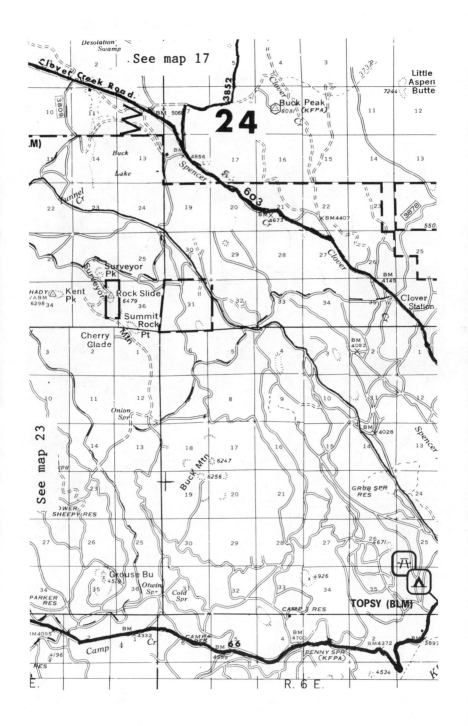

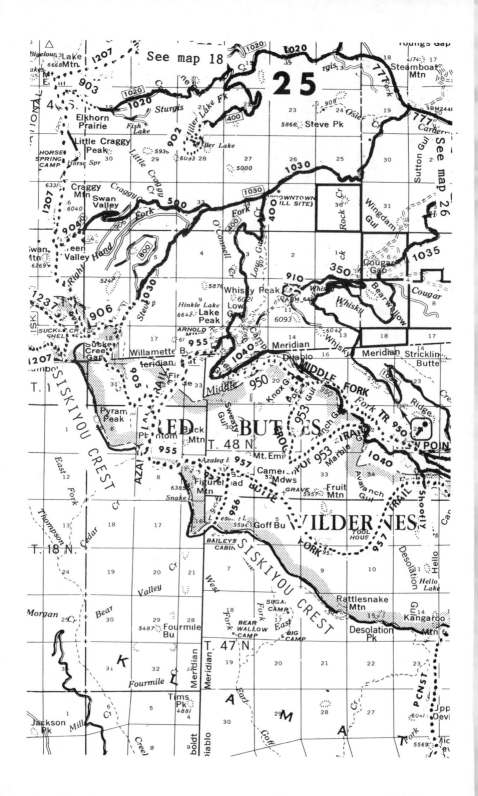

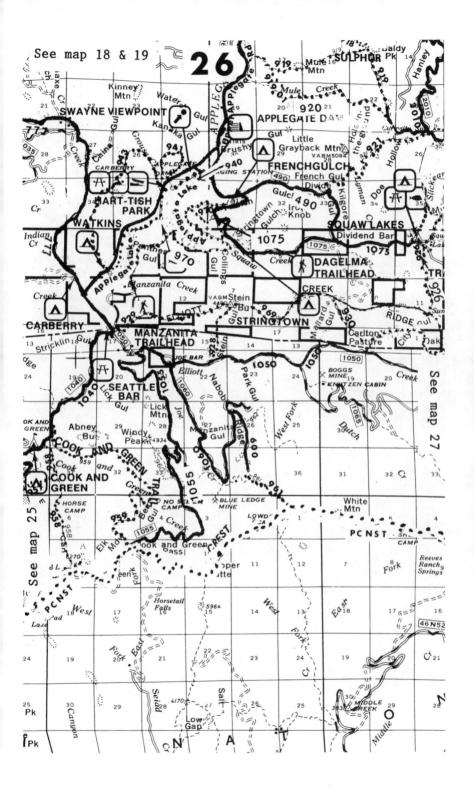

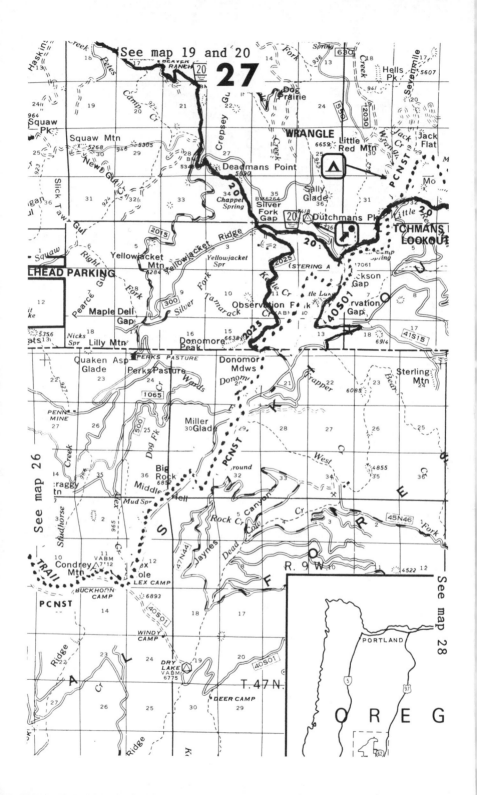

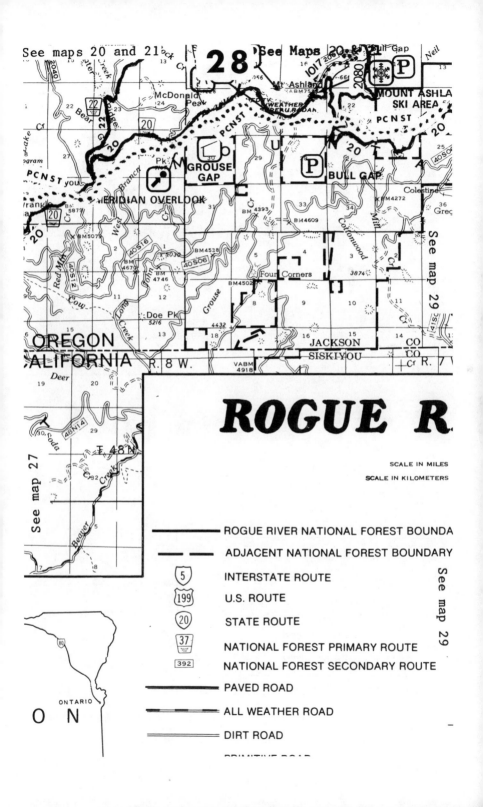

See maps 20 and 21

28

See Maps 20-21

Bull Gap

Neil

P

13

Mt Ashland
VABM 75

MOUNT ASHLA
SKI AREA

McDonald
Peak

WEATHER
FIBER U.S. DAM

PC N ST

PCN ST

GROUSE
GAP

U

P

BULL GAP

20

25

PCN ST you

MERIDIAN OVERLOOK

BM 4393

BM 4272

Colestine

Gre

36

20

BM5875

BM 4609

Cottonwood

See map 29

Red Mtn

40516

5030

BM4538

40506

BM
4679

BM
4746

BM4502

Four Corners

3874

Grouse

Cow

Long Creek

Doe Pk
5216

4432

Four Corners

JACKSON
SISKIYOU

CO
CO

Cr R.

OREGON
CALIFORNIA R. 8 W.

VABM
4918

Deer

See map 27

48N14

T. 48 N

Coda

Creek

Beaver

ROGUE R

SCALE IN MILES

SCALE IN KILOMETERS

See map 29

———— ROGUE RIVER NATIONAL FOREST BOUNDA

– – – ADJACENT NATIONAL FOREST BOUNDARY

(5) INTERSTATE ROUTE

(199) U.S. ROUTE

(20) STATE ROUTE

[37] NATIONAL FOREST PRIMARY ROUTE

[392] NATIONAL FOREST SECONDARY ROUTE

═══ PAVED ROAD

═══ ALL WEATHER ROAD

═══ DIRT ROAD

ONTARIO

O N

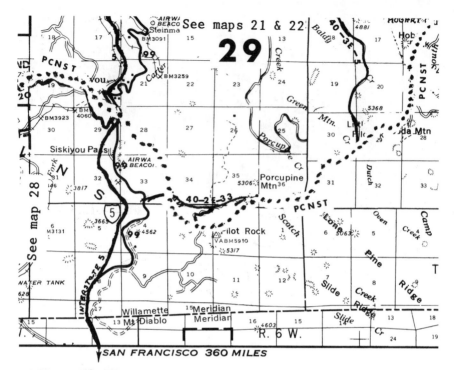

See maps 21 & 22

29

See map 28

SAN FRANCISCO 360 MILES

IVER National Forest

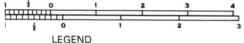

LEGEND

Y ▢	ROGUE RIVER NATIONAL FOREST	
▢	ADJACENT NATIONAL FOREST	
▢	BUREAU OF LAND MANAGEMENT	
▢	STATE LANDS	

FOREST SUPERVISOR HEADQUARTERS

RANGER STATION

FOREST SERVICE STATION

PACIFIC CREST
NATIONAL SCENIC TRAIL
(Closed to Motorized Vehicles)

See Map 28

CAMPGROUND

PICNIC AREA

FISHING

LAUNCHING RAMP

WINTER RECREATION

NATURE TRAIL

TRAIL SHELTER

WINTER PARKING
(FEE AT SOME AREAS)

POINT OF INTEREST